FIVE-STAR
LEADERSHIP

Also by Patrick L. Townsend and Joan E. Gebhardt

Commit to Quality

*Quality in Action: 93 Lessons in Leadership,
Participation, and Measurement*

FIVE-STAR LEADERSHIP

The Art and Strategy
of
Creating Leaders at Every Level

Patrick L. Townsend
Joan E. Gebhardt
Foreword by Nancy K. Austin

John Wiley & Sons, Inc.

New York • Chichester • Brisbane • Toronto • Singapore • Weinheim

This text is printed on acid-free paper.

Copyright © 1997 by Patrick L. Townsend and Joan E. Gebhardt

Published by John Wiley & Sons, Inc.

Library of Congress Cataloging-in-Publication Data

Townsend, Patrick L.
    Five-star leadership : the art and strategy of creating leaders at
every level / Patrick L. Townsend, Joan E. Gebhardt ; foreword by
Nancy K. Austin.
        p.   cm.
    ISBN 0-471-01288-2 (cloth : alk. paper)
    1. Leadership.   2. Employee empowerment.   3. United States
Marine Corps—Management.   I. Gebhardt, Joan E.   II. Title.
HD57.7.T69   1997
658.3'14—dc20   96-35909
                                                                    CIP

Printed in the United States of America

10 9 8 7 6 5 4 3 2 1

CONTENTS

FOREWORD

One sticky July day a dozen years ago, I opened the windows in a cramped conference room and settled down to listen to an audiotaped speech about leadership. With the heat shimmering outside, the speaker presented his ideas as if they were cool drinks. "The one piece of advice which I believe will contribute more to making you a better leader," he said quietly, "doesn't call for a special personality, and it doesn't call for any certain chemistry. Any one of you can do it. And that advice is that you *must* care." His was the kind of voice that made you want to listen forever. It belonged to Lieutenant General Melvin Zais, former commander of the U.S. Army's blood-and-guts 101st Airborne Division. The beneficiaries of his remarks were the graduates of the Armed Forces Staff College, the school founded fifty years ago to train officers from all branches of service. That day, as I listened, I realized that everything I thought I knew about military leadership was wrong.

Like many people, I had always believed that leadership in the armed forces came down to one essential equation: rank equals authority. When your first name is General or Major or Lieutenant, an order barked is an order obeyed—or else. Why wrestle with slippery concepts like trust and loyalty when you've got a lockstep chain of command to lean on? But as Pat Townsend and Joan Gebhardt show in this remarkable book, behind the military's disciplined, combat-ready carapace is a core sensibility that transcends old models about what military leadership is and does. This is a book that zeroes in on the heart of leadership—and, not incidentally, followership—at its honorable best.

Presented here are leaders of all stripes—from Civil War General Joshua Lawrence Chamberlain to Sgt. 1st Class Michael T. Woodward to Florence Nightingale—as a rich resource for leaders everywhere, civilians and officers, neophytes to chief executives. In Chapter 4, for example, you can sneak a peek at the fourteen-point backbone of the Marine Corps' leader training, a roster that begins with integrity and ends with judgment. In between, you'll encounter other hallmark traits of gallant leadership, including courage ("Stand for what is right, even in the face of popular disfavor."), tact, and unselfishness. Big as these ideas are, Townsend and Gebhardt succeed in making the leap from a colonel's command post to a soldier's foxhole to the supervisor's cubicle seem a very short span indeed.

The best part of the book, for my money, centers on the art of encouraging innovation and initiative throughout an organization just like yours or mine. "Creative talent," the authors say in Chapter 5, "is too precious to waste. Squashing even one person's innovative impulses might well discourage others from ever speaking up, and at that point, the organization loses countless new and exciting ideas." An attractive image, but one notoriously difficult to indulge in the heat of battle. Again, the authors provide real-world touchstones. If you have a thing for lists, you'll love this one from the Marines, called "sixteen traits of creative people." Among them: openness to experience, a delight in the challenging and the unfinished, and (hooray!) a good sense of humor. But as Townsend and Gebhardt also understand, creative people almost by definition shake things up to a fare-thee-well. They are mighty, unpredictable, and destabilizing forces in the kind of environment (Army, Navy, Air Force, Marines) that most of us assume thrives on control and coercion.

Well, we were mistaken. The military, like IBM or General Motors or Nordstrom, has survived and prospered because it is comprised of people willing to force changes on themselves, even when it means abandoning what has served them well in the past, and even when it hurts. What's key is to nurture the sort of leadership, at every level, that encourages and supports smart people with the vigor to push for changes they think make sense. If that describes you, here is your handbook.

—Nancy K. Austin

PREFACE

In today's corporate environment, managers and nonmanagers face each other across an ever-narrowing gulf. Employees at all levels find their responsibilities and authority realigned, often with the result that they are expected to do more with less. The aftermath of these inexorable shifts has been to leave a vast number of employees alarmed, puzzled, or just plain tired.

This book can help. It is more than a bare-bones leadership course; call it a manual of coping skills. The lessons provided are based on the premise that individuals can bring their personal strengths to bear to make an ever-changing workplace intelligible. The leadership philosophy and practical tools presented teach employees to analyze situations and avoid the leading causes of stress, namely confusion and powerlessness. Anyone who has an eye on the executive suite, including front-line supervisors, middle managers, and less-than-senior executives, will find this book indispensable, as will nonmanagement employees who are called upon to be decision makers without positions of authority.

Most of all, the book illuminates a fundamental truth about leadership: *Leadership is a behavior, not a position.* It invites everyone from CEOs to clerks to work in cooperation to instill leadership at every level. The best leaders know that in addition to developing their own leadership skills, they have a responsibility to develop leadership in others. Ideally, as each individual is encouraged to take full advantage of his or her own talents, work life will become more productive, more rewarding, and—quite possibly—more fun for everybody.

ACKNOWLEDGMENTS

Ten years ago when we wrote our first book, we were asked to delete a chapter on leadership because our editors were not convinced that leadership had anything to do with the subject of quality. We want to begin with a special thanks to our publisher, John Wiley & Sons, Inc., for letting us tackle what we believe is the most important issue in quality and business today: the need for leadership at every level. They deserve kudos for letting us use an unusual source for insights into personal leadership behavior.

Our goal was to provide a *practical* guide to leadership: a guide that encouraged action. After two years of research, we came to the conclusion that, stereotypes not withstanding, the clearest, most concise, most humanitarian expressions of leadership theory were put forth by the United States military. We hope you'll agree that by combining military theory with corporate examples, we've captured the best of both worlds.

To be sure we stayed anchored to a "civilian" perspective, we brought two individuals on board: Keith Buffo, a marvelous editor, who worked through every word with us, and Linda Zambarano, a psychologist, who provided useful comments throughout, listened to moanings and misgivings, and read the darn-near finished product. We also owe a debt of gratitude to "almost-military" John Mellecker, who attended a Marine Corps Platoon Leaders Class before going civilian and ending up as an executive in financial services. He contributed in several ways: as an invaluable resource for Chapter 4, as a devil's advocate in the book's earliest stages, and as a reader.

Thanks to others—both civilian and military—who gave encouragement at the start and ideas and material along the way: Ray Ashcraft; Lt. Badkin, USMC; Bruce Basaraba; Major Bean, USMC; Jackie Bryant; Joe Byrnes; Sharon Conner; Sally Davenport; Jeff Dennard; Mary Imbornone; Dr. Brent James; Commander Pat Kelly, USCG; Bob Knezovich; Christy Linder; Paul Manoogian; Captain Hector Marcayda, USMC; Myles Noel; Mary Ann O'Mara; Chief

Master Sergeant O'Neil, USAF; Master Chief "Otto" Ottoviani, USN; Gunnery Sergeant Payson, USMC; Joe Posk; Captain Keith Poulin, USAF; Mary Price; Kevin Rohan; Captain Philip Shevis, USMC; Dr. Marion Steeples; Karen Thompson; and Keith Taylor, our favorite quality observer and phrase-turner.

Particular thanks go to five Marines at the Marine Corps Recruit Depot in San Diego, California, who in a conversation early in this effort assured us that our memories of the caring essence of Marine Corps leadership were accurate: Gunnery Sergeant William E. Hazelwood, Gunnery Sergeant Michael Walker, Gunnery Sergeant Edward T. Sax, Staff Sergeant Robert E. Farmer—and their boss who organized the meeting, Captain Sean T. Moore.

Many thanks also to the Marines Pat was privileged to serve with who provided inspiration and lessons in leadership, especially Skip Bartlett, Dan Blaul, Dan Carpenter, Larry Dorsa, Ed Dwyer, Marvin Geisler, Robert Hunsberger, Bob Keller, Ed Kurdziel, Paul Lessard, Mike McDonald, Bud McFarlane, Bruce Pifel, Mark Rainer, Elsmere Randall, Don Rosenberg, and Charlie Spadafora. From the other services, there were Frank Feild and Glen Skulborstad from the Army, Thad Sandford from the Air Force, and Jack Wheeler from the Navy. And both of us have special admiration for Susan Goddard-Dooley, USMC, one of the few female officers and leaders we are privileged to know. She makes us aware of how much richer the armed services are for expanding the number of females in the military. Thanks, too, to Willis Reed, NBA, whose leadership example is unparalleled.

The book has a bias toward the Marine Corps, although there is material from all of the services. This is perhaps unavoidable because Pat spent twenty years wearing the eagle, globe, and anchor insignia and still considers himself a Marine; Joan was married to him for sixteen of those years. He would like to say many thanks to the leadership instructors whose classes he attended during twenty years in the Corps and four years in Naval ROTC: He doesn't remember your names, but some of the information did get lodged between his ears and stayed—honestly. Joan would like to say thanks to Gunnery Sergeant Marvin Geisler, who promised to take care of Captain Townsend in Vietnam—and did.

1

LEADERSHIP AT
EVERY LEVEL

A new reality has emerged in the last twenty years, one that redefines effective leadership within organizations: the Quality Revolution. It took the Quality Revolution to demonstrate how valuable the ability to make decisions and build consensus, once thought to be solely the province of management, could be when deployed throughout an organization. Organizations succeed with quality when they encourage everyone to aspire to the kind of autonomy and personal growth usually associated with leadership and, in effect, create leadership at every level.

Make no mistake: The Quality Revolution represents the first major shift in the manager-employee-result relationship since the beginning of the Industrial Revolution, and no one has been free of its impact. Like it or not, in an international economy where every second counts, leadership skills must be mastered by *everyone in the organization* if the organization is to survive. Personal and corporate success in the twenty-first century depend not only on developing the ability to lead, but also on recognizing and developing leadership in others. That's what this book is all about.

THE QUALITY REVOLUTION

The Quality Revolution changed the way in which work is accomplished in quality-driven organizations, both in the United States and abroad. To comprehend what a profound change there has been and what it means for leadership, a brief history of the Quality Revolution

1

is in order. Dr. Joseph M. Juran, who dubbed the twentieth century the "Century of Productivity," predicted that the twenty-first century will become the "Century of Quality," and the change is more than a matter of semantics.

The roots of the Quality Revolution lie in post–World War II economic conditions. The United States emerged from the armed conflict with its economy essentially intact. As a result, its products found a ready market virtually free of competition. Even if a product wasn't totally reliable, it was superior to what the rest of the world could make; and, besides, what Americans bought from each other all had about the same degree of reliability. Everyone more or less broke even. Rather than viewing shoddy production as a flaw, two words were used to elevate it to a virtue: *planned obsolescence*. According to this philosophy, keeping up with the Joneses and replacing old products with new was the way to keep an economy humming. Products that lasted forever were considered vaguely déclassé, somehow undesirable. Productivity was the key, and "productivity" in this case meant lots of products made quickly.

Across the Pacific, the Japanese were fashioning an alternative philosophy of production with the help of American renegades such as Dr. W. Edwards Deming, Dr. Joseph M. Juran, and Dr. Armand Feigenbaum—all broadly ignored by the vast majority of U.S. business giants until the 1980s. As early as 1950, the Japanese institutionalized this approach by creating the Deming Prize, a national quality award named after Deming in recognition of his influence. In Japan, "quality" was broadly defined as providing goods that were manufactured with minimum waste,ppp, designed to last, attractive to the customer, and competitively priced. It is reported that the Japanese thought they were learning "the American way" under American mentors using American business practices as a prototype.

Progress was slow. Initially, "Made in Japan" was synonymous with novelties and gimcrack goods; even as late as 1957, the first Toyopet (later Toyota) exported to America had a top speed of 35 mph and petered out on the hills of San Francisco. Yet, within twenty years, Japan had become a major source of goods for American consumers; and the Japanese were as surprised as the Americans that their product quality was on a par or superior.

The rest of the world paid scant attention to Japanese competition until it became obvious that quality made money. By then, other countries—including the United States—had a lot of catching up to do. Their collective response became the Quality Revolution, as companies worldwide began to look for ways to use the quality tools utilized in Japan to build and sustain a competitive advantage.

Once the Quality Revolution got rolling, it proceeded quickly. The British established a national quality award in 1984; the United States awarded the Malcolm Baldrige National Quality Award for the first time in 1988. The American Society for Quality Control, which administers the award, received 12,000 requests for applications that year. By 1991, the number of requests had risen to 240,000. Today, Baldrige Award clones have sprung up throughout the United States at state, local, and corporate levels. Not only companies, but governmental entities apply for their own versions of the Baldrige Award. Abroad, countries as far flung as Sweden and Brazil have developed award criteria using the Baldrige as a pattern. During this same period, ISO 9000, a set of international quality standards, burst onto the scene in Europe and spread worldwide. Clearly, quality gained an impressive hold on the economies of the world in a relatively short period of time.

There were a few surprises along the way. The first was that quality on the Deming/Japanese model underwent considerable modification as it made inroads in the West. In the almost forty years between the first Deming Prize and the first Baldrige Award, quality became less dictatorial and more democratic. Briefly stated, the Deming Prize laid down prescriptive criteria, a roadmap of the only route to quality. The Baldrige criteria were descriptive, a combination destination and compass, with a request for information on possible routes. Unfortunately, ISO 9000 settled for presenting evidence that a trip, almost any trip, was made, without assuring that the destination was reached. A company could get certification if it made concrete life preservers—as long as it made them the same way every time.

The second surprise was that quality conferred enormous benefits beyond making money. It made a lot of people—consumers, employees, and shareholders—happy. It also enabled organizations to conduct their affairs in an ethical manner by creating the capacity to deliver on promises. Most organizations began by believing that the primary reason to invest the time, money, and effort necessary to define, implement, and sustain a quality process was the bottom line; many soon changed their minds. Companies found that focusing on quality *for quality's sake* yielded better results than obsessing over financial data. FedEx, a Baldrige Award winner in 1991, operates under the banner "People, Service, Profit," with profit a deliberate third, and Ritz-Carlton Hotel Company, winner in 1992, says flatly, "Profit is the residue of quality."

FREDERICK TAYLOR REVISITED

The major surprise in the Quality Revolution was that the dramatic shifts in the international marketplace were accompanied by sweeping changes within organizations themselves. No change was more complex—or overdue—than the reversal of the principles of Frederick Taylor, the management guru of the early twentieth century. As Juran has pointed out, Taylor's theories were appropriate (or at least defensible) for his time. By focusing on productivity, his theories facilitated the rapid shift from an agricultural society to a manufacturing society in the United States and elsewhere.

When looking at Taylor's theories through the prism of quality, however, they appear outdated and more than a little dangerous. His time-and-motion studies reduced the complexities of production to mind-numbing, machinelike routines. It was Taylor who made the statement, "Any change the workers make to the plan is fatal to success," reflecting his view that input from anyone other than the management of an organization was of little value, if not worthless. There is no contradiction in noting that the first warden at Alcatraz, James A. Johnston, looked to Taylor when designing the prisoners' routine for that high-security facility.

With a Taylor approach, management was concerned with only a small portion of the individual worker's capabilities. A Taylorist could ignore any and all abilities and attributes above and beyond the single set of skills that fit the precise job description/requirements as designed by management; there was no need to deal with workers as complete, complex individuals. The waste of human potential was staggering, and remains so for those who still embrace Taylor's philosophy.

It was an accident of history that Taylor stayed in vogue for so long. His theories were dominant when the Great Depression hit the United States and the rest of the world in the 1930s, bringing economies worldwide to a virtual halt. By default, they continued to dominate when the need to fuel war production took over U.S. industry in the 1940s and the object was to get lots of equipment to the war zones as quickly as possible. When World War II ended and the United States had the only undamaged industrial base of any size in the world, the U.S. economy was unchallenged. If a U.S. company could get something into a box, it could find someone to buy it. The system worked.

During the period when Taylor's assumptions were sufficient for the job of running the nation's business, something else happened to perpetuate his dictums: Business schools and MBA programs came of age. By the late 1950s, MBA schools had cast Taylor's management theories into academic concrete—seemingly ignoring the fact that post-war circumstances represented a transitory period in the world marketplace, one that would pass as soon as the rest of the world rebuilt their economies. As early as the mid-1960s, it should have been obvious that U.S. managerial style, which appeared to stand astride world commerce like a giant bronze colossus, had feet of clay. The carefully formulated, never-miss approaches missed: They resulted in products and services that, while arguably as good as they used to be, were no longer competitive. Customers demanded more. Oddly, almost another two decades passed before management schools conceded that productivity alone was not enough to keep a company's goods and/or services in the game.

A LABORATORY FOR LEADERSHIP

As organizations experimented with various internal structures to respond quickly to customers' requirements, documented options for participation developed, ranging from well-run suggestion systems at the "low end" to self-managed work teams and high-performance work teams on the "high end." Over time it became clear that *any structure could be successful* as long as it routinely involved a very high percentage of both management and nonmanagement employees (ideally,

100%), and as long as the organization diffused decision making throughout the organization. Where those two conditions were not met, the results were disappointing.

This was true of the early effort to use Quality Circles to improve quality in the United States. In a rough adaptation of Japanese Quality Control Circles, U.S. terminology dropped the word control, but the way the circles too often played out, the word could have remained. In a weird reversal of Taylor, employee participation was almost exclusively nonmanagement. Taylor's obsession with management control, however, remained. Participation was guided into neat little constructs with assigned problems, circles were directed by facilitators/overseers, and solutions were subject to management review. Power stayed at the top; participation within organizations was set at 10 to 15 percent, shutting out the majority of employees in the process; and enthusiasm quickly waned.

Countless suggestions systems also failed to live up to expectations. Among the host of reasons was that few employees participated. When they did, they rarely received training as to what constituted a worthy idea—or even how to fill out a suggestion form. Not surprisingly, many ideas submitted were not implemented. Then, too, management often failed to peek into the suggestion box on a regular basis.

Total Quality Management (or what was called in the medical field—for reasons lost forever in semantic fog—Continuous Quality Improvement) also fell short more frequently than it succeeded. For the most part, TQM relied on a few individuals and/or a few select teams to make decisions that affected the entire organization. Although christened "total" because "We told everyone to get better and we told them how to do it," TQM in these instances was business as usual with a quality face. Genuine change requires quite a different use of the word total, one in which everyone has the opportunity to have an impact on the organization. Quality is not something you do *to* someone or *for* someone—quality is something you do *with* someone.

After nearly two decades, it became clear that leadership and quality were inextricably linked. In *Principle-Centered Leadership,* Stephen Covey referred to leadership as the "glue that holds Total Quality together" and as the "catalyst that makes the rest of Total Quality work." If leadership and quality are not flip sides of the same coin, they were at least struck in the same mint.

Leadership at every level makes possible the creation of an integrated quality environment in which ever-improving products and/or services are not only achievable, but inevitable. Any blend of elements that invites leadership also promotes quality: vigorous activity, flow of communications/information, mutual support, explicit common goals, and delegation of appropriate authority throughout the organization. Everyone must have permission to "fall forward," that is, make mistakes so long as the effort is well-intentioned and shows an attempt at progress in the right direction.

At the same time, quality is more likely to take root—and to send its roots deep—in an organization in which leadership itself is actively pursued and practiced. A public commitment to improving not only the leadership skills of management, but also the skills of subordinates goes a long way toward institutionalizing quality improvement. Against this background, leaders who know how to foster leadership in others, no matter where they are in the hierarchy, will be in demand throughout the "Century of Quality."

WHERE MANAGEMENT AND LEADERSHIP PART

If the Quality Revolution has redefined leadership for our times, what is the new definition? This book takes two primary approaches to answering that question: defining leadership relative to its cousin concept, management; and defining it in absolute terms as a stand-alone concept.

An informal poll can illuminate the difference between leadership and management. If possible, ask members of any organization to list the adjectives that come to mind when they hear the word leader, then to list the ones that come to mind when they hear the word manager. (No preamble or prompting allowed.) Most likely, leader will evoke words such as bold, daring, inspirational, innovative, effective, and caring; manager will put folks in mind of such adjectives as stuffy, slow, multilayered, bureaucratic, and overcontrolling. Having done that, ask a separate set of people from the same organization to list adjectives describing the organization as a whole. A comparison of the new list with the previous lists can yield a thumbnail sketch of the state of leadership in the organization.

What is probably more significant is that few, if any, of the people asked to complete the poll will question the validity of the exercise. Everyone accepts that leadership and management are somehow different. Techniques taught in MBA schools are for the most part management, an essential part of a leader's tool kit, but not the whole story. Perhaps the easiest way to express the concept is that management is a subset of leadership. British author John Adair sums it up eloquently in *Training for Leadership*, a book based primarily on his work with the military:

> Far from occupying a remote corner in "industrial sociology" or "industrial relations," leadership is *the* integrating concept, relating and binding together those subjects which are loosely grouped together as "Management Studies" in business schools and universities.

Management is a relatively straightforward proposition; leadership is not. Management strives for objectivity; leadership goes beyond objectivity to incorporate the profoundly personal into the equation. Management can be memorized; leadership requires experimentation, renewal, and awareness. Management is about skills; leadership is about skills coupled with character. British Field Marshall Lord Slim was quoted in a United States Air Force training manual as saying:

> There is a difference between leadership and management. The leader and the men who follow him represent one of the oldest, most natural, and most effective of all human relationships. The manager and those he manages are a later product with neither so romantic, nor so inspiring a history. Leadership is of the spirit, compounded of personality and vision—its practice is an art. Management is of the mind, more a matter of accurate calculation, statistics, methods, timetables, and routine—its practice is a science.

The difference between leadership and management can be traced to the relationships between people. It does not overstate the case (or it overstates it only slightly) to say that while managers care that a job gets done, leaders care that a job gets done—and they openly care about the people doing the job. One way to look at it is that a manager is a potential leader who hasn't finished evolving yet. And it takes self-confidence. Only the self-confident can lead; the insecure are doomed to manage. The operative differentiation is trust, both of oneself and of others. Without trust, there can be no self-confidence, nor confidence in the abilities in others—and no leadership.

Empowerment comes out of confidence in the ability of others. It is essential to leadership. Known mockingly to many in the corporate community as "the E-word," empowerment was added to the quality vocabulary primarily by the book *The Empowered Manager* by Peter Block, first published in October 1986. By 1988 it was a hot topic and courses on empowerment abounded; by 1989 it was a cliché, taken over almost exclusively by motivational, feel-good speakers. This track record obscures the fact that empowerment was, and is, a valid concept, one that went awry in large part because Block never offered an un-adorned, solid definition that people could apply under a variety of cir-cumstances.

Empowerment is nothing more than *the granting of authority equal to responsibility,* and nothing less. Far from some threatening call to do your own thing, empowerment entails spelling out authority, responsi-bility, and accountability. Competent leaders push authority to the ap-propriate level. Whoever is blamed, whoever is identified as the person whose inappropriate action caused the problem, is entitled to the au-thority to fix the problem. If the authority is not forthcoming, the re-sponsibility ceases to exist. It is unfair to assign responsibility without sufficient authority.

In organizations where authority and responsibility are misaligned, empowerment is impossible. Often this is a result of happenstance. An upward drift of power over time is a natural phenomenon in most orga-nizations, unless there has been an ongoing effort by leaders at every level to prevent it. This drift can usually be traced to one of two sources: (1) a person's tendency to take one or two of his or her favorite decisions along with him or her upon promotion, or (2) a manager's usurpation of a subordinate's power upon the occasion of an error. To correct the drift, a leader must look at each of the decisions he or she makes and ask, "Who will be held accountable if this doesn't work?

Who really is responsible for getting this done?" In short, "Who gets the blame if this goes wrong?"

Accountability is only part of the issue. Giving credit where credit is due is the rest. While *leaders* assure that the people responsible for good work receive the kudos, many *managers* are all too willing to take the credit for themselves. Among the sure signs of deficiency in the leadership abilities of senior management is taking undue credit—or crediting the wrong people when something worthy of praise occurs.

Although it sounds like the logical thing to do, it is actually very difficult for many managers to empower subordinates. For managers grown used to micromanaging, pushing power down to a lower level introduces two possibilities, neither of them attractive from the managers' viewpoint. One possibility is that the subordinate might make a mistake or two; the other is that the subordinate might do a better job. Again, trust and self-confidence are essential.

Given the admitted risks, why would anyone empower employees? Where's the gain? One reason was alluded to above: By empowering subordinates, leaders increase the odds that the job will be well done, mainly because it will be done by somebody close to it who better understands it and who truly has to live with the results. The more subtle reason, but perhaps the one with the strongest personal appeal, is that anyone who empowers her or his subordinates has more time. Once free of making decisions that should be made by subordinates, an individual is able to devote personal time and energy to wrestling with decisions and challenges appropriate to her or his position in the organization. If, for instance, a senior works a forty-hour week but uses 10 percent of her or his time making decisions belonging to subordinates, that amounts to a free half day a week—once authority has been redistributed.

Empowerment is not just the right thing to do, it is good business and it has a personal payback. It is also essential to creating leaders at every level. As the reader moves through the following chapters, he or she is urged to think of the information presented in the context of both "How can I use that to improve my skills?" and "How will I pass that on to my subordinates?"

Informed businesspeople have a fundamental grasp of the difference between management and leadership—and of the inexorable link between leadership and quality. In a very real sense, management and productivity are what happen by default in functioning organizations. They deal with yesterday and, at best, today. Leadership and quality are two linked concepts that focus on the future.

COSMIC VIEWS OF LEADERSHIP

To fully appreciate the depth and breadth of the meaning of leadership today, one must consider it not only in relationship to management, but also as a standalone concept. Here's where cosmic questions arise, not infrequently degenerating into how-many-angels-fit-on-the-head-of-a-pin disputes. A central point of debate among current authors and givers of seminars on leadership revolves around the question, "Is leadership an art or a science?" Max De Pree's popular quick-read book, *Leadership Is an Art,* put this question at center stage. Field Marshall Lord Slim, quoted above, also came down firmly on the side of leadership as an art.

Casting the discussion in either/or terms may be viscerally satisfying, but it is unlikely to lead to improved leadership skills. Like two other questions surrounding leadership—"Is it rational or emotional?" and "Is it innate or acquired?"—the answer is "Yes." Yes, leadership is an art; yes, it is a science. Yes, it is rational; yes, it is emotional. You get the idea.

For leadership to be purely scientific, humans would have to be capable of acting as totally rational beings while following definable patterns. Although this was argued as the basis of management theory for most of the twentieth century, it is obviously false. People are not machines. In fact, given the variability in the output of machines (the beginning point of much of what Deming taught), it has been argued that machines aren't "machines" either. Even a machine's performance cannot be predicted without taking variation into account.

On the other hand, viewing leadership only as an art has other problems. While it is true that the dictum "If it feels good, do it!" received a good bit of publicity in the United States in the 1960s, a society (or a business organization) based on such a notion would rapidly disintegrate. Humans who rely on emotion-based or instinct-driven decisions and actions are dangerous—even when they happen to do the right thing *this* time. An element of judgment is essential to good leadership.

Leadership is not simply an art (emotional/instinctual) or a science (rational/acquired), although there are those who practice leadership as one or the other. Solely rational attempts to influence the actions of others are called management; efforts that are limited to emotional appeal are called rabble-rousing. Both are attempts to oversimplify one of the most intriguing of human relationships; both are pointless and ultimately destructive.

Leadership is a blend of the rational and emotional, the innate and acquired, the ideal and practical. Both Mr. Spock of *Star Trek* and Commander Data of *Star Trek: The Next Generation* frequently marveled at the irrational things humans do in the practice of leadership. Spock was easily Captain Kirk's intellectual better, and Data could rattle off information far more quickly than Captain Picard; yet, the shows' creator, Gene Roddenberry, recognized that being smarter and more logical were not enough to merit command. In both cases, the captains' rational abilities were augmented by emotional capabilities, a characteristic looked on with disdain by Spock and appreciation by Data.

The debate about art versus science also colors opinions on how good leaders come to power. Are power and good leadership synonymous? Do good leaders always rise to the top in an organization? Are people automatically equipped with the information, ability, and personality to perform well when promotions occur? Experience suggests that none of these questions can be answered in the affirmative, but anyone who is not actively working on leadership skills acts as if any or all of them were true.

The leaders-are-born-not-made school refuses to die. It is comforting to assert that not only is it not "my fault" if I am not a natural leader, it is also impossible to do anything about it. Unfortunately, that won't hold up. This point was directly addressed in a World War II–era book, *Leadership for American Army Leaders:*

> Thus the theory that leaders are born and not made is the saw of the defeatist, for acquaintance with the things that produce morale is one of the vital elements of leadership that any reasonably intelligent and forceful man can acquire, no matter

how inexperienced he may be or how little he may know to begin with about the practical problems of leading men.

The first chapter of that book, "Leadership Can Be Learned," also states that, "Some leaders have an instinctive knowledge of human nature. These are the natural leaders. To the others but two roads to leadership are available: experience and study." A concerted effort to master leadership skills can surpass natural ability alone.

The emotional component of leadership is often the most difficult to master; like Spock, many managers find emotions incomprehensible. Tom Peters refers to the demographic group WOM (White Older Males) as a group that has had a difficult time adjusting to the new workplace. For decades, Taylor and MBA schools held out the promise that business was fundamentally rational—a predictable and sensible world needing only enough information to be *sure*. This promise was bolstered by countless spreadsheets and investment strategies. By contrast, emotions were viewed as slippery, something to be indulged in at home . . . as an option.

Leaders, however, need to be aware of the emotional impact they have on the people around them and subordinate to them. While a leader might make a rational decision to do something (e.g., "I will go to visit that department"), the visit will provoke an emotional reaction and a memory. Unintended consequences always accompany rational decisions.

Balance can be elusive. Decisions must make the trip from the head to the heart in order to be believable. At the same time, decisions must make the trip from the heart to the head in order to be useful. Knowing that something difficult is the right thing to do and the will to forge ahead are two different things, just as feeling good about what you are doing is a separate consideration from deciding the right thing to do.

As with leadership, quality is made up of both emotional and rational components. When efforts to instill quality have died, their demise is usually due to senior management's failure to recognize and incorporate a balance of rational and emotional components. It is impossible to win employees' loyalty and redouble dedication through entertaining activities or exhortations in the absence of a coherent long-term philosophy and structure. It is equally impossible to make significant gains by relying on stacks of charts and rampant reengineering without regard for the human response. When the need to recognize employees' successes is dismissed with "We don't have to say thank you. They were just doing their jobs," quality is doomed.

A LIFETIME OF LEADERSHIP

Learning leadership is an ongoing process. Consciously or unconsciously, thoughts and ideas are continually integrated with responses and instincts into leadership practice. Reason and emotion—the mix varies from person to person and from day to day within each person. The results can be either positive or negative. It is just as easy to ingrain poor leadership habits as it is to incorporate good ones.

The most efficient way to precipitate learning is practice. Leadership skills improve through study and experience. Reading lays the foundation; use develops proficiency. The basics in the following chapters are presented as a prelude to action. Any self-improvement quest benefits by mastering—or reviewing—the basics. Reading them is like the warm-up before exercise: stretch, reach for your toes, be sure you are ready for the long run ahead. Otherwise, you might create more problems than you solve. Then get on with it.

It may help to think of change as coming from the outside in, rather than from the inside out. Internal conviction can follow action. Does that mean that insincerity can carry the day? (Or as broadcaster and journalist Daniel Schorr once opined, "Sincerity. If you can fake it, you've got it made.") Blatant insincerity will show through, but as long as behavior is in the context of an overall effort, even a halfhearted try is likely to be accepted. Practice of provably effective behavior can come before emotional acceptance; well-informed content, intellectually accepted, can precede total commitment and personal integration.

An example of commitment following action comes from the Ragsdale-Fuller Pontiac-Cadillac dealership in Auburn, Massachusetts, where decorous signs state DON'T FORGET THE TEN FOOT RULE. If you ask a salesperson, he or she will tell you (somewhat sheepishly) that it is the boss's rule that, "If you come within ten feet of someone, you should greet them." It's an artificial device. Technically, it means nothing. But customers at Ragsdale-Fuller always feel as if the staff are

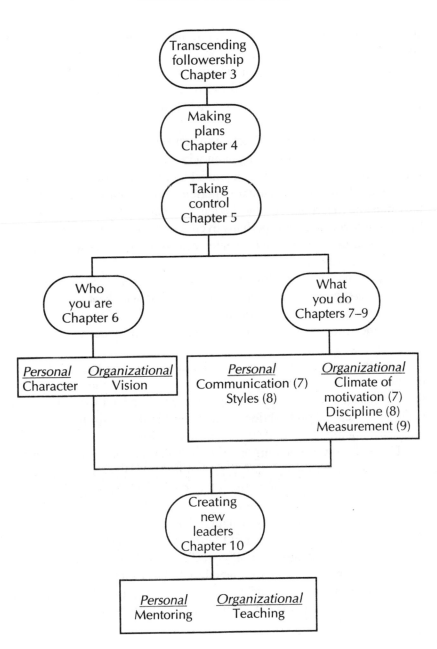

Figure 1.1. A plan for creating new leaders

glad that they are there, and the staff have found that people smile back—making it well worth the effort of remembering the ten foot rule. It wouldn't work if it wasn't in the context of a larger effort. Ragsdale-Fuller's staff is well trained and the receptionist sits right next to the front door, welcoming everyone with a "How can we help you?" and an offer of coffee.

To use an old phrase, "Practice makes perfect." The practice analogy is particularly apt. Learning cannot be limited to theory; experience is imperative. No one becomes a pianist by reading about it. As lessons accumulate both from personal experience and from outside sources, they must be incorporated into the leader's personal style. No one will be a legendary leader, nor perhaps even a particularly good one, on his or her first effort, but without repeated efforts, proficiency and commitment never develop.

Leaders who are working on their own leadership skills are encouraging leadership in others. It's as simple as that. The best way to teach leadership is by conscious, informed example. If the goal is to create other leaders, the only way to accomplish it is to model the behavior desired.

Too few organizations devote time and money to helping leaders develop their own leadership skills, much less make the transition to their responsibilities as mentors and teachers. Leadership skills, when taught, rely heavily on traditional corporate paradigms for their inspiration, teaching old skills to deal with new situations.

This book gives you corporate models that are based on an up-to-date assessment of the relationship between followers and leaders. It also integrates a noncorporate model, one in which developing leaders at every level has always been recognized as crucial to the success of the organization: the military. Chapter 2 introduces this underutilized resource, providing a realistic (and perhaps surprising) fund of leadership theory and practice. A look at the flowchart in Figure 1.1 illustrates the continuum from followership to the highest expression of leadership: creating new leaders. This is the journey every modern leader must make and it is the pathway through this book.

2

BENCHMARKING IN CAMOUFLAGE

Quality theory teaches organizations to look beyond surface differences for genuine similarities and to borrow, borrow, borrow. When Baldrige Award–winner Xerox wanted to improve its customer service, it benchmarked its telephone operation against that of L.L. Bean, even though the two companies had vastly different business operations. When the dairy industry wanted to refine its method of transporting milk, it looked at the American Red Cross's procedures for transporting blood. Corporate America has long been aware that the military offers a rich legacy of leadership theory and practice, but efforts to tap *its* lessons have met with mixed results.

Previous attempts to present the military as a model for civilian businesses have drawn primarily from grand strategy, often including some statement along the lines of "Business is like war!" Nonsense. The military's mission is a unique one and the analogy is weak. Anyone who has been in a war knows that there are vast differences between competition and combat. Business is not like war and won't be until one competitor calls in an air strike on another's reception area, there are shrapnel divots in the walls of the executive dining room, and casualty totals are a regular part of the annual corporate report. Worse, implying that businesses exist in a perpetual state of emergency too often gives poor leaders an excuse for continuing questionable leadership behavior.

Even respectable efforts such as Sun Tzu's classic *The Art of War* and William Peacock's *Corporate Combat* focus on the strategies leaders use to overcome adversaries. While some incontestable similarities do exist between military and civilian leadership at the strategic level,

17

the more genuine and intriguing similarities occur at the day-to-day level. *The Art of War* assumes that loyal and competent forces are available to defeat opponents; little is said about how to win that loyalty and create that competence. This is where military leadership has the most to contribute.

The salient characteristic of military leadership is that its principles, values, and techniques have been publicly debated, refined, and recorded for over twenty-five hundred years. As a result, the military has measurable success in converting leadership concepts into programs that produce effective leaders. It does so consistently, taking even eighteen-year-olds and transforming them into decision makers. Fortunately, precisely because it has systematically compiled a historical record of successes and failures, the military's "secrets" for creating leadership are easily accessible.

This chapter examines the military as an ideal benchmark for developing leadership skills. It is divided into three parts. The next two sections are written specifically for readers who feel a certain ambivalence about using the military as a source for interpersonal skills. The middle sections lay out the philosophy of military leadership and take a look at the structure that supports it. The closing sections examine the points at which quality theory and military leadership theory coincide.

OVERCOMING AMBIVALENCE

From a historical perspective, Americans have always been ambivalent about the military. The first president, George Washington, was a general; the third, Thomas Jefferson, was openly hostile to standing armies. Before attaining the presidency, Jefferson fumed about the increase in enlistments to fight the Indian campaigns:

> ... [E]very rag of an Indian depredation will ... serve as a ground to raise troops with those who think a standing army and a public debt necessary for the happiness of the United States and we shall never be permitted to get rid of either.

Early in his tenure of office, the Regular Army numbered 248 officers, 9 cadets, and 3,794 men, but Jefferson objected to even these modest numbers on both financial and philosophical grounds, preferring to rely on militias and citizen-soldiers until war was actually declared. Of the distinction between the civil and the military, he said that it was "for the happiness of both to obliterate [it]."

Ambivalence about the military has also pervaded the last half of the twentieth century. From World War II to the Korean War, from the conflict in Vietnam to the Gulf War, Americans ran the gauntlet from positive to negative perceptions of the military and back again. In a 1994 Harris poll, the military was rated as the most trusted institution in America, which was not to say that cynicism about the military disappeared. Applying the adjective militaristic to someone or something is still not a compliment.

Among the barriers to using the military as a resource for personal leadership skills are the stereotypes that "military leadership" and "authoritarianism" are synonymous and that "military types" are somehow different from "civilians." Neither is the case, but it is easy to see how both stereotypes came into existence. Another distancing factor comes from the practice of using exclusively male pronouns in virtually all military manuals. Given that women have only recently appeared at all levels of the command structure, this reflects a historical reality. Some recently published military manuals do employ inclusive, gender-neutral language, but the fact remains that the vast body of literature is stuck with biased language that obscures its validity.

Popular perception of the military comes primarily from four sources: personal experience, "sea stories," the popular media, and historical texts. Unfortunately, personal experience is not as universal as it once was. Where experience does exist, however, leaders have adapted military techniques to a civilian setting. Fred Smith, CEO of FedEx and a former marine, based his company's Guaranteed Fair Treatment on the Marine Corps' Request Mast, which enables service personnel to ask to talk over a matter with a senior officer.

At several points in our nation's history, suggesting the military as a resource for leadership would have been redundant. For veterans, military leadership traits and knowledge were a part of their tool bag when they joined the civilian workforce. If the execution of those principles slipped over the years, it could be traced in large part to ignoring one of the military's guiding rules: periodic leadership schooling is necessary as a person progresses through the ranks. Today, the common experience of young men and women entering the workplace is a tour of duty not at Fort Swampy, but at the local McDonald's. Ray Kroc, McDonald's founder, set the stage for a giant that spans the globe, but the leadership lessons picked up by osmosis in one or two summers at a fast-food emporium are not a match for those gained from formal instruction during two to twenty years spent in the military.

Current lack of military experience is so commonplace that Phil Strub, the Pentagon's film liaison, told *USA Today* reporter Andy Seller, "Today, we have to assume that the audience knows *nothing* about the military." As a result, the Department of Defense has changed its criteria for cooperating with filmmakers. Although the Pentagon tolerated portrayals of villainous military men in films such as *Top Gun* and *The Sands of Iwo Jima* when the audience had sufficient familiarity with the military to recognize that the figures represented were the exception rather than the rule, these films would no longer receive Department of Defense support if they were made today.

A prevalent secondhand source of opinions about the military are stories told by veterans, referred to in the navy as sea stories. These involve amazingly inept (or merely odd) officers and senior enlisted men (and, now, women) as central characters. As a rule, these stories are pretty amusing ("Remember the general who put all the horses on a diet after he passed the corral and decided they were too fat?"), but the cumulative effect can be somewhat misleading. Stories are told about the unusual, not the usual. The unexpected is what makes any story interesting and worth repeating for the umpteenth time.

To the detriment of the military's reputation, the single most unusual experience anyone has in the military is boot camp; and while "My drill instructor once put us in the dumpster and forgot us" will be greeted with hoots of laughter by fellow vets, the majority of uninitiated civilians, without experience or context, can only respond with numbed disbelief. Boot camp is, admittedly, where some—but not all—leadership principles are put on hiatus in the interest of time. The military accepts boot camp as a special situation in which the paramount requirement is to integrate individual identities into a new culture. If drill instructors didn't actually invent the concept of "tough love," they have raised it to an art form—and all to a good purpose. Accelerated acclimatization is essential because the military's turnover rate is kept intentionally high, both to keep the organization young and to preserve the enthusiasm and the questioning so important to its vitality.

Leadership training does, however, take place at boot camp. Both the recruits and their drill instructors (DIs) are required to master all the theoretical aspects of leadership, even when all its facets are not consistently modeled. Abuse of power is not tolerated and DIs who cross carefully defined lines are punished. As of a few years ago, for example, the fine at Marine Corps boot camps was $50 per profane word for swearing at or in front of recruits.

As for the popular media's contribution to stereotypes, the greatest barrier to understanding what actually happens in a military situation is simply time and space. There just isn't enough of either in a movie, or even in most books, not to mention a news blurb, to paint a complete picture of the relationship between a military leader and his or her followers. To be truthful, the act of leadership that stirs the observer's blood is almost always an authoritarian one. Authors have no interest in describing or portraying the hundreds of acts of participative and delegative leadership that build a strong relationship between a military leader and subordinates. Those acts aren't exciting. In fact, taken one at a time, they aren't even particularly interesting. But they are vital.

Imagine John Wayne (or the Sheen of your choice) standing at the bottom of a hill with a group of warriors gathered around him. "Follow me!" he cries and races up the hill to glory, followed by an inspired and dedicated band. That is unquestionably an act of authoritarian leadership. And it is thrilling to watch or to read about. "Follow me" commands obedience, however, only when there is a bond between the leader and the led, a bond forged by other types of leadership. If followers do not believe in what the leader is fighting for, if they don't trust in the leader's judgment and expertise, if they are not a cohesive unit, then the leader is going to be very lonely on that heroic charge.

There will always be tension between the press and the military, mainly because both consider themselves guardians of the rights of a free society. They do, however, share a number of values, among which are an appreciation of strong character and effective leadership. On August 25, 1995, *USA Today* printed a story about a stewardess as a follow-up to an airplane crash in which an amazing twenty-four out of twenty-nine people survived. It read in part:

> Passengers credit [Robin] Fech, 37, with keeping them from panicking when the plane faltered after it lost a left engine.
> They say her demeanor was that of a drill sergeant as she

tested passengers one by one to make sure they knew how to brace themselves and calmly pointed out the exits as the crippled plane lurched toward a hayfield.

"I think because of her, everyone in the cabin was calm," said Air Force Maj. Chuck LeMay, a passenger. "There was no screaming, no yelling."

In the nine minutes between a loud bang and the crash itself, Fech never raised her voice and made all the passengers demonstrate the doubled-over crash position, correcting them when they did it wrong, he said.

As the turboprop grazed treetops and sharply descended, she pointed out exits. She told some passengers to switch seats so the most able-bodied were near the emergency exits.

After the crash, Fech, her face bloodied, pulled passengers from the wreckage, and she didn't sit down until the emergency workers arrived, LeMay said.

"She just did an absolutely fantastic job."

Comparing Ms. Fech's behavior to that of a drill sergeant in this context was clearly meant as a compliment. Even more interesting, the comment was accurate: She trained the people who were her responsibility, she tested their knowledge, she exercised judgment to keep them safe (moving the able-bodied), she modeled the behavior she wanted (keeping passengers calm and alert through her example and the force of her own personality), and she stayed at the job until it was done. In short, for that period of time she was the epitome of a drill sergeant.

AMERICA'S FINEST CITIZEN-SOLDIER

Historical texts have often been kinder to the military than accounts written contemporaneously, and one notable fact accounts for this phenomenon: There have been no military coups in U.S. history. The Constitution spells out a relationship between the civilian and the military branches of the government in which the civilian branch has the ultimate authority. The military has always respected that authority. When General Douglas A. MacArthur disagreed with President Harry

S. Truman during the Korean War, Truman dismissed him in 1951, and despite mass public demonstrations when MacArthur returned to the United States, there was no constitutional crisis.

While skepticism about the military has served the United States well, the need for some kind of effective fighting force has never been in question. Admiration for the citizen-soldier is embedded in the nation's psyche. The Minuteman is the ultimate symbol of the Revolutionary War, and no figure better personifies the idea of the citizen-soldier than Civil War General Joshua Lawrence Chamberlain. He embodied the Jeffersonian ideal: He was indifferent to the military in times of peace, but when he heard his nation's call, he answered and he served and, when the war was over, he went back to civilian life. Chamberlain was an entrepreneur, a teacher, a president of Bowdoin College, and a governor of Maine in times of peace, and a military man when the need arose. Any discussion of leadership drawing even in part on U.S. military experience is incomplete without knowing something about his background and character. The broad strokes of his military career appear here, and he will be referred to in other chapters of this book as well.

Until the Civil War began, General Chamberlain was a professor of rhetoric at Bowdoin College in Maine—an occupation that could qualify for entry into a thesaurus as an alternative phrase for civilian. He believed passionately in the rights of all men to be free, although he had actually seen very few black people in his life; and he believed that the Union should be preserved. Early in the war years, he volunteered to help organize a regiment of men from Maine to meet the most recent quota sent to the state from the federal government.

Such was the system at the time that he was offered the command of the regiment by the governor of the state. Chamberlain turned the governor down, saying that he did not know enough about the military, either as a leader or as a technical expert, to merit the position of commanding officer; he was appointed second-in-command as executive officer. Once the regiment was formed, it joined the Union army, and Chamberlain set himself a course of study. He organized classes using West Point graduates and other career officers as instructors, and then attended the classes. On his own, he pored over every book he could lay his hands on about any aspect of the military. Equally important, he got to know his men and their capabilities, both as individuals and as a unit.

By the time the Battle of Gettysburg took place, Chamberlain was a colonel and the commanding officer of the 20th Maine Regiment. As luck would have it, his unit was given responsibility for the far left flank of the Union line—a position that Chamberlain, thanks to his studies, immediately assessed as both crucial and vulnerable. Between attacks by the Southern forces, he gave the command for his men to execute a sideward shift of troops to better protect their flank, a difficult maneuver under the best of circumstances. Because of the training he had given his men and because of their trust in him and his judgment, the Maine soldiers took up their new location quickly and met the next attack. Without this successful tactic, historians feel, the Confederate forces would have had a very real opportunity to overrun Chamberlain's unit and perhaps endanger the entire Union position. When the unit was low on bullets, Chamberlain instructed the men to fix bayonets and charge. This they did, breaking the back of the Confederate offensive in their area.

Chamberlain's strategic acumen was matched by personal bravery. At the Battle of Quaker Road in Virginia on March 29, 1865, he displayed heroism that defies belief. Recently promoted to general, Chamberlain (the only recipient of an on-the-field-of-battle promotion to general in the Union army during the entire war) was recovering from earlier wounds when the action occurred. As reported in the Army's *Leadership Manual (FM 22-100):*

... [A] bullet passed through the large muscle of his horse's neck [the horse was also recovering from wounds suffered while carrying Chamberlain into a previous battle], hit a metal mirror in his shirt pocket, penetrated the skin, followed his ribs around to his back, and came out the other side of his coat [with enough force, it was reported, that it knocked another man off his horse]. Horse and rider slumped, bleeding profusely.

When he regained consciousness, Chamberlain saw the entire right of his attacking brigade retreating, about to panic. Hat gone, blood all over his chest and head, he spurred his bleeding horse to the center of the retreating troops—ordering them to turn and attack. Awed by his courage and will, they attacked and won the battle.

After the tide of battle had been turned, Chamberlain, riding across the rear of his troops, was applauded by both Union and Confederate soldiers.

Chamberlain expected a great deal, both of himself and his troops. And he understood men. Chamberlain was quoted in Alice Trulock's biography entitled *In the Hands of Providence:*

> But, as a rule, men stand up from one motive or another—simple manhood, force of discipline, pride, love, or bond of comradeship—"Here is Bill; I will go or stay where he does." And an officer is so absorbed by the sense of responsibility for his men, for his cause, or for his fight that the thought of personal peril has no place whatever in governing his actions. The instinct to seek safety is overcome by the instinct of honor.

During the Civil War, General Daniel E. Sickles said to Chamberlain, "General, you have the soul of a lion and the heart of a woman." His sensitivity to the emotions of others was demonstrated at Appomattox, where he was personally chosen by General Ulysses S. Grant to receive the surrender of the Confederate army forces in the area. Trulock's biography sets the scene:

> At the surrender, Chamberlain saw the once great Confederate Army, dejected in defeat, starting to march past his division. Feeling deep respect for the great Confederate soldiers, Chamberlain shocked the world by ordering his division to present arms [thus, offering a salute to his defeated enemy]. This gesture of human compassion sparked pride and an answering respect from the Confederates. Those who were there thought Chamberlain's gesture a fitting end to the tragic struggle to save the Union.

Chamberlain's explanation for his action was "Honor facing honor."

There is no question that Chamberlain was a extraordinary man who brought personal attributes of unusual strength to the task. Acting on a conscious decision, he learned to be both a master tactician and one of the finest leaders in military history. His exploits and triumphs, his relationship with his men, his dedication to a cause in which he believed, and his continual self-improvement can serve as examples for leaders in any line of endeavor. An army manual on leadership states simply:

> We can develop leaders like Joshua Chamberlain in our schools and in our units. *You* can become this kind of leader, and you can teach your subordinates to be this kind of leader. This is your challenge and responsibility.

THE BASIS OF MILITARY LEADERSHIP

"You do realize, sir, that leadership is all about caring." It wasn't a question; it was a definitive statement made by Gunnery Sergeant William E. Hazelwood, who at the time had responsibility for the leadership instruction at the Drill Instructor School, Marine Corps Recruit Depot, San Diego, California. It was the first thing he said in response to a request from one of the authors of this book to talk about leadership and how it is taught at the school. The straightforward phrasing and the sincerity behind it go a long way toward explaining why military leadership theory is a valuable resource for nonmilitary men and women aspiring to be leaders.

The military nurtures the connection between caring and action in many ways. It tells stories establishing a standard for compassion, even on the battlefield, as this description of an action by General Joshua Chamberlain during the battle of Gettysburg demonstrates:

> In hard-hit Company H, Chamberlain found the recumbent form of Private George Washington Buck. He had a gaping chest wound, and the flowing blood was fast draining his life away. In winter camp at Stoneham's Switch [before Chamberlain had assumed command] the young soldier had been unjustly reduced to the ranks from sergeant on the word of a bullying quartermaster. As his colonel bent down to him, Buck's face brightened, and he whispered a request that his mother know he had not died a coward. Thinking of a way to right the wrong done Buck and to recognize his bravery too,

Chamberlain immediately promoted him again to sergeant for his "noble courage on the field of Gettysburg." The boy, only twenty-one, died knowing he had been exonerated, and his honor restored.

One of the strongest recognitions of the importance of caring is reflected in the highest honor given to any member of the military: the Congressional Medal of Honor. The medal is almost always bestowed for acts of heroism beyond rational explanation. Jumping on a grenade to save the lives of others and dying in the process is not a rational act; it is a gesture of pure love.

Building a cohesive unit is another act of caring. Consider the following excerpt from a Marine Corps document, "Band of Brothers":

- All Marines are entitled to dignity and respect as individuals, but must abide by common standards established by proper authority.
- A Marine should contribute 100% of their abilities to the unit's mission. Any less effort by an individual passes the buck to someone else.
- A unit, regardless of size, is a disciplined family structure, with similar relationships based on mutual respect among members.
- A blending of separate cultures, varying educational levels, and different social backgrounds is possible in an unselfish atmosphere of common goals, aspirations, and mutual understanding.
- Every Marine deserves job satisfaction, equal consideration and recognition of his accomplishments.
- Knowing your fellow Marine well enables you to learn to look at things "through his eyes" as well as your own.

The application of these precepts to a nonmilitary unit may be as simple as substituting "associates of Firm XYZ" for "Marines." That would be a starting place for a fruitful discussion of organizational ethics, ethos, and expectations, and no leadership training is complete until such a discussion takes place.

There is no doubt that the degree of emotional closeness implied in the foregoing excerpt is rare in a nonmilitary organization. To be honest, it is not always achieved in military units; for the most part, however, military leadership promotes intimacy to a greater degree than its civilian counterpart. This intimacy comes relatively easily in times of war; in times of peace, it must be consciously pursued.

American military units located outside the United States have at least two advantages for establishing cohesion: (1) units are usually stationed in a small physical setting, and (2) there is a decreased number of competitors for the attention of members of the "military family," as many of these tours are unaccompanied by spouses and children. An *in loco parentis* aspect to the relationship is added by the age of the junior enlisted men and women—and the very real possibility that many of them are away from home for the first time. It is also not unusual for a young newly commissioned second lieutenant to counsel an older noncommissioned or enlisted man or woman on finances or personal problems. Both leader and led tend to know a great deal more about one another in military organizations than in civilian ones.

As important as it is to care about troops, no one denies that the military has a higher priority: accomplishing the mission. One veteran of Vietnam and a variety of peacetime assignments recalls that the first time he heard about leadership priorities, he reasoned, "Well, that must be the difference between the military and the civilian worlds. In the civilian world, taking care of the employees must be number one, while accomplishing the mission is number two." Now retired from the military and the veteran of over a decade in business, he believes that taking care of people often does not even make the list in the civilian world: "Even worse, in a lot of organizations, the sole mission is to make the owner rich—that's a tough one to win emotional commitment to. The strange thing is that those companies in which taking care of their own people really is an obvious priority—be it number one or a strong number two—are, by and large, doing very well."

Is it ethical to place taking care of the troops second to accomplishing the mission? In combat, winning the war (or enforcing the peace) is the military's job—even if it means placing lives in jeopardy. In times of peace, lives are never knowingly placed at risk. Perhaps the most succinct explanation of the interplay of the priorities for a military leader was given by one of the leadership instructors at the DI school:

"A small unit leader's job in the Marine Corps is to prepare subordinates to fight and to lead them into the fight—and to bring them back."

In war or in peace, leadership principles are the same, but the crucible of a battlefield serves to remind everyone of the essential nature of leadership. In the words of John Adair, "The *underlying* principles of leadership are the same [in combat and in peace]. Indeed it could be argued that the crisis element of war serves to reveal the essential nature of leadership more clearly." As one of the DIs said in response to a question about the relationship between a leader and the led in combat, "There needs to be candor, honesty, simplicity. There can be no white lies, no games. The battlefield demands honesty."

RELATIONSHIPS BETWEEN THE RANKS

There will always be a rank structure in the military and a corporate structure in the civilian world, just as there will always be strategic and personal leadership. And there will always be choices about how that structure is invoked. The pre–World War II book *Leadership for American Army Leaders* by Colonel Edward L. Munson Jr. discussed some of the choices facing military officers:

The wise officer will set a middle course, a common-sense course. At one extreme, unfortunately, is the unreasonable martinet, imbued with exaggerated ideas of rank and authority, using his conferred status to impress subordinates with his military and social superiority, assuming a caste which has no place in American institutions. At the other extreme is the officer who neglects or ignores the distinction that prevails in all armies between officers and men, the officer who permits familiarities that, unless he is an extraordinary leader indeed, will destroy his prestige. Enlisted men understand and appreciate the reasons and the necessities which generally prevent undue familiarity, and, except in the most unusual cases, have little but contempt for the officer who, forgetting his own place, deliberately crosses the dividing line into *their* terrain.

Executives set the tone. In the military, that tone is expected to be one of mutual respect. Colonel Munson cautions, "The inexperienced often feel that politeness in a military leader implies softness; or worse, that from a subordinate it indicates bootlicking. Nothing is farther from the truth. Real courtesy is simply common everyday civility."

As quoted in *Love 'Em and Lead 'Em* by retired army colonel Paul Malone III, General of the Army and President Dwight D. Eisenhower had this to say on the topic of leadership: "I happen to *know* a little about leadership. . . . You do not *lead* by hitting people over the head. Any damn fool can do that, but it's usually called 'assault' and not 'leadership.' . . . I'll tell you what leadership is. It's *persuasion* and *conciliation*—and *education*—and *patience*."

The previous chapter referred to quality as something you do *with* someone—not *to* or *for* someone. In the military, the great leaders subscribe to the same philosophy. Consider a quote from a gentleman who was in the army during World War II and subsequently wrote extensively on General George S. Patton: "No man served under General Patton, he was always serving with us."

The glue that holds units together is mutual trust. There is always the possibility that the senior person is going to have to order the junior person to go into harm's way someday—perhaps never to return. Senior personnel trust junior personnel to obey those orders, and junior personnel trust that their lives will not be jeopardized unnecessarily. That mutual recognition of the possibilities does not bar respect, or even friendship, between the ranks.

Mutuality and trust do not preclude authoritarian action in times of emergency. In the military, subordinates know when they are at war and when they aren't. The same is true in the civilian world: People know when there is a crisis afoot. If they don't know, then the leader has failed in his or her responsibility to communicate. If subordinates—military or civilian—do not think there is a crisis meriting an autocratic decision, their reaction is not going to fit what the boss believes is appropriate. Crying "wolf" does not enhance a senior person's position. The rule of thumb is simple: If everything is a crisis, nothing is a crisis.

Civilians who depend on the stereotype of the martinet to explain leadership in the military see the military as having a natural advantage, according to Adair:

Some managers assume that leadership is "easier" in the armed services than in industry. "We have no Queen's Regulations," lamented one. But this is an unrealistic assessment. In fact there are advantages and disadvantages as far as leadership is concerned in both fields. For example, the serviceman rarely sees an "end product" to his labours; it is often difficult for him to regard his tasks in tangible, worthwhile or profitable terms, a factor which may contribute to a lack of enthusiasm on the job.

There is no doubt that the military does have some advantages, but they are not what the majority of civilians imagine, nor are these advantages confined to the military environment. In the military, the basic mission is clear: to fight the nation's battles in order to keep the country independent and its people free of foreign domination. As part of this mission, the military consciously seeks and cherishes camaraderie. Ironically, just as the civilian workforce was being separated from its managers by Frederick Taylor's dogma, the military developed a tremendous appreciation of the interconnectedness of the ranks. Describing the impact of the War to End All Wars, a Marine Corps manual states, "World War I made a great change in the relations between officers and enlisted men in the military services. A spirit of comradeship and brotherhood in arms started in training camps and on battlefields."

Overall, however, the military's advantages are cosmetic. Civilians can and do build esprit de corps; compelling mission statements abound. What is more striking are the similarities between civilian and military organizations. Three separate master's degree theses written at the United States Naval Postgraduate School in Monterey, California, used *In Search of Excellence,* the enormously popular book by Tom Peters and Bob Waterman, as a jumping-off point. Peters, a navy veteran, convinced American businesspeople that they could compete successfully with the Japanese or anyone else. The book drives home leadership lessons and principles, both implicitly and explicitly. Using Peters's and Waterman's characteristics of excellent businesses, the theses looked for differences and similarities in military units. One thesis addressed "Excellence in the Surface Navy," while the other two looked at army units and air force units.

Not surprisingly, the fit was nearly perfect. What set nonmilitary organizations apart from their competitors and peers also worked in military organizations. Effective leadership in both organizations had a great deal in common. The navy report included this assessment:

> The phrase we heard over and over again when an officer or an enlisted man was asked to describe his captain was, "He acts like a human being and he treats others as human beings." One got the feeling listening to these junior officers and enlisted men describe their captains as human beings, that this was one of the highest compliments that a junior could bestow on his senior.

MAKING LEADERSHIP HAPPEN

Civilian organizations often fail to provide leadership training. The database for the influential book *Leaders—The Strategies for Taking Charge* by Warren Bennis and Burt Nanus was a series of interviews with ninety recognized leaders. Not only did *none* of the ninety interviewees have any military training, none is quoted as claiming to have had any formal leadership training whatsoever. By inference, these powerful and successful people came to be called leaders by dint of their own will, knowledge, natural ability, and self-education in the art and science of leadership. The military has long known that it cannot settle for a random selection process for its leaders. Waiting for leaders to develop naturally is out of the question when the penalty for error is swift and permanent, as it is in combat. The military schedules leadership training for everyone, and in today's rapidly moving nanosecond business world, businesses would do well to do the same.

Leadership training—formal and informal—consciously pursued and spread throughout a civilian organization does not guarantee financial success any more than leadership training in the military guarantees success on the battlefield. What it does—in both cases—is raise the odds of success to a point worth betting on. A leadership void is insupportable in either a military unit or a business division. Training leaders is the military's third priority. According to General Carl E. Mundy Jr., former commandant of the Marine Corps, "The Commandant of the

Marine Corps is directly responsible to the Secretary of the Navy for establishing and maintaining leadership standards and conducting leadership training within the Marine Corps." This responsibility is not traditionally spelled out for CEOs.

To ensure a continuous supply of leaders, leadership training is an ongoing part of the military experience. Training falls into four categories, two formal, two informal. Leadership courses and evaluations, the two formal approaches, are systematically employed. Informally, personnel receive mentoring and are expected to learn from their experiences. In addition, leadership is always on the list of possible topics when a group of military folks sit down to talk—even if it is only to criticize the lack of it in a senior.

Service members combine attendance at schools with correspondence courses to sharpen leadership skills. All personnel receive formal leadership training lasting anywhere from three days to six months (or longer) with every second or third promotion, not counting the leadership component of technical schools. In technical schools, the odds are good that an individual will hold a leadership billet and receive an evaluation of her or his performance. Correspondence courses supplement live courses on leadership. Facts are spelled out, emotions identified and described, and mnemonics by the hatful offered. A central precept in correspondence courses and regular classroom sessions is that study is the prelude to action.

The military's promotion system is advantageous for the military in general, if not always for particular individuals. The system is strictly "up or out." As a person moves from place to place and unit to unit, evaluations are collected at the service headquarters in the Washington, D.C., area. Every personal evaluation has a leadership segment. As a rule, service members are evaluated—and, hopefully, counseled—on their leadership abilities at least twice a year. Promotion boards consider an individual's track record, depending on the person's rank and number of years of service. One doesn't apply for promotion; when a person has the appropriate number of years in rank, his or her record is automatically put into the to-be-considered pile. Exact procedures vary, but the baseline policy is that if a person is passed over for promotion two successive years, they have no choice but to get out of the service. The system isn't perfect, but it serves to keep capable people moving up the ladder and to prevent the military from having to put up with a large number of people who are content at their current rank, wanting nothing more than to live and let live. Not surprisingly, the selection percentage drops at each successively higher rank.

Another advantage that the military has in nurturing leadership talent is a by-product of its size and its habit of moving its people from place to place with regularity: No one need fear that mentoring will lead to subordinates bumping the mentor out of the organization and into the breadline. A far-away promotion board makes promotion decisions, and an equally distant figure makes decisions on where personnel will be sent. Seniors are not directly replaced by up-and-coming subordinates.

Writing in the Autumn 1990 issue of *Organizational Dynamics*, Jay Conger pointed out how sensitive the issue of mentoring can be:

> ... [I]t is difficult for others with leadership potential to develop in the shadow of such [strong] leaders. For while they may actively coach their subordinates, I suspect that it is extremely difficult for them to develop others to be leaders of equal power. Leaders simply enjoy the limelight too much to share it so when they ultimately depart, a leadership vacuum is created.

Military leaders are free to train and mentor others without fearing that they are setting themselves up for cutthroat competition.

The military takes the responsibility to mentor seriously. Rear Admiral William Leahy viewed developing subordinates pragmatically: "You may be the boss, but you're only as good as the people that work for you." Retired Captain Thomas Osborne, who served with Admiral Leahy, calls him "that rare kind of leader who lets the men and women that work for him, and put their life on the line every day, receive the recognition."

Mentoring rounds out empowerment in that it not only grants authority to accomplish tasks as appropriate, but also encourages organizational juniors to seek further authority and become leaders in their own right. Mentoring supplements training, ensuring that juniors are prepared to act as effective leaders. Neither authority nor responsibility can simply be dumped on a subordinate. Technical knowledge and leadership skills must be both taught and guided.

In order to lead and let lead, military leaders have developed a degree of tolerance for error. No aspiring leader is going to get everything right the first time. Mistakes are going to be made. The goal is to ensure (1) that no long-term damage is done to the unit, (2) that any stumbles constitute stumbling forward, and (3) that learning situations really do yield lessons. This is what makes mentoring overwhelmingly important. Senior leaders cannot and do not assume that a subordinate understands why things didn't work out; left to his or her own devices, his or her next guess might be even worse. After all, if a subordinate already knew a better way to do it, she or he would have done it that way in the first place.

Mentoring takes an unusual twist in the military: Enlisted personnel, technically junior, act as mentors to young officers. Many a dewy-eyed twenty-two-year-old has graduated from ROTC or officer candidate school with shiny gold lieutenant (or ensign) bars and a sterling piece of advice: Find an NCO (a noncommissioned officer) and *learn everything you can about leadership*. As one sergeant major cautioned his newly commissioned son, "Today, you pin on your rank. In five years, you'll really be an officer." Older, experienced, accustomed to dealing with troops, the NCO ranks are the backbone of the military in a way that middle management in corporate America is not.

Experience is the final element of leadership training. The military is basically a young organization. Careers over twenty years are the exception, not the rule. As a result, very young people are often given a great deal of responsibility: Twenty-five-year-olds are routinely entrusted with millions of dollars of equipment and hundreds of lives. The Gulf War brought to the national attention dozens of stories about young military leaders taking on enormous responsibility and the corresponding authority and distinguishing themselves in the process.

MILITARY LEADERSHIP AND QUALITY

Evaluating military leadership theory using the criteria developed during the Quality Revolution illustrates a remarkable overlap. One characteristic of military leadership has already been alluded to in this chapter: documentation. Military leadership theory is based on capturing and applying best practices. In this, the military foreshadows one of the fundamental principles of quality improvement. A distinguishing attribute of a well-implemented quality process is the presence of accumulated knowledge. Improvements are captured as part of a continual effort to change and grow, distributed throughout the organization, and used either as the platform for incremental improvement or to prepare the organization for a quantum leap in a new direction. Organizations without a quality process may be quite successful, but their improvements are single occurrences that may or may not be recorded, may or may not be spread throughout the organization, may or may not be used as a basis for change, and may or may not be remembered a year—or a week—later.

The reason the military developed its passion for writing things down is obvious: the nature of their mission. In the civilian world, there is the ever-present concern about getting laid off. In the military, the concern is about being laid to rest. This same concern is the basis of leadership at every level. The military recognized long ago that leadership was not confined to that one person at the top of the chain of command. There does, indeed, need to be a leader in charge of the ten thousand (or the hundred thousand), but there also needs to be someone designated and trained as a leader when only two people are present. The Quality Revolution came to the same conclusion.

Where the military appears to fall short in terms of the Quality Revolution is in its old-fashioned hierarchy. At a time when there is so much call for reengineering in the civilian world, when promises to flatten the organization roll back and forth across the industrial landscape, how can the rank structure be defended? Primarily because it is used, for the most part, as a communications channel. "Getting out the word" is considered an extremely important thing to do in the military, a value that quality shares.

The military has always used what quality now calls self-directed work teams. Working under broad directives, these teams give a great deal of power to people who are maturing in both experience and age. Military units are left to their own devices at every level of the chain of command. From a team of recruiters in a town far from headquarters to a behind-enemy-lines special combat team to the captain (often a junior officer fresh out of the Coast Guard Academy) and the crew of a cutter intercepting a ship at sea, small units are expected to make independent decisions with a very real impact.

As the world situation changes, the military is constantly reevaluating the right thing to do, which is a basic tenet of reengineering. The military can no more ignore changes in the broader culture than can a business. In a Marine Corps manual discussing leadership training, the following warning is given:

> While today's young Marine is as effective a fighting man as our country has produced, he is more challenging to lead for two reasons: the complexity of the skill he must be taught in order to perform his duties and his varying values and attitudes, brought about by the rapid social change which has taken place in the past 15 to 20 years.

An example of reengineering done right (and before the term was coined) was the reshaping of the U.S. military from the defeated group that left Vietnam to the professional force that fought the Gulf War. The military, too, faces gender issues, racial tensions, educational deficiencies, drug abuse, budget cuts, and reductions in force (downsizing). Its inescapable advantage is that its people are trained to work in teams to determine how to do things right once the right thing has been defined.

Beyond team independence, exercising individual initiative is also embedded in the military chain of command, especially in the U.S. military. A Marine Corps manual phrases it concisely:

> The objective of military leadership is "the creation and maintenance of an organization which will loyally and willingly accomplish any reasonable task, assigned or indicated, and will initiate suitable action in the absence of orders."

Anyone who doubts that American soldiers will initiate suitable action in the absence of orders should reread the story of the landing at Normandy during World War II. On the fiftieth anniversary of the invasion, news commentators often marveled that the loss of the titular leader of any one unit did nothing to slow the attack. As each man fell, the next senior man stepped forward and assumed command. Decimated units re-formed under men with little rank and less experience and fought their way off the beach, using routes and methods never dreamed of by the planners of the assault. In most units, the nominal title of "the one in charge" went in succession to several people before the day was over. One newsman went so far as to observe that the Germans were incapable of the same flexibility. Trained to wait for orders, they wasted amazing amounts of time as Americans overwhelmed their defenses. Often, when senior officers were killed or wounded, German units became immobilized.

While the accolades were all well deserved, the fact is that the heroic actions so apparent at Normandy were in the tradition of U.S. military leadership. Since the early days of the Revolutionary War, the idea of stepping into the breach, of acting in the best interests of the common cause despite the lack of specific directions, has been a trademark of the American military man and woman. There has always been the "cowboy" in the U.S. military, with the willingness to take the bull by the horns when necessary. Authority equal to responsibility, the key phrase in empowerment, is the basis of military leadership.

Not all suitable actions are dramatic. Under assault and trapped with several others in a room in Grenada, one U.S. Army lieutenant used his phone credit card to place a call to Fort Bragg, North Carolina. The call was patched through to an artillery unit in Grenada, which responded with fire support. That kind of inventiveness has gotten the U.S. military out of a lot of potentially painful situations.

One of the pieces of Marine Corps history that all marines learn early in their enlistment is the story of the commandant of the Marine Corps who left his post in Washington, D.C., and went where the action was. In 1836, Commandant Archibald Henderson sent half of the Marine Corps to the Florida-Georgia area to take part in the war against the Creek and Seminole Indians. The legend is that he simply left a note tacked to his door in the building that is still the office of Marine Corps Headquarters in Washington, D.C. The note read GONE TO FLORIDA TO FIGHT INDIANS. He was gone from June 1836 through June 1837, and the marines he personally led were major contributors to the victories of those campaigns.

Looked at from a modern business point of view, Colonel Henderson's actions are interesting. In mid-1836, he was the appointed leader of the Marine Corps. His office was in D.C., but the main action of his organization and half his people were several hundred miles to the south. What did he do? He went to where the action was, placed himself in danger, and personally led his men into combat. This example of being obviously and personally involved in an organization's biggest challenge echoes a basic tenet of quality theory.

DR. DEMING AND MILITARY
LEADERSHIP THEORY

No one had a greater impact on the Quality Revolution than Dr. W. Edwards Deming. His Fourteen Points are, of course, one of the foundation stones of both the American and the Japanese Quality Revolutions. Consider the analysis of Deming's Fourteen Points published in the *Marine Corps Gazette* as part of an ongoing discussion of the application of quality principles and procedures to the military. The author is a Marine Corps officer named Captain James F. Brownlowe. Before looking at each of the points individually, he states his proposition:

> TQL [Total Quality Leadership, the Department of the Navy's quality process], when applied by the small unit leader, is nothing more than fundamental leadership principles. If we focus on the 14 points of TQM [Total Quality Management] from which TQL is derived, as they apply to the small unit leader, we will see that it is not something new, but a reaffirmation of sound military leadership principles.

Captain Brownlowe's complete article can be found in Appendix A. Excerpts from his analysis of four of Deming's points show how military leadership theory parallels Deming's philosophy:

Constancy of purpose

As successful military leaders, we have instilled in our troops the notion that there is a direction our unit must take to accomplish the mission assigned. Initiative should be encouraged from the bottom up and everyone should know his part of the plan. . . .

Cease dependence on inspection to achieve quality

[E]very small unit leader knows that inspections do not guarantee quality. Pride, trust, training, example, and attitude ensure quality. . . .

Institute leadership

The successful unit leader will not overly supervise his troops and will allow them to perform the tasks they are capable of with minimum supervision. . . .

Eliminate slogans, exhortations, and targets. Eliminate numerical goals

The leader knows that trendy slogans such as "Be all you can be" and "The few, the proud, the Marines" may be great for recruiting posters, but they do little to foster unit morale or mission accomplishment. He knows that the best motivator for his troops is for him to provide them with the best opportunities for success by conducting realistic training, knowing their problem areas, and exhibiting his personal devotion to the unit's success.

The captain concludes his article with this sentence: "The 14 points can be best summarized by three simple lines quoted by Army Maj. C. A. Bach in an address to new officers in 1917: *'Know your men, know your business, know yourself.'* "

Captain Brownlowe is not the only one to find common ground with Deming. A statement by Captain Samuel B. Griffith, USMC, anticipated Deming's oft-repeated statements that 85 percent or more of all quality problems are the fault and responsibility of management, and that workers do the best they can considering the material, education, and management they are given to work with. In northern China in 1937, Captain Griffith observed, "Wars and battles are not lost by private soldiers. They win them, but don't lose them. They are lost by commanders, staffs, and troop leaders, and they are often lost long before they start." Even Napoleon held the opinion, "There are no bad regiments, only bad colonels."

A VISION FOR THE FUTURE

If the first rule of benchmarking is to borrow, borrow, borrow, a succinct vision of leadership is worth borrowing. The United States Coast Guard Academy has devoted a great deal of time and effort to the development of a leadership curriculum for its students. Commander Patrick T. Kelly, chief of the Leadership and Character Development Branch at the academy, led a committee that established the following "Leadership Outcomes":

Upon graduation, midshipmen of the United States Coast Guard Academy shall:

1. Demonstrate understanding and usage of leadership theories when serving in a leadership position.
2. Demonstrate moral and ethical judgment.
3. Demonstrate the ability to direct and develop others.
4. Demonstrate facility in functioning up, down, and across a chain of command.
5. Demonstrate the ability to function as an effective team member.
6. Demonstrate respect for all persons one interacts with as part of one's role and areas of responsibility.
7. Demonstrate professional decision-making ability.
8. Demonstrate professional communication ability.
9. Demonstrate an ability to self assess their leadership ability.
10. Describe a personal framework of leadership that integrates the Core Values of the Coast Guard.

Substitute "Organization XYZ" for "Coast Guard" in the tenth objective and the result is a set of objectives that could serve well for the leadership training program of any organization. Even the core values are applicable. As defined in 1994, they are honor, respect, and devotion to duty. The Coast Guard supports these core values with the "Four C's": character, competence, commitment, and community.

3

BUILDING A STRONG FOUNDATION: FOLLOWERSHIP

Leadership has its complement in followership. The significance of this fact was underscored in a comment by former Speaker of the House Sam Rayburn: "You cannot be a leader, and ask other people to follow you, unless you know how to follow, too."

This should come as no surprise. No one begins as a leader, either in his or her personal life or in the business world. Willingness to guide others is meaningless unless it is accompanied by willingness to learn. Everyone starts as a student of leadership—consciously or unconsciously—or as the object of someone else's leadership efforts. One Marine Corps manual puts it this way:

> To be an effective leader, you must be a good follower and set the example for your Marines. . . . As a young Marine, you spend most of your formative years following and demonstrating signs of leadership. Through your study and in your attempt to abide by the leadership principles, you tend to copy the style or methods used by your past and present leaders. If you, as a follower, could command a combination of good features that you have observed in your leaders, you would be the ultimate leader. . . .

The split between leaders and followers (or between managers and nonmanagers) has never been as tidy as Frederick Taylor and many current observers of the work scene have taught or implied. If "leader" is synonymous with "thinker" or "decision maker," and "follower" with "implementer" or "doer"—what, then, do you call a vice president who has just received specific goals for his or her part of the business plan? Organization charts, indeed, can obscure function. Is the president of the company a leader 100 percent of the time?—not when groups such as boards of directors or customers are considered. Is a nonmanagerial customer service person always a follower?—not when he or she makes an independent decision to solve a customer's complaint. Realistically, everyone in the company has to be prepared for a dual role: sometimes a leader, sometimes a follower.

And while many discussions are limited to a bipolar choice between being a leader and being a follower, there are times when everyone "just pitches in and gets it done": It's called teamwork. At these times, the roles of leader and follower can change so frequently that they're not worth labeling. The benefit of teamwork is that people who are not normally comfortable with being labeled leaders will assume the role whenever their skills are called for as team members.

Everyone is simply a pair of hands some of the time; conversely, the distribution of brains is one per employee. Virtually everyone shifts back and forth between the role of thinker and the role of doer, between being a manager and being one of the managed, between being a leader and being a follower. When New Mexico Senator Jeff Bingaman and his staff wanted to explore the topic of quality, they scheduled a two-day workshop to design procedures for their offices in D.C. For those two days, Senator Bingaman sat in as a member of the class, unavailable for phone calls or meetings. His attendance ensured that everyone else was there; his participation ensured that the workshop was a success. After a second workshop in Taos for the New Mexico staff, the two staffs created a more effective approach to serving their constituency, which they dubbed "Quality con Queso." Literally translated, the phrase means "Quality with Cheese"; more figuratively, it expresses a goal of quality with something extra. Blurring the line between those designated as "leaders" and those lumped under the title of "the led" enables everyone to function at his or her full potential.

GUIDELINES FOR FOLLOWERSHIP

What is not immediately obvious is that effective followership requires skills of its own. The United States Coast Guard Academy considers followership so important that it devotes a full year of its leadership curriculum to the topic. Writing in the U.S. Army journal *Infantry*, Sergeant First Class Michael T. Woodward offered the following opinion:

> [Followership] needs to be nurtured and fostered as leadership has been. Leaders are useless without followers, marginally effective with apathetic followers, and most effective when the followers are as professional in their attitude toward followership as the leaders are about leadership.

Followership is not only a prerequisite to leadership, it is also a continuing role. Exemplary followers demonstrate an ability to become good leaders—while continuing to be good followers.

That being the case, it behooves organizations to train for followership. Ignoring followership could be likened to putting a disproportionate share of a symphony orchestra's training budget into locating and cultivating splendid first chairs for each section. The first chairs may well be the finest in the land, but if minimal time and effort have been invested in recruiting, understanding, and training the rest of the musicians, the result ain't gonna sound so good.

Followers are entitled to know what is expected from them. The military provides a list to enable followers to take a personal inventory of their followership skills, and leaders can use it as a springboard for discussion. A list is an excellent way of taking stock of personal attributes as a prelude to change. When looking at a list of principles, characteristics, or whatever, the trick is for the reader to realize that he or she already knows some of them or does some of them—and can make choices based on the options presented.

Formulated at the United States Army Infantry School, the "Guidelines for Followers" are presented here with additional commentary. By comparing each of the ten guidelines on followership to the leadership lists in the following chapter, it is possible to glimpse something of the relationship between the two.

1. *Know yourself and seek self-improvement.* Self-assessment is never easy, although it does get easier with practice. The important thing is to *decide to take action and then do it.* An author of any periodic evaluation is an excellent source of information and specific suggestions on how to improve. Corporate and public libraries also have a plethora of self-test surveys available. Self-assessment need not be self-derogatory; it should lead to a specific plan for improvement. In areas of competence, the plan should be about how to move from being merely competent to being great.

2. *Be technically and tactically proficient.* While the previous point dealt primarily with "soft" skills and attributes, the question at hand here is, "How are your technical skills? Do you know your job? Do you know how to apply your skills in various situations?" Again, continual improvement, not self-flagellation, is the objective.

    Followership is the joint responsibility of the individual and the organization. If a person doesn't know how to perform a task, his or her ability to be a follower will be severely impaired. Ideally, an organization will provide or arrange for training. Continual learning as the basis for developing proficient employees/followers is in perfect harmony with the urgings of everyone from Tom Peters to President Clinton's Secretary of Labor, Robert Reich.

3. *Comply with orders and initiate appropriate actions in the absence of orders.* The first part of this guideline fits the stereotype for a follower: comply with orders. The second half takes it out of the realm of robotics. The effective follower doesn't let opportunities slide by just because the leader of the moment isn't around; he or she becomes the leader of the moment. In fact, one of the basic tenets of Marine Corps leadership is that whenever two marines of whatever grade are together, one is in charge.

    Failure to comply with orders is a problem for any organization. Even when you have the best, if no one follows orders, there's chaos. Take an example from the world of sports: In the early 1990s, General Manager Willis Reed assembled a group of talented players for the National Basketball Association's New Jersey Nets. He then added Bill Fitch, a championship-level coach, to the mix. The team went nowhere. Several of the players rejected their role as followers to the point of refusing to enter games when directed to do so by Fitch. Fitch quit at the end of two miserable seasons; three members of the team made the 1994–95 *Sports Illustrated* "All (Bad) Attitude Team" and were subsequently traded; and Reed began to rebuild.

4. *Develop a sense of responsibility and take responsibility for your actions.* Good followers, particularly those actively working on their leadership skills, know that being a follower does not mean one can hide comfortably behind that role and avoid responsibility. Accepting the blame for jobs poorly done is the flip side of accepting credit for jobs well done; a person can't reasonably expect to do the latter unless he or she is willing to do the former.

5. *Make sound and timely decisions or recommendations.* The more useful data available, the more fact-based decision making played out successfully at lower levels, the greater the chance that every follower will be able to be decisive at her or his own level.

6. *Set the example for others.* If the organization is going to continue to exist, much less be successful, new followers must always be in training, and the best training is training by example. Every observable action is a potential example, intentionally or not.

7. *Be familiar with your leader and his job, and anticipate his requirements.* The intelligent leader makes adherence to this guideline easy by guaranteeing that key followers know details of his or her job and his or her preferences. Even in athletics, it is impossible for a group of people to be a team unless the members of the team know the coach's game plan; otherwise, it is just a bunch of folks who happen to dress alike. The same basic rule applies in the workplace as well.

8. *Keep your leaders informed.* Effective communication flows in all possible directions at all times. Just as the leader needs to keep his or her followers informed about "the world out there," followers must keep the leader informed about "the world in here"— and exactly what the unit's current capabilities are.

9. *Understand the task and ethically accomplish it.* Individuals should never violate organizational or personal ethics—even if it

means disobeying orders. They must, however, be prepared for scrutiny. In healthy organizations, ethical conduct is rewarded.

10. *Be a team member—but not a yes man.*   A good follower holds a mirror up to the leader when necessary. If the only thing a leader wants to hear is "Yes, you've made another brilliant decision," the organization is headed for trouble. Once a decision is made (assuming there are no ethical problems), there is an obligation to execute the plan, but prior to that moment, questions such as "Can we go back over point three again? If I understood it correctly, I don't think it is the best we can do" are very much in order.

Guidelines for Followers

1. Know yourself and seek self-improvement.
2. Be technically and tactically proficient.
3. Comply with orders and initiate appropriate actions in the absence of orders.
4. Develop a sense of responsibility and take responsibility for your actions.
5. Make sound and timely decisions or recommendations.
6. Set the example for others.
7. Be familiar with your leader and his job, and anticipate his requirements.
8. Keep your leaders informed.
9. Understand the task and ethically accomplish it.
10. Be a team member—but not a yes man.

COMING TO TERMS WITH FOLLOWERSHIP

Just as not everyone aspires to fill the first chair of an orchestra section, not everyone aspires to a leadership role. In his book *The Power of Followership,* Robert Kelley states that for many people the role of follower is a conscious choice. The reason for making such a decision is the attractiveness of any of several "paths of followership": Apprentice, Disciple, Mentee, Comrade, Loyalist, Dreamer, and Lifeway.

The best followers, according to Kelley, are the ones he identifies as "Exemplary Followers," those who are both actively engaged with their leaders and their environment and who exhibit independent, critical thinking. The argument that "I was just following orders" is not one that is ever advanced by an exemplary follower. In addition to choosing whom they follow, they choose when to stop following someone.

Kelley points out that it isn't enough to be either a critical thinker or an active follower alone. Without the combination, both can degenerate into destructive tendencies: A passive critical thinker becomes an alienated follower, and an active uncritical thinker becomes a conformist follower. Kelley's assessment of the importance of the role of followers is encapsulated in his pointing out that "without his armies, Napoleon was just a man with grandiose ambitions," while his description of the rights and responsibilities of exemplary followers is best summarized by his observation that a "nation of exemplary followers makes a government of wolves impossible." Followers are not sheep; they are the ones who, according to Tom Peters, do the honest work.

Leaders must come to terms with the fact that while it is their responsibility to create new leaders, some followers are just not interested in the role. Example and moral suasion won't shift them. Training leaves them cold. It's frustrating, but past a certain point, as Adair cautioned in *Training for Leadership,* it's up to the individual:

> [Any] course . . . cannot *teach* leadership: it can only provide opportunities for the students to *learn* for themselves. Thus there is an important "take it or leave it" element in the course: in this field the "sacred right of rejection" has to be guarded at all costs.

Protecting the right of rejection in the real world means leaving people at their current level—as long as the individual continues to contribute to the organization.

Fewer followers might opt out if they didn't find the prospect of leadership overwhelming. The publishing industry has a lot to answer for in this regard: All but a precious few of the current books on leadership are aimed at those aspiring to the ranks of what could be called "capital-L" leadership. This is leadership in the classic, heroic sense of individuals who see beyond the horizon, make bold decisions, affect hundreds of lives, and inspire all. It is leadership as practiced by individuals at the top of the corporate pyramid. When books gather information solely from studies of CEOs or presidents of thriving organizations (or, for negative examples, CEOs or presidents of failing organizations), everyone else involved in the organization becomes a leader wanna-be.

This, of course, implies that the joys, the challenges, the problems, the exhilarating accomplishments, what Warren Bennis and Burt Nanus call "a sense of adventure and fun," and the quiet satisfaction that a leader experiences are available only to strategy makers. Nothing could be further from the truth. There is also what could be called "small-l" leadership, more modest in scope, but equally important and with equal rewards. It occurs when individuals interact in day-to-day operations throughout an organization. Small-l leadership is exemplary followership with superior skills. Anyone can aspire to small-l leadership; everyone must master small-l leadership to be an effective capital-L leader. And for the majority of the men and women drawing a paycheck, capital-L leadership is a spectator sport while small-l leadership is a participation event.

Capital-L leadership is essential in the marketplace; it is also crucial in setting a vision, getting things started, and maintaining support of small-l leadership. Decisions at the top commit resources. For small-l leaders, however, the hot question is not "What bold move can I make in the marketplace today?" or "Where should resources go?", but rather "What can I do to increase the odds that Phan, Sally, Maria, Chris, Fran, and Amar will work to accomplish what we need to accomplish?" Finding the answer to the latter can be every bit as challenging as finding the answer to the former. People are as volatile as the marketplace—and their actions, or reactions, are more immediate and more personal.

Because of the shift in the economies of the developed countries from manufacturing to service, organizations have a vested interest in moving employees past followership to small-l leadership. Leadership at every level is *the* make-or-break issue in service quality. In a comfortably paced, inside-our-building manufacturing operation, everyone's work could be overseen by a duly trained (or, perhaps, dully trained?) manager. In today's highly competitive service economy, it is impossible for senior management to either monitor or double-check every act affecting a customer. Even in manufacturing, an increased need for speed and flexibility makes hoarding authority at the top indefensible.

The equivalent to capital-L leadership and small-l leadership in quality theory and practice is addressed by asking two questions: "Are we doing the right things?" and "Are we doing things right?" Doing the right things is seen as the province of high-level decision makers and senior management—capital-L leadership in action. The tools available include value analysis, process analysis, blueprinting, and reengineering. Doing things right is the responsibility of every employee at every level. It is enacted through individual initiative, suggestion boxes, quality teams, self-managing work teams, or other constructs with similar names. Put one way, capital-L leadership gets everyone looking in the same direction; small-l leadership ensures that everyone steps off on the same foot.

The most effective followers are almost always those whose goal it is to be small-l leaders (and possibly capital-L ones). That ambition can pave the way from one role to the other, an evolution that is more an expansion of capabilities than it is a transition from one state to another separate state. A Marine Corps manual offers the following on the topic of the relationship between leadership and followership:

- Every follower is potentially a leader and every leader is also a follower.
- The most effective follower is that individual who has proven leadership abilities and who is loyal, dependable, obedient, and dedicated to uphold his responsibilities and perform his duties to the best of his ability, as well as exert positive influence upon his comrades.
- Followership must be an integral part of our philosophy, for it is the base upon which future leaders are tempered, and its enhancement among subordinates will ensure that professionalism is keyed to all levels—followers as well as leaders.
- The most effective leader is a good follower. He sets the example of followership/leadership for his subordinates. His subordinates are watching his example, and as a leader he can only expect them to provide the same degree of

"followership" that he exhibits by his example of leadership and followership.

Sergeant Woodward defines followership in terms of its primary responsibilities:

> Followership can be defined as a process in which subordinates recognize their responsibility to comply with the orders of leaders and take appropriate action consistent with the situation to carry out those orders to the best of their ability. In the absence of orders they estimate the proper action required to contribute to mission performance and take that action.
>
> Inherent in the above definition of followership is a high degree of self-discipline. The follower must have a personal commitment to the successful completion of his unit's mission. The most effective follower is the one who accepts the necessity of compliance and who is committed to placing the needs of the unit above his own needs.
>
> An effective follower needs more than self-discipline. Competence is a requirement and requires continual self-development . . . acquired competence among followers leads to responsibility, an important characteristic of followership professionalism.

Woodward acknowledges the fluctuating role of followership when he advocates that followers step forward and take charge in "the absence of orders." Being a good follower is not a passive role, but it does not require giving up a personal life. When Woodward talks about placing the needs of the unit above personal needs, he is speaking about commitment to the organization, not advocating becoming a workaholic.

The self-discipline Woodward refers to as a prerequisite for followership is analogous to self-confidence as a prerequisite for leadership. Both require self-knowledge, an awareness of environment and options, and conscious choices. What is seen as self-discipline in a follower can easily be taken as self-confidence in a leader. The parallel is not surprising, considering that most people move back and forth between the two roles.

Followership takes character, commitment, energy, and judgment. Woodward summarizes its relationship to leadership succinctly:

> Effective leadership requires followers who are more than Pavlovian reactors to their leaders' influences. When followers actively contribute, are aware of their function, and take personal pride in the art of followership, then the joint purpose of leadership and followership—higher levels of mission accomplishment—is achieved effectively.

THE INTERACTION BETWEEN LEADERSHIP AND FOLLOWERSHIP

The interaction between leadership and followership is like the tango. While a certain amount of technical expertise can be acquired in isolation, it isn't until another person is involved that any judgment can be made concerning competency. A tango offers an infinite variety of ways to successfully display one's expertise, depending on mastery of style, internal fire, and the abilities of the follower. It also, unfortunately, provides an infinite number of ways to fail, even when one person is technically proficient.

Trust is as important as technique. Imagine, for instance, that Fred Astaire asked a complete stranger—a lady who had no idea of who he was or his talents as a dancer—to dance the tango. No matter what the lady's abilities, the dance would no doubt start cautiously, with her confidence in his talents growing as he led her around the dance floor. As her trust increased, she could relax and follow his lead, perhaps even trying steps she had never tried before.

If, however, Fred asked someone who *did* know who he was to dance, someone with minimal skills of her own, the trust issue is more ambiguous. A great deal depends on the self-confidence of the lady. Would she immediately give herself over to his lead, trying to follow his every suggestion? Could she dance and learn at the same time? Or would she clutch, paralyzed by lack of faith in her own abilities? Imagine dancing with Fred Astaire! Even Debbie Reynolds confessed unease in her autobiography: "At first I was afraid that I wouldn't follow him correctly. However, with Fred, you couldn't *not* follow because he led you. Even a klutz could look great with Fred Astaire." His ability to put a partner at ease despite her initial misgivings was due to more than just his technical expertise. Ginger Rogers related in her autobiography that the great thing about Fred was that he was an interesting conversationalist, someone who could talk and dance at the same time.

The analogy between leaders and led is fairly easy to follow when the focus is on Fred Astaire as the epitome of a knowledgeable, accomplished, and humane leader, worthy of trust. One result of pushing leadership down a corporate ladder, however, is that people end up constantly changing roles, acting as leaders one moment and followers the next. When functioning as followers, leaders aren't suddenly struck stupid. Nor are subordinates always less knowledgeable than those in leadership positions. In short, how about looking at it from Ginger Rogers's point of view?

By conventional definition, when a man and a woman engage in ballroom dancing, the man leads. Imagine that someone who had no idea who Ginger Rogers was asked her to dance the tango. Assume, too, that she accepted and went onto the dance floor, hoping that this guy danced better than his plaid sport coat insinuated. If Ginger's partner were genuinely competent, the traditional roles would see them through. If not, the couple could have an awkward time of it. A good follower usually accommodates even the most heavy-handed lead while preventing actual collisions, but if the gentleman were oblivious to the fact that dancers on the floor seemed to want to go in different directions at different speeds, Ginger could either begin a sentence with, "Listen, Bozo" or she could accept her fate, try to follow his lead, and hope nobody was injured in the process.

If, however, the gentleman knew Ginger's reputation or figured out that she was the better dancer, the whole tenor of the relationship would change. By convention, he would still be the "leader," but he would pay close attention to any signals from her. She could make him look good. And while he would enjoy the best tango of his life, Ginger would undoubtedly appreciate his awareness of her talents and his willingness to take suggestions. When a leader appreciates a subordinate's talents, it's a win-win situation.

When Fred Astaire escorted Ginger Rogers onto the dance floor, of course, the ingredients were perfect: competence on both sides and complete trust. As she once said, "You could put yourself in his hands and trust to his feet." When they danced, the result was a thing of beauty that has rarely been matched and has never been surpassed. Part of what made Astaire-Rogers such a marvelous sight to behold was the viewers' knowledge that they were watching an extraordinary pair of dancers who blended their strengths into an unbeatable combination.

WHAT LEADERS MUST DO

Leadership is in the eye of the follower. In their book, *The Leadership Challenge,* authors James Kouzes and Barry Posner had this to say: "Asking leaders about their personal best is only half the story. . . . A complete picture of leadership can be developed only if we ask followers what they look for and admire in a leader."

Marines judge leadership like some people judge wine—they are connoisseurs. One of the benefits is that subordinate and senior-level leadership is under constant, active evaluation. Continual self-improvement is all but mandatory under such conditions. What do marines look for in leaders? Because each of them is in training to be a leader, they are a tough crowd. A list from one of their manuals reflects this:

- Marines want to be led, but they soon become impatient with dull or unimaginative leadership.
- Marines expect their leaders at all levels to be competent, but they often have a "show me" attitude until it becomes self-evident.
- Marines will uniformly support enthusiasm, sincerity, and determination, even if it is reflected in tight, firm discipline.
- Marines can spot selfishness a mile away.
- A good horse deserves a loose rein. Train 'em right, and then give 'em room to operate. Don't suffocate initiative.

To instill initiative, a Marine Corps manual suggests the following for developing subordinates:

- Encouraging subordinates to become innovative and self-starting.
- Setting a positive example that could be emulated.
- Giving responsibility to subordinates and holding them accountable.

Followership, leadership, and quality are built on the same foundation: trust, initiative, and continuous improvement. From a follower's point of view, the three are closely related. Followers take the initiative when they trust leaders to back them up. Continuous improvement is the result. The topic of initiative will be covered more fully in Chapters 4 and 5.

All leaders have the responsibility to teach and guide their juniors. Military sources put that responsibility third in importance for a leader, superseded only by accomplishing the mission and taking care of the troops. As individuals develop as leaders, they must remember that they are always serving as an example.

The actions of a real person override lessons in a book almost every time. Both acts of commission and acts of omission can be taken as examples. Avoiding a decision, letting something slide by, deciding to not decide—all these are acts of omission that not only retard a person's growth as a leader, but also serve as examples for followers. Followers may fail to differentiate between what is worth emulating and what isn't, resulting in a jumble of disconnected ideas with equal weight. When they do, there's no telling what will surface when the need to act arises.

Leaders are responsible for building trust within organizations. According to the Marine Corps, trust binds leaders and followers together:

Consequently, trust is an essential trait among leaders—trust by seniors in the abilities of their subordinates and by juniors in the competence and support of their seniors. Trust must be earned, and actions that undermine trust must meet with strict censure. Trust is a product of confidence and familiarity.

Confidence among comrades results from demonstrated professional skill. Familiarity results from shared experience and a common professional philosophy.

A Marine Corps manual offers five ways to strengthen trust:

- Strive for forceful and competent leadership throughout the entire organization.
- Inform people of plans of action and reasons whenever it is possible and practicable to do so.
- Endeavor to remove causes for misunderstanding or dissatisfaction.
- Assure that everyone is acquainted with procedures for registering complaints—and of any subsequent action taken.
- Build a feeling of confidence so that subordinates ask for advice and assistance freely—not only in professional matters, but also for personal problems.

Trust requires leaders to recognize that just as leaders have individual styles, so do followers. Anyone in a senior position who proudly proclaims "I treat all of my people exactly the same" is confusing leader-follower relations with policy. In spite of treating Employee A exactly like Employee B, it is quite possible to smash the self-esteem of Employee B while hardly ruffling Employee A. Is that a problem? You bet it is. Each follower must, to a degree, be treated uniquely to fulfill the twin objectives of accomplishing the mission and taking care of subordinates.

As more organizations move toward the goal of creating exemplary followership and beyond, leaders will have to consider not only the job-defined capabilities of employees, but also their preferences, dreams, and competencies. Leaders must know the full range of the strength and liabilities of each individual in order to create an environment that makes it possible for each person to bring all of his or her capabilities to bear.

4

TAKING STOCK
BEFORE TAKING STEPS

The major premise of this book is that people grow into leadership. During periods of growth, there may be conflict between a person's beliefs and actions—a somewhat uncomfortable state of affairs. According to three British theorists, Andrew Kakabadse, Susan Vinnicombe, and Ron Ludlow, in *Working in Organisations,* this disconnect isn't a matter for panic: "For a manager to be a good leader . . . it is not necessary to change his inner core values, but he must be able to change his style of interpersonal interaction to fit the variables of the situation."

Is this hypocrisy? Not really. Hypocrisy refers to performance *falling short* of professed standards. If the situation is reversed and performance *exceeds* personal beliefs, the word hypocrisy does not apply. Suppose, for example, someone is convinced that it is perfectly all right for him or her to have several drinks before getting behind the wheel of a car. The person justifies this position by saying that he or she has an excellent driving record, feels perfectly fine, and has always gotten home safely. If that person decides *not* to drink and drive based on scientific studies and societal norms—even without changing the basic conviction that it is safe to do so—society quite accurately labels the action as responsible behavior or self-discipline. And the results speak for themselves: one less impaired driver on the road.

Changing behavior with or without changing hearts is, however, possible only if desirable behavior is identified. People who are power junkies may always be power junkies at heart. If, however, they recognize that their behavior is counterproductive, they can learn to restrain themselves. Over time, positive feedback might even result in a change of core values.

The military is straightforward about asserting what makes a good leader. Reflection on the elements of leadership is encouraged; navel-gazing (no pun intended) is not. The goal is to apply knowledge. As one Marine Corps manual states without apology:

> The elements of leadership discussed in the following chapters are based upon sound psychological premise. That they exist is enough for our purpose; from whence they spring and why they exist is relatively immaterial. They will be studied from the viewpoint of their results rather than that of their origins, lest their analysis become obscured or entirely hidden in theoretical abstractions.

In a sense, the military's approach is like teaching people to drive without bothering to review the laws of relative motion. It works. Others have done it using these guidelines. Taking someone through a detailed course, replete with Socratic discussions, research, and graded experience in the "real world," might possibly produce a more sophisticated leader upon graduation than military training does. Such an approach, however, is a luxury no military service of any country can afford—nor can most businesses. Military schools rely on mentoring, subsequent experience, and periodic schooling to complete the process begun in basic training.

Military leadership materials are designed to meet the challenge of teaching students who vary in experience from eighteen-year-old, not-quite-high-school graduates to fifty-year-old general officers with advanced degrees and years of combat and noncombat experience. In addressing both these groups, the military uses lists as a teaching tool, breaking leadership down into easily digestible pieces. The guidelines for followers in the previous chapter is one such list. Lists of leadership traits, leadership characteristics, leadership principles, and leadership styles can be found in a single army manual. The plethora of lists speaks to their flexibility. Some lists assume that students are early in their careers and nothing can be taken as a "given" in terms of knowledge or experience. The same ideas are reframed or reviewed in lists for senior officers, maintaining a common vocabulary to facilitate open discussion between the ranks.

Appendix B contains lists from military and nonmilitary sources. The enormous variety evident in these lists reflects the fact that what one sees as central to leadership depends on where one is standing and where one expects to go. While lists of military origin include "courage," some nonmilitary lists refer to "courage of convictions," a similar, but not identical concept. The existence of so many distinctive points is one more testimony to the complexity of leadership. Two people can study the same lists and have parallel careers, and the results can be very different, albeit highly effective, leaders. Consider General Colin L. Powell and General H. Norman Schwarzkopf. Both eminently successful army generals, they come from widely dissimilar backgrounds and have developed substantial differences in style.

MAKING FULL USE OF THE LISTS

Lists such as those in this chapter or in Appendix B are of no use if they are reduced to just-in-time tools to be pulled out in case of an emergency. The lessons must be discussed, digested, practiced, and integrated into a leader's thinking and behavior prior to a critical moment. In fact, a leader's reputation is established during all the individually mundane interactions she or he has with subordinates, peers, and seniors—all of whom act as "press agents." That reputation either aids or impedes a leader in successfully meeting a crisis.

The full range of the leadership challenge was presented in a very valuable and readable self-published book *Love 'Em and Lead 'Em* by Paul Malone III. Malone uses a list of ten roles to define what constitutes a good leader:

- The leader as an *executive* serves as a coordinator of group activities.
- The leader as a *planner* serves to influence the ways and means a group achieves its assigned goal.
- The leader as a *policy maker* serves as a work group re-

presentative to higher levels in establishing goals and policies.

- The leader as an *expert* serves as a source of information and skills.
- The leader as *external group representative* serves as a work group representative in dealing with other groups.
- The leader as *purveyor of rewards and punishments* serves as a recognizer of excellence and a disciplinarian.
- The leader as *arbitrator and mediator* serves as judge and conciliator of conflict within a group.
- The leader as *exemplar* serves as a model for the behavior of other work group members.
- The leader as *symbol* of the group serves as a focus for group unity.
- The leader as *scapegoat* serves as a target of criticism when things go wrong.

Leaders must shoulder all these expectations, regardless of the size of the group—from a four-person team in the mail room to a multi-million-dollar organization. Some of these roles are automatic; others require concerted study, practice, spirit, and perseverance.

LEADERSHIP IN TWENTY-FIVE WORDS OR LESS

In studying these lists, sometimes the relationship between an item and the broad concept of leadership is obvious; sometimes it is not. To put items in perspective, it helps to have a brief, clear, useful definition of leadership as a handy reference. Chapters 1 and 2 looked at leadership through the prisms of quality, management, and the military, exploring a number of its aspects in the process. Something slightly different is called for here, something brief, a touchstone for putting material in context. With this in mind, weigh the following definitions.

The simplest definition of a leader is, obviously, "someone with followers." It's certainly brief enough and it appears clear enough. All you have to do to check your own leadership abilities is look over your shoulder. If there are people following you, you must be a leader. There are two problems with this definition. First, it fails the "usefulness" test: It offers no lessons, or even any hints, on how to become a leader. Even worse, this definition is open to fraud and blatant misinterpretation. More than once in world history, a politician waited on the sidelines to see which way the crowd was going and then ran around to the front, giving the appearance of leadership—perhaps even convincing himself or herself in the process.

C. A. Gibb got closer to the heart of the matter. In *Training for Leadership*, John Adair cites a 1952 study conducted by Gibb that lays out the components that form the basis of a good definition:

> . . . [A]ny comprehensive theory of leadership must incorporate and integrate all of the major variables which are now known to be involved, namely (1) the personality of the leader, (2) the followers with their attitudes, needs, and problems, (3) the group itself . . . (4) the situations as determined by physical setting, nature of task, etc. . . . No really satisfactory theoretical formulation is yet available.

While Gibb gave up on a definition, Adair offers his own viewpoint, which emphasizes the view of leadership as dialogue, not monologue:

> One may suggest provisionally that leadership is the measure and degree of an individual's ability to influence—and be influenced by—a group in the implementation of a common task. This circumscribes three important aspects of the leadership function: the individual, the group, and the task: and indicates leadership as a functional relationship between these three basic variables.

Gibb and Adair, though accurate, are inclined to be wordy. An ideal definition of leadership would be easier to carry around in the head: something in twenty-five words or less that covers the same concepts. The most elegant definition these authors have come upon was offered by John Mellecker, an executive in a financial services organization and an admitted leadership junkie:

Leadership is the creation of an environment in which others are able to self-actualize in the process of completing the job.

This definition is imbued with a sense of mission, an insight into what actually creates a chain of leadership—and it underscores the need to keep the goals of leadership firmly in mind. Mellecker restates the essential characteristic of leadership already identified: A leader cares that a job gets done—and he or she cares about the people doing the job. As a convenient touchstone for putting lists in context, this definition would be hard to beat.

FOURTEEN LEADERSHIP TRAITS

Leadership lists are presented somewhat differently in each of the armed services. The marines use fourteen leadership traits and eleven leadership principles to teach leadership. The army identifies nineteen leadership traits and eleven principles, and the air force has six traits and ten principles. The differences are superficial, usually having to do with sequence and wording.

The lists presented in this and the following section are hybrids: the fourteen leadership traits and eleven leadership principles identified by the Marine Corps are combined with observations from analogous lists published by other services, a dash of common sense from two military childhoods (army and navy), and a twenty-year career in the Marine Corps. For the most part, military jargon has either been "translated" or dropped—with a few exceptions.

Keep in mind that these lists can serve both as an inventory of current assets and as the basis for a personal plan of action. If a person decides that it is not worth his or her effort to correct a particular deficiency, he or she must offset this shortcoming with outstanding performance in other areas. While it is possible to rise to the top in both military and civilian organizations without attention to one or more of the traits and principles on these lists, it requires enormous compensatory strengths elsewhere—and even then the leader can expect criticism in the area he or she chooses to ignore.

The Marine Corps defines "traits" as "personality traits," while "principles" are "fundamental guidelines a leader uses in the selection of appropriate actions and orders." Together, the two lists cover the basics, providing an inventory of what makes a leader. The Marine Corps text states simply, "The traits and principles of leadership are the yardsticks [people] use to determine their own leadership abilities and those of juniors." Millions of members of the military have memorized these lists or ones like them at various points in their careers.

Considering the leadership traits first, the Marine Corps views this list as a guideline. No marine considers these traits as the be-all-and-end-all of leadership. Again, context is vital:

> Possession of these traits does not guarantee success. . . . Although these traits are a good guide for determining the desired personality to be developed as a leader, the mission, the personalities of subordinates, and the situation will have a direct effect on what traits the leader must apply.

In this section, each leadership trait is accompanied by recommendations for how an individual might strengthen his or her abilities in that area. These recommendations are *quoted directly* from *Fundamentals of Marine Corps Leadership (MCI 03.3m)*, a correspondence course for noncommissioned officers, because translating or omitting portions might invite the question, "I wonder what else was there?" A few points (e.g., "In the field, your Marines eat before you do") may have little relevance to the civilian world; but quoting them highlights the fact that the majority are directly applicable.

As you go through the lists, remember to think about how each item contributes to "the creation of an environment in which others are able to self-actualize in the process of completing the job."

1. *Integrity.* Anyone who says that it is possible to have a little integrity is not being completely honest. Attempts to practice integrity part time are hypocritical and forfeit virtually any chance of engendering trust in seniors or subordinates. Indicators of integrity include habitually placing honesty, sense of duty, and

sound moral principles above all else. The recommendations given by the correspondence course are exercises for developing the habit of integrity:

- Practice absolute honesty and be trustworthy at all times, not only with yourself, but with others. Never shade the truth.
- Be accurate and truthful in all statements. Don't tell your superiors only that which you think they want to hear. Tell it as it is—but tactfully.
- Stand for what you believe, even if the belief is an unpopular one.
- Place honesty and duty above all else.

2. *Knowledge.* Know your job, know your people, know yourself. Continuous learning is a common theme in today's discussion of how to ensure success in the twenty-first century. Knowledge doesn't happen accidentally. Individuals have the responsibility to develop a deliberate program of education that ranges from reading newspapers to studying technical manuals to discussing leadership (and other issues) with colleagues. Nothing gains the confidence and respect of subordinates more quickly than demonstrated knowledge, both general and specific. Knowing the strengths, weaknesses, and preferences of one's subordinates is another component of this trait. The guidelines offered for improving this trait are straightforward:

- Read all kinds of articles and take courses.
- Listen to experienced people.
- Ask questions.

3. *Courage.* To quote directly from one Marine Corps manual: "Courage is that trait which enables you to recognize and to fear danger and criticism, while at the same time allows calm and firm action. It exists in a moral as well as a physical sense. Moral courage means knowing and standing up for what is right in the face of popular disfavor. Thus, a leader accepts blame when at fault." Having the courage of one's own convictions, being ready to take the heat from above or below, is sometimes painful in the short run. A lack of courage is damning in the long run:

- Place duty over your personal desires or feelings.
- Look for and readily accept responsibilities.
- Speak in a calm tone; keep an orderliness in your thought processes; don't make any physical danger or hardship bigger than it really is.
- Stand for what is right, even in the face of popular disfavor.
- Never blame others for your mistakes.
- Recognize fear but control your emotions.

4. *Decisiveness.* "A positive approach, little waste of time, objectivity, time analysis, and sound evaluation of suggestions from others all contribute to decisiveness." The manual counsels that a "wise leader gets all the facts, weighs one against the other, then calmly and quickly arrives at a sound decision." Remember that a "leader keeps in mind that many solid ideas originate at the subordinate level." In today's business climate, the upward flow of ideas common to a quality process is not an excuse for indecision, but a way to capture the best information to make timely and accurate decisions.

The failure to be decisive is readily noticed and obscures other strengths. Recall that when supporters of President Bill Clinton questioned why he was not getting credit for some of his accomplishments in the first two years of his administration, the most frequent response was that he appeared to be indecisive. So common was this perception that a poll taken on the Internet by the comic strip *Doonesbury* settled on a waffle as the symbol for President Clinton. Four guidelines lead to decisiveness:

- Form the habit of considering several points of view for every problem.
- Learn from the mistakes of others.
- Force yourself to make a decision and then check the decision to see if it is sound.
- Talk to people and practice making your conversations logical and clear.

In short, the keys to becoming a decisive leader are practice and experience—not impulsiveness.

5. *Dependability.* Dependability is defined as "the certainty of proper performance of duty." Personal considerations are secondary to duty and high standards are a must. While this trait includes the "willing and voluntary support of the policies and orders of the chain of command," the manual is careful to emphasize that it "does not mean blind obedience." The potential for conflict is addressed by advising that leaders "should first listen to suggestions from their subordinates" and that, once a decision to proceed is made, "subordinates must make an effort to attempt to achieve the highest possible standard of performance." As the Quality Revolution has confirmed, decisions based on input from those involved in implementing practical applications are more likely to be carried out in a dependable way. Several developmental tools are offered:

- Practice honest thinking and avoid making excuses.
- Accomplish the assigned task, regardless of the obstacles.
- Always be prompt and do all tasks to the best of your ability.
- Be careful about making promises and personal deals. But when you have made them, build a reputation for keeping them.

6. *Initiative.* "Action in the absence of orders" runs counter to the common military stereotype, yet the presence and value of this trait has been proven repeatedly in combat. As mentioned in the second chapter, American willingness to exercise initiative during the World War II landing at Normandy carried the day. Far from "training out" initiative, the services explicitly teach that it is a key trait. The relatively simple act of encouraging initiative may be all that is needed to see a growth in its practice in any organization.

As a Marine Corps manual states, "Closely associated with initiative is resourcefulness—the ability to deal with a situation in the absence of normal resources or methods." The key to initiative is identified as the capacity "to recognize the task and accomplish it, using the resources at hand." The ability to anticipate is another critical aspect presented, paralleling the movement from correction to prevention in the quality movement. Developing personal initiative requires a particular mindset:

- Develop and maintain a state of mental and physical alertness.
- Look for tasks to be done and do them without being told.
- Practice thinking and planning ahead.
- Anticipate situations before they arise and have a plan already developed.

For a more complete discussion on the topic of initiative, see Chapter 5.

7. *Tact.* "A decent regard for the rights and feelings of others is essential to leadership," according to General of the Army George C. Marshall as quoted in an Air Force leadership manual. The importance of tact is a matter of some discussion—and more than a few jokes—in a community in which rough-hewn bluntness is sometimes equated with toughness. In fact, teaching materials specifically state that inexperienced people may "wrongly feel that politeness in a military command is a sign of weakness." The story most often informally told to demonstrate the importance of tact concerns a senior officer aghast at the behavior of one of his subordinates. Receiving word that the mother of one of the troops in his unit had passed away, the senior officer instructed the First Sergeant to inform Private Jones of his loss. The First Sergeant immediately called for a formation of the entire unit and announced, "Private Jones, your mother kicked the bucket."

The senior officer counseled the First Sergeant at length afterwards, pointing out that while what he had done was, admittedly, an honest and efficient way of conveying the news, it lacked a certain finesse. He suggested that the First Sergeant temper his style when passing sensitive information and soften the blow by coming to the heart of the matter in an indirect manner.

Several weeks later, Private Rodriguez's father passed away. The senior officer again directed the First Sergeant to inform Rodriguez of his loss—and reminded him about their conversation. The First Sergeant called for a formation and announced,

"All those troops whose father is alive, take one step forward . . . not so fast, Rodriguez."

While the joke is a groaner, the fact that it has been told thousands of times in every branch of the military indicates an awareness of the issue. Tact is defined as "the ability to deal with others in a manner that will maintain good relations and avoid offense"; lack of tact crushes spirit and initiative. The value of tact may be summed up in the statement, "All orders given will be obeyed but those given with courtesy will be obeyed willingly. Even in emergency situations where orders must be abrupt and rapid, there is no room nor need for discourtesy." Tact is applicable both up and down the chain of command and is especially challenging when delivering criticism:

- Be considerate. Develop the habit of cooperating in spirit as well as in fact.
- Study the actions of successful senior NCOs [noncommissioned officers or the military equivalent of front-line supervisors and middle managers] who enjoy a reputation for being able to handle Marines successfully.
- Check yourself for tolerance and patience. If at fault, correct your habit.
- Apply the Golden Rule: Do unto others as you would have them do unto you. It is vital to teamwork.
- Let no Marine, superior or subordinate, exceed you in courtesy and consideration for the feelings of others.

8. *Justice.*   Fairness and impartiality are the hallmarks of justice. In the 1970s, a squad leader was asked by a senior Department of Defense official how many of his marines were black and how many were white. His reply was, "All my marines are green, sir." To quote directly and completely from one manual: "The just military leader gives rewards and punishments according to the merits of the case in question. Impartiality is exercised in all judgment situations, and prejudice of any kind is avoided. Because each decision is a test of fairness which is observed by subordinates and superiors alike, the leader must be fair, consistent, and prompt. Individual consideration should be given in

each case." A leader's practice of justice is under constant review by those above, below, and at the same organizational level:

- Search your mental attitudes to determine prejudices. Then seek to rid your mind of them.
- Learn to be impersonal when imposing punishment or giving rewards. Be absolutely impartial when performing these duties.
- Search out the facts of each case.
- Analyze cases that have been decided by leaders who have the reputation for justice.
- Study human behavior.
- Be honest with yourself.
- Recognize those subordinates worthy of commendation or award. Don't be known as one who hands out only punishment.

9. *Enthusiasm.* Enthusiasm is defined as the "display of sincere interest and exuberance in the performance of duty." Why follow someone who doesn't care about where she or he is going? Enthusiastic leaders are said to be "optimistic, cheerful, willing to accept the challenges of their profession, and . . . determined to do the best job possible." Success breeds enthusiasm, and enthusiasm is contagious:

- Explain "why" the mission must be accomplished, time and situation permitting.
- Understand, know, and believe in your work.
- Tackle all tasks with a cheerful "can-do" attitude.
- Believe in your mission, no matter what it is.

10. *Bearing.* While at first glance this trait may appear to have scant, if any, application outside the world of officers standing at attention in starched uniforms looking down broken noses at intimidated inferiors, the areas included under the heading "bearing" merit further investigation. Bearing is more than simply looking good; beyond general appearance and carriage, bearing includes conduct. One Marine Corps manual cautions, "Frequent

irritation, loss of temper, and vulgar speech indicate a lack of self-control or self-discipline and should be avoided." It also states, "Dignity, which implies a state of being honorable and which requires the control of one's actions and emotions, is also an essential element in a leader's bearing and should be cultivated." Developmental tools for the trait of bearing emphasize personal control:

- Practice control over your voice, facial expression, and gestures.
- Demonstrate calmness, sincerity, and understanding.
- Master your emotions so that you control them and they do not control you.
- Speak simply and directly.
- Never reprimand subordinates in the presence of *their* subordinates.
- Observe and study leaders who enjoy a reputation for good bearing.
- Know and adhere to regulations concerning dress, grooming, and conduct.
- Demand the highest standards of yourself and subordinates.
- Avoid indiscriminate use of coarse behavior, profanity, and vulgarity.

11. *Endurance.* This is not simply the ability to run further or carry a heavier pack than anyone else; it includes psychological toughness as well. The definition given is, "Mental and physical stamina measured by the ability to withstand pain, fatigue, stress, and hardship." Mental endurance refers to the ability to think straight even when fatigued or depressed. Ways to increase mental and physical endurance combine a healthy lifestyle and a challenge:

- Avoiding excesses that lower both physical and mental stamina.
- Keeping physically fit by exercise and proper diet.
- Learning to stand discomfort by undertaking hard physical tasks.

- Forcing yourself to study on occasions when you are tired and your mind is sluggish.
- Finishing every job regardless of the obstacles.

12. *Unselfishness.* "The unselfish leader is one who does not provide for personal comfort and advancement at the expense of others." Part of this is giving credit where credit is due. People in senior positions who hog credit and rewards for themselves, or who build palatial facilities for themselves while forcing juniors to "make do," have no right to act surprised when no one wants to follow them. To develop unselfishness, focus on subordinates:

- See that subordinates have the best that can be obtained for them under the circumstances.
- Try to understand the problems, military or personal, of subordinates.
- Put the comfort, pleasures, and recreation of subordinates before your own. In the field, your Marines eat before you do.
- Give credit to subordinates for jobs well done and ensure that any recognition from higher commands is passed on to the deserving Marine or Marines.

13. *Loyalty.* Loyalty and longevity are not inextricably linked. In the corporate world, loyalty is often equated with a forty-years-in-one-building-followed-by-a-gold-watch career. The majority of the men and women who join the military have careers of less than four years. One Marine Corps manual defines loyalty as "Faithfulness to your country, the Corps, the unit, to your seniors, juniors, and to your peers." Espousing faithfulness to country is not unique to the military; "Made in America" is a rallying cry for many a consumer. Calling for loyalty to a person's immediate business organization, seniors, juniors, and peers also rings true.

The oft-repeated phrase "loyalty is a two-way street" is ignored at great peril. A second Marine Corps manual adds, "Your reputation spreads far and wide if it is based on actions taken to protect subordinates from abuse. Loyalty means supporting the views and methods the unit employs, but it doesn't mean becoming a 'yes man.' Every action you take must reflect loyalty to every area where you owe allegiance."

Disagreement is not disloyalty. When subordinates express concern to seniors, they are exhibiting initiative and dependability. What is disloyalty is to take those same concerns to *their* subordinates once a decision has been made. The manual's recommendations reveal the complex claims on loyalty:

- Be quick to defend subordinates from abuse.
- Never give the slightest hint of disagreement with orders from seniors when giving instructions to subordinates.
- Practice doing every task to the best of your ability. Wholeheartedly support your commander's decisions.
- Never discuss the personal problems of subordinates with others. Keep them confidential.
- Stand up for your country, the Marine Corps, your unit, and your fellow Marines when they are unjustly accused.
- Never criticize seniors to subordinates.
- Do not discuss command problems outside the unit.
- Be loyal to your seniors and subordinates. Support the lawful policies of senior officers whether you personally agree with them or not. Remember loyalty is a two-way street.

14. *Judgment.* This "ability to weigh facts and circumstances logically in order to make decisions . . . [includes] anticipation of situations, avoidance of hasty decisions, and the application of common sense," as well as technical knowledge. Leaders without the personal knowledge necessary for solving a problem must be prepared to confer with experts. Often the experts are the subordinates, those more closely involved in completing the task. The leader may have the responsibility and the authority to make decisions, but few decisions need to be authoritarian. A mix of participative and delegative decisions increases the odds that decisions will be timely and accurate:

- Practice making estimates of the situation.
- Anticipate situations which require decisions in order to be prepared when the need arises.

- Avoid making rash decisions.
- Approach problems with a common sense attitude.

Fourteen Leadership Traits

1. Integrity	8. Justice
2. Knowledge	9. Enthusiasm
3. Courage	10. Bearing
4. Decisiveness	11. Endurance
5. Dependability	12. Unselfishness
6. Initiative	13. Loyalty
7. Tact	14. Judgment

ELEVEN LEADERSHIP PRINCIPLES

The companion list to the list of leadership traits is the list of eleven leadership principles, the guidelines for appropriate actions and orders. One manual cautions, "The fact that every leader has not always made full use of each one of these principles does not make them any less valid. Although their application may vary with the situation, a leader who disregards them risks failure."

1. *Be Technically and Tactically Proficient.*   Know how to do your job, both in theory and practice. Scoring high on a written test in a classroom is just the beginning; a leader also has to be "tactically proficient," that is, able to apply his or her knowledge in a rapidly changing environment. One manual points out, "Subordinates recognize that leaders must know their job to generate confidence, trust, and respect in them. . . . Do not fool yourself. You may fool your superiors, but YOU CANNOT FOOL YOUR PERSONNEL."

2. *Know Yourself and Seek Self-Improvement.*   A leader must assess current strengths and weaknesses and set out specific plans of action for improvement. Self-evaluation using these lists and performance evaluations at work can both be valuable. Continue to seek technical knowledge. Avoid bluffing. As one manual states, "bluffing is like a malignant disease; it keeps eating away

until all confidence is consumed." This second leadership principle complements the first: Become knowledgeable and stay knowledgeable.

3. *Know Your Marines and Look Out for Their Welfare.* This principle has a wider range of implications in a military organization than in a civilian one, but it is valid in both settings. The difference is one of degree rather than kind. Become acquainted with subordinates, recognize individual differences, know something about employees' lives outside the office, be available to talk about nonjob-related topics—gather information to help individuals grow on the job. Any support offered with regard to personal matters should be restricted to listening and directing the individual to the appropriate professional.

4. *Keep Your Personnel Informed.* People who know why they are doing something not only do a better job, but also are more apt to develop better ways of doing whatever that something is. Withholding information can make initiative downright dangerous, resulting in good-faith efforts that lead to disaster. Well-informed workers carry on in the event that lines of communication are interrupted, but don't expect initiative on the part of subordinates if knowledge is hoarded at the top.

Obviously, there are emergency situations when there isn't time to explain why a job must be done, although no one likes working in the dark. In those cases, a leader is drawing on the reserve of trust he or she has built up by keeping subordinates informed in the past. In the words of one Marine Corps manual: "Blind obedience to orders can sometimes be just as bad as disobedience to orders. The job might get accomplished, but the morale of your unit will drop and in the long run your unit will falter." Trust can be replenished by offering a full explanation at the first opportunity.

5. *Set the Example.* Leaders set the personal and professional standards for their organizations by their performance. Speaking to the Senior Division of the Royal Military Academy Sandhurst, Great Britain's Queen Elizabeth II cautioned the newly commissioned officers to, "Remember that the best and purest form of leadership is example: that 'Come on' is a much better command than 'Go on.' " Only if a leader's standards are high can he or she

rightfully expect any subordinate to perform to those same standards. One litmus test before acting is the question, "Would I want my people to do this?"

The importance of this principle was highlighted by the Quality Revolution. One question provides an insightful critique of the leadership component of a quality effort: "Of the last ten decisions announced by senior management 'in the name of quality,' how many directed a change in the behavior of any member of senior management?" If the answer is three or four or less, the leadership offered is suspect. Make sure that subordinates know when senior managers do change for the better. How can anyone follow an example they don't know is there?

6. *Ensure that the Task Is Understood, Supervised, and Accomplished.* As with so many aspects of interpersonal relationships and of quality efforts, balance is called for. Leaders should give clear, concise directions, and they should supervise their subordinates to insure that the directions are properly executed. The degree of supervision requires judgment. A Marine Corps manual cautions against micromanagement:

> Develop individual initiative in subordinates by allowing them to develop techniques on their own. . . . Do not supervise by telephone but do not oversupervise. You must check the finished product, but do not stand over [your people's] shoulders and watch every move they make. Oversupervision makes people nervous and leads them to believe that they are not trusted. Offer guidance, but then allow them to use their own initiative to get the job done. After they complete the job, offer suggestions that might make their work easier. There is nothing wrong with offering advice or instructions while they are actually working; however, give the opportunity to try before you jump in. Doing this will also help you because your Marines will be contented, and at the same time training to take your place.

Training someone to take your place is a fearful specter in many civilian organizations, but the Quality Revolution suggests you do just that. The alternative is to ration training and hoard information. You want someone who can take your place, whether they do so or not.

7. *Train Your People as a Team.* At any level of an organization, teamwork is essential. People who are excluded, or who are allowed to withdraw, subtract from the potential of the unit. Training may be in the form of specific classes and exercises or may come from informal discussions during which each member of the team becomes familiar with the strengths, weaknesses, and preferences of other team members. A common method used in the military to promote teamwork is to have people switch roles for a designated period of time. Chapter 8 provides additional information on how to build and motivate teams.

8. *Make Sound and Timely Decisions.* Akin to the leadership trait of decisiveness, this principle revisits the need for a leader to make logical decisions (even under trying conditions) and to take advantage of opportunities as they occur. An indecisive leader naturally creates lack of confidence, hesitancy, and indecision among his or her juniors. How can one improve? "The ability to make sound and timely decisions can be acquired by constant study and by training in making estimates without fear that [senior managers] may consider such action as a vacillation." One interesting thought is that "not telling your unit immediately about changes that have occurred is as bad as being a vacillating leader." Changes are not of themselves bad; change is at the heart of a quality process. Surprises, on the other hand, are rarely welcomed outside the context of birthday parties.

9. *Develop a Sense of Responsibility Among Subordinates.* This cannot be done unless the leaders are willing to pass along authority appropriate to responsibility, and neither will it be welcomed unless leaders habitually give credit where credit is due. Having others do the jobs that they have been trained to do, are fully capable of doing, and are being paid to do is the only way to build self-confidence and self-esteem. Here is the greatest opportunity for "creation of an environment in which others are able to self-actualize in the process of completing the job." The immediate benefit to leaders is time: They are free to turn their attention to other tasks.

10. *Employ Your Command in Accordance with Its Capabilities.*
Any good leader knows the capabilities of his or her organization
and strives to assign objectives within its reach. While it is possible to expand capabilities through challenge, be careful not to set
people up for failure. It brings about the collapse of morale, discipline, and efficiency. Stretch goals are of no use if everyone
stretches until they break.

There may be rare situations in which an organization must
be pushed without hesitation beyond current capabilities. Compensate by conscientiously adhering to other principles, such as
keeping your personnel informed, setting the example, and making sound and timely decisions. A leader who knows his or her
people knows what is within stretching distance and what is beyond the breaking point.

11. *Seek Responsibility and Take Responsibility for Your Actions and
the Actions of Your Unit.* This principle is paramount. One
Marine Corps manual discusses it in depth:

> (a) Leaders must be quick to take the initiative in the
> absence of instructions from their superiors by seeking re-
> sponsibility. In this manner, the leader develops profes-
> sionally and increases his potential ability. Proper
> delegation of authority is a sound attribute of leadership.
> The leader holds subordinates strictly responsible for re-
> sults and rarely for methods of procedure. Such action by
> the leader creates cooperation. Reluctance to delegate au-
> thority often is a mark of retarded growth in leadership.
>
> (b) The leader of a unit is responsible for all the unit
> does, or fails to do. The leader recognizes and acknowl-
> edges this responsibility on all occasions. Any effort to
> evade this responsibility destroys the bond of loyalty and
> respect that must exist between the leader and subordi-
> nates.
>
> (c) The Marine who does just enough to get by, does not
> advance or achieve. You must carefully evaluate a subordi-
> nate's failure. Make sure shortcomings are not due to an
> error on your part; then, salvage the Marine when possi-

ble—replace him when necessary! Never be afraid to accept criticism. It can help to improve you and your unit.

Another Marine Corps manual also puts it forcefully:

> Acting as a *buffer* to protect subordinates is a key responsibility of any leader. Leaders must avoid "passing the buck." Leaders must, if necessary, act from the courage of their convictions, even when such a position runs counter to the policy of seniors. Leaders must accept full responsibility for their actions, as did the Commanding General, 1st Marine Division, in Korea.

The latter reference is to General Oliver P. Smith, USMC, who refused an order by General Douglas A. MacArthur, USA, to string out his troops in the rush to the North Korean border. General Smith was subsequently vindicated. His behavior reflected a number of leadership principles: He was tactically and technically proficient, he knew his men and their capabilities, he made a judgment call as to what constituted their breaking point, and he protected subordinates at the risk of his career.

Eleven Leadership Principles

1. Be Technically and Tactically Proficient.
2. Know Yourself and Seek Self-Improvement.
3. Know Your Marines and Look Out for Their Welfare.
4. Keep Your Personnel Informed.
5. Set the Example.
6. Ensure that the Task Is Understood, Supervised, and Accomplished.
7. Train Your People as a Team.
8. Make Sound and Timely Decisions.
9. Develop a Sense of Responsibility Among Subordinates.
10. Employ Your Command in Accordance with Its Capabilities.
11. Seek Responsibility and Take Responsibility for Your Actions and the Actions of Your Unit.

MASTERING THE GESTURE

One of the authors' heroes is Aubrey K. Reid Jr., the president of the Paul Revere Insurance Group at the time it instituted its highly successful Quality Has Value process in 1984. Tom Peters deemed Quality Has Value the best quality process in North America in 1986; and the company was a finalist for the Baldrige Award in 1988, the award's inaugural year (no service company won until FedEx in 1990). The quality process saved the company $16 million in the first five years, while its market share grew from 11.8 percent to 18.4 percent.

Reid was the master of the gesture. Whether dishing up ice cream sundaes to say thank you to employees, visiting with new employees over a welcome-to-Paul-Revere breakfast, or making a heartfelt speech at a year-end celebration, his personal concern for the people who worked for and with him earned respect and affection throughout the organization. The success of Quality Has Value was in no small measure due to his leadership.

Reid was the inspiration for the authors' own list of desirable leadership traits:

1. Integrity
2. Technical competence
3. Passionate belief in the goal
4. Consideration for people
5. Unwillingness to ask others to do what one would not personally do
6. Trust in others to follow one's example
7. Mastery of the gesture, large and small
8. Little tolerance for incompetence

There is, of course, overlap between many of the points above and issues raised in other lists; the seventh attribute, "Mastery of the gesture, large and small," however, is peculiar to this list. A powerful form of empathy, the gesture is often overlooked.

A gesture is a shorthand means of communication that conveys a message in concentrated terms. In the British book *Training for Leadership,* Field Marshal Lord Slim is quoted as having told the following story from his World War II experiences:

I indulged in a little bit of theatricality . . . myself. When any of the forward formations had to go on half rations, as throughout the campaign they often did, I used to put my headquarters on half rations too. It had little practical effect, but as a gesture it was rather valuable, and it did remind the young staff officers with healthy appetites that it was urgent to get the forward formations back to full rations as soon as possible.

As a further example, consider General Bill Creech and his astounding turnaround of the Air Force's Tactical Air Command between 1978 and 1984. First publicized by Tom Peters and Nancy Austin, General Creech's accomplishments in leading TAC—an organization with an annual budget of $35 billion—from not-ready-for-combat status to the Air Force's highest readiness rating is well worth investigating. To communicate a clear, consistent message and rallying cry to over 115,000 men and women in a hurry, Creech often used symbols and gestures.

On a visit to one of his units, he noticed that the supply sergeant's chair terminated in three casters and a block of wood. Four-star General Creech had the chair boxed and sent to TAC's Langley, Virginia, headquarters—where he held a ceremony and awarded it to the three-star general who headed logistics. Creech told the general that he could get himself a new chair *after* he had the supply system running smoothly—which didn't take long.

Within days, every person in TAC had heard the story and other support functions got the message: "The units close to the action are your customers. Treat them with respect or answer for the consequences." The story became the basis of a self-fulfilling prophecy that things were bound to get better with Creech in command.

American history offers some incredibly moving gestures. General George Washington single-handedly quelled an uprising of U.S. Army officers outraged over their post–Revolutionary War treatment, which included the withholding of wages. As he began his speech, General Washington pulled out his glasses saying, "Gentlemen, you will permit me to put on my spectacles for I have not only grown gray, but almost blind in the service of my country."

5

PRESCRIPTION FOR PROGRESS: INITIATIVE

"Tired? Listless?" A half-remembered radio advertisement of the 1940s touted a little pink pill guaranteed to cure all ills. More recently, the blahs have met with a different prescription: exercise. Doctors aren't too fussy about the form the exercise takes; there are benefits to almost anything that gets the body moving. Exercise is recommended to prevent such major health threats as heart disease, diabetes, and osteoporosis; it is also linked to a more positive outlook on life. Studies find that even smokers who exercise live longer than smokers who don't. This is no magic pill, just consistent individual effort.

So what has that got to do with leadership? While exercise goes a long way toward relieving physical stress and improving the quality of life, a hostile work environment would seem to call for something more than a long walk. Yet once again, consistent individual effort makes all the difference. A mental equivalent to physical exercise is available to anyone who cares to utilize it: initiative. It's better than a little pink pill.

This chapter looks first at how an individual can bring his or her own initiative to bear even in the most unencouraging of corporate environments. It then examines how organizations (and individuals within organizations) can encourage initiative in others. Along the way, initiative is linked to three personal traits: industry, innovation, and self-confidence.

Initiative is the bridge between followership and leadership. Neither follower nor leader can escape the necessity of developing personal initiative, although organizations, unfortunately, stifle it all the time. Initiative enables employees to establish a degree of control over

83

their own lives—whether they expend the effort to improve the workplace or move on to greener pastures or apply their talents in their personal lives. One thing is certain: The more individuals are sure of, and comfortable with, their own abilities, the more initiative they exercise.

The *American Heritage Dictionary* describes initiative as "The power, ability, or instinct to begin or to follow through energetically with a plan or task; enterprise and determination." This sounds appealing. Who wouldn't want to go through the day brimming with enterprise and determination? Developing initiative, however, may require a radical change in behavior—sort of a personality transplant. It is definitely not for the faint of heart.

One way to gain the courage to begin is to evaluate the current work environment. Being realistic about what can and cannot be accomplished under existing conditions can bestow peace of mind—and freedom to act. Some organizations really do not encourage initiative; others may welcome it without actively encouraging it. Identifying opportunities to exercise initiative can be a source of confidence. In *Leading Marines (FMFM 1-0),* commandant of the Marine Corps, General Carl E. Mundy states, "Courage can be misunderstood. It is the ability to know what is, or is not, to be feared."

Exercise is not a universal panacea; neither is initiative. There will still be impersonal bosses, routine tasks, and economic downturns; but as with exercise, anyone with a strong sense of what he or she can accomplish through his or her own volition will be in a better position to deal with negatives. Initiative is the way to empower oneself. The alternative is helplessness, fear, and loss of pride in a job well done—that's the perfect prescription for depression.

THAT CRITICAL FIRST STEP

Initiative can be broken down into incremental steps. Decide to become a better leader; acquire this book; read the first four chapters. Presto!— the first stirrings of initiative . . . not enough in itself, but an excellent start. Follow-through is as important. The dictionary definition of initiative refers to "a plan or task," and it is easiest to begin with tasks that focus on something that can be accomplished in the absence of anyone else's approval or consent: self-development.

Does everyone have to go through the unquestionably clumsy business of self-development? Do "natural leaders"? What follows is a passage from John Adair's book on training:

> In discussing the results or effects of leadership training, it is perhaps important not to compare the top 10 per cent of leaders who command naturally with the more "average" who, newly conscious of the requirements of leadership, deliberately set about supplying the necessary functions. Officer cadets, understandably, prefer the natural leader, little realizing that often this kind of ability can become either fixed at a certain level or ceiling, or become rigid and stiff with advancing age and changing circumstances. In fact, leaders on all points of the continuum of leadership ability in order to grow have to pass through a period of "artificiality" or self-consciousness, as they awkwardly apply theory to practice, or reflect upon their experience in new terms.

While some people are naturally more comfortable with introspection than others, it behooves everyone to develop a degree of self-awareness. Too often reflection gets short shrift. Times of reflection—even if only for a short period during the work day or work week—are essential to maintain focus on what is important. It is extremely difficult to learn leadership on the run: On the run, a person does what he or she already knows how to do. General Joshua Chamberlain, the citizen-soldier first mentioned in Chapter 2, had periods of reflection forced upon him each of the six times he was wounded and sent to the rear to recuperate. (He even returned to Maine a couple of times to recover from his more serious wounds.) Each time he used part of his recovery period to assess his progress in becoming an accomplished combat leader and to set new goals and plans for himself.

Self-development requires self-examination. Note in the following "Leader's Code" from a Marine Corps manual that knowledge of oneself is given very high priority:

> I become a leader by what I do. I know my strength and my weakness and I strive constantly for self-improvement. I live by a moral code, with which I set an example that others can

emulate. I know my job and I carry out the spirit as well as the letter of orders I receive.

I take the initiative and seek responsibilities, and I face situations with boldness and confidence. I estimate the situations and make my own decisions as to the best course of action. No matter what the requirements, I stay with the job until the job is done; no matter what the results, I assume full responsibilities.

I train my men as a team and lead them with tact, with enthusiasm, and with justice. I command their confidence and their loyalty; they know I would not consign to them any duty that I myself would not perform. I see that they understand their orders, and I follow through energetically to insure that their duties are fully discharged. I keep my men informed and I make their welfare one of my prime concerns.

These things I do selflessly in fulfillment of the obligations of leadership and for the achievement of the group goal.

Although this "Leader's Code" came from a military manual, nothing in it is unique to a military organization (with the possible exception of the male bias).

An Army manual offers a commonsense, four-step approach using strengths and weaknesses to develop leadership skills:

Step 1: Identify your strengths and weaknesses in specific areas (see below)
Step 2: Set goals
Step 3: Develop plans to achieve goals
Step 4: Evaluate. For each goal write out two or more ways of evaluating progress towards the goal.

As with other sequences, such as Dr. Deming's Plan-Do-Check-Act cycle, this process can be used continuously. Ideas garnered in the process of step 4 can be used to return to step 2 to set new goals. Since strengths and weaknesses have a way of changing as you grow, it also pays to go back to step one occasionally.

Beginning at step 1, the army's *FM 22-100* (1983) identifies a half-dozen areas for self-examination:

- Beliefs, values, and ethics
- Character traits

- Knowledge—of yourself, human nature, your job, and your unit
- Directional skills such as problem solving, planning, decision making, and goal setting
- Implementing skills such as communicating, coordinating, supervising, and evaluating
- Motivating skills such as teaching, counseling, and applying the principles of motivation

In a sense, moving toward becoming a better leader means tackling everything on this list at once. Self-knowledge requires analyzing beliefs and communication skills. Character traits impact how well an individual teaches and counsels others. But a plan for improvement can focus on one or two items at a time.

Step 1 is usually downright difficult. Looking back at the word *enterprise* in the definition of initiative on page 84, it is itself defined as, "An undertaking, esp. one of some scope, complication, and risk." The risk here is exposure—few people enjoy making a list of their negatives. Less threatening, although often equally difficult, is making a list of positives, although both lists are equally important. Concentrating only on weaknesses invites paralysis. Beyond ego preservation, a list of strengths provides substantial clues for putting together an improvement plan. How were strengths acquired? Were they adapted from models? Were they a matter of learning from mistakes? How can those strengths be used in the future?

Initially, review your favorite books and articles on the topic of leadership to help identify personal strengths and areas to be worked on. Once these lists are compiled, it gets riskier: The next step is to seek the opinions, suggestions, and observations of others. Soliciting input is easiest where a system of "360° evaluation" is in place, but in a traditional workplace, the most recent written evaluation can be a jumping-off point. Alternately, a list of leadership traits can be presented to fellow employees with a request to identify what they view as two or three strengths and two or three areas needing improvement in your leadership style. Even without additional commentary, the accumulation of the outside opinions combined with self-analysis yields two things: (1) a list of points to address, and (2) some idea of how to prioritize that list.

Honesty—brutal honesty—is required. The most accurate information is gained by asking a wide variety of people and analyzing assessments by "group," such as senior, peer, and junior. Perceptions of others can be compared with your own assessments of strengths and weaknesses. Does the world view your actions and abilities the same way that you do? Is there consistency by group? By gender? By race? Does everyone senior see you one way while everyone junior sees a completely different person? Do seniors, for example, list "loyalty" as a strength, while juniors list "loyalty" as an area needing improvement? Be prepared for a surprise or two.

Even organizations can be surprised. The business school at St. John's University was confounded when a workshop for staff and faculty on internal improvements took an unexpected turn. The evening before, consultants who were to teach the workshop met with a graduate class to identify students' concerns. More than twenty issues were identified, many of them areas that the business school leaders were already prepared to address: lighting in the parking lot, availability of food for the evening students, scheduling snags. But the concern that topped the students' list was not even on the current staff and faculty to-do list: Teach professors how to teach. Professional development classes held in the past had been ill-attended, leading the administration to believe that they were unimportant. Once professors realized that student/customers ranked teaching skills as a top priority, enrollment in future classes jumped dramatically. So did customer satisfaction.

Step 2 requires setting goals for each desired improvement. Resolving "to do better" is not enough—these are not New Year's resolutions. If decision-making skills are weak, studying logic or Statistical Process Control or the Ishikawa Fishbone cause-and-effect diagram might be in order. If that material is familiar, investigating benchmarking, value analysis, and reengineering can provide insight into powerful tools for changing processes. If the area requiring attention is the ability to communicate, goals might include improved public speaking skills, writing skills, listening skills, and increased vocabulary. Here again, seeking the opinion of others is virtually always a good idea. Are the goals realistic? Will attaining these goals be beneficial to the organization? Or at least to the individual?

Step 3 is the logical outgrowth of step 2. After setting a goal, make a detailed, written plan on how to reach it. For many people, it may seem strange to sit down and put pen to paper detailing future actions.

The temptation is to say to oneself, "I don't need to write that down; I'll remember that!", or "Well, of course, that's a given so I won't bother writing it down." Keep in mind that growth is uncharted territory. If a map of some sort isn't necessary, the road probably stays a bit too close to home.

Tasks to "get from here to there" must not only be identified, but also prioritized. Conditions necessary to carry out each task must be established. Using the preceding examples, subtasks for decision making might include reading a book or taking a course through in-house corporate training or a local college. Improving public speaking skills might include joining the Toastmasters Club, Dale Carnegie, or a local theater group. Probably some combination of options is in order. The point, of course, is to make conscious choices about specific actions. Once more, input from others can be valuable. Are there other options available that aren't yet on the list?

Step 4 is a natural outgrowth of the previous steps. In some respects, this is much the same as step 3—from a slightly different perspective. Write down desired results. Include "hard" measures where possible: deadlines, grade points, and milestones, such as becoming chairperson of a committee for decision making or making a presentation at every third staff meeting for communications. Evaluation is the only way to track progress.

THE FRATERNAL TRIPLETS: INDUSTRY, INNOVATION, SELF-CONFIDENCE

Bringing initiative to bear on the job is somewhat more complex than embarking on a course of self-development. Where initiative is valued, there are ample opportunities to practice, but unfortunately, this is not always the case. Nevertheless, there are still things that can be done in the absence of changes in the workplace. While it may be impossible for individuals to change the conditions under which they labor, *it is possible for them to change their response to those conditions.* The first step is to analyze what is and is not possible in the current situation.

One of the interesting things about the dictionary definition of initiative is that it makes no mention of innovation or creativity, beyond a somewhat elliptical reference "to begin." And yet in popular parlance, the word initiative is used to imply a "something more than," a spark, a cleverness. Even in the military, initiative takes on that cast. An army manual could not be more clear: "Discipline is instant and willing obedience to all orders, and in the absence of orders, to what you believe the order would have been. Here is the essence of true initiative."

The military is not advocating clairvoyance. Its policy is to keep all personnel informed about details of specific missions, including what resources are available to accomplish the task. What it expects is responsible action coupled with judgment—not just slogging ahead. Personnel are required to use all the resources at their disposal to the greatest effect. Initiative is a blend of perspiration and inspiration—of industry and innovation.

Perhaps the simplest way to look at it is to imagine a "black box," where leaders can see inputs and outputs, while what goes on inside the box is hidden. Leaders decide on the mission. They also decide on things like allocations of personnel, time, funds, and equipment. The people in the black box are expected to use the inputs to produce the outputs, *but how they do that is up to them*. That is the essential characteristic of initiative. Within the black box, the ones who perform the task are the "boss." Not only do they have the responsibility, they have the authority—or at least they should have.

It doesn't always work out that way. Take the case of a secretary at Holy Cross College. She used her knowledge of computer technology to streamline record keeping in her department. With the help of a work study student, she wrote a software program that enabled information to be printed in a number of different ways by making a single change. Prior to that, each file, each index, and each list had to be retyped from scratch. Her boss had no objections. There was no change in inputs (other than the software) and no change in output (other than speed).

On a separate issue, her boss was inclined to look at already-typed correspondence and request that letters typed on large stationery be transferred to small stationery—or letters typed on small stationery be transferred to large stationery. When queried prior to typing which size she preferred, the inevitable response was, "Do what you think best." In a vain attempt to encourage clearer communication, the secretary asked for a meeting. While the boss recognized that there was a problem, she assured the secretary that time would take care of it, making the comment, "You'll soon learn to read my mind."

This is a classic dilemma. In the first instance, the secretary made her own work environment less hectic by exercising initiative; in the second, no initiative was possible. The boss clearly did have an opinion on the output, although she said that she didn't. The result was that accurate work was often done twice. The disconnect was severe enough that the secretary's yearly evaluation contained the comment "asks too many questions," yet there was no recognition that, overall, work was processed in roughly one-third less time.

What are the secretary's options? First, she can use the extra time she generated to retype correspondence. Second, she can accept that there will always be a degree of disharmony between her and her boss. Third, she can look for another job—and that's what she did.

Before applying for a job in the Theater Department, she visited the secretary whose job was being posted and asked her to describe the workload. Concluding that here, too, was an area that required computer support (not to mention a typewriter with an erase key!), she made a request for new equipment part of the job interview and promised that the flow of work would improve. She got the position. Her former boss offered this bit of advice during the exit interview: "Just observe for a year before you start making recommendations." (Some people don't ever get it.)

Where initiative was applauded, the secretary was able to negotiate with professors for a no-same-day-service policy, enabling her to prioritize work with greater accuracy and leaving time both to desktop publish programs for students' projects and clean out twenty-five years of department archives. By making both inputs and outputs negotiable, the Theater Department modernized its office procedures to everyone's satisfaction.

Like most instances of initiative that drive an organization forward, this secretary's experience was not made up of earth-shaking events. But it provides an example of someone who understood the job's requirements and believed that grabbing the moment and getting something done benefits the organization, bosses, and customers (in this case, the students), as well as oneself. This same dynamic holds true throughout an organization. Senior vice presidents who allow junior vice presidents to exercise their initiative are also using the black-box approach. Seniors and juniors working as a team allow for the natural combination of industry and innovation, particularly when an innovative idea comes from one person and the willingness to act comes from some other person or from the group as a whole.

The relationship between self-confidence and successful action is somewhat of the chicken-and-egg variety. Self-confidence leads to action. Successful action leads to more self-confidence. Even in the department where initiative was not welcome, the secretary was able to take pride in her ability to muscle the work around and her basic self-confidence was unimpaired, although even the strongest ego eventually falters when faced with a steady stream of negative feedback. A pre–World War II army manual puts it this way:

> Initiative and willingness to assume responsibility are direct products of self-confidence and will-power. To do well just what he is told to do but never initiate anything himself—to drag along with his interest solely on his pay check and on keeping out of possible trouble—these are the traits of military deadwood, the symbols of timidity, laziness, and mediocrity.
>
> Initiative does not belong exclusively to the leader. It is essential in all ranks and grades. The commander must foster initiative among his subordinates by giving them duties commensurate with their rank and then letting them work out the details and finish the job unaided. A company commander who is a busybody and who will not trust his subordinates, who handles all details of the orderly room, the kitchen, the supply room, who is the corporal of every squad in training and battle, not only narrows his own vision and ability, forming the hindering habit of attention to petty detail, but kills the pride, the spirit and ambition, the initiative, of every man in his unit.

Recognizing and encouraging initiative throughout an organization is particularly important in service industries where "moments of truth" (Jan Carlzon's marvelous phrase—and the title of his book about his success with Scandinavian Airline) abound. It takes confidence and skill to deal with an irate or needy customer when time is of the essence and it is vital that the person on the scene behave "in the absence of orders." Sharon Conner recalls a vacation in Puerto Rico when the batteries for her insulin pump stopped working on a Sunday. After a frantic search for replacements, she and her husband arrived at a K-Mart in San Jermain just after closing. Tapping on the glass, she got the attention of the store manager, who opened the door, listened to the problem, escorted them to the camera section, and found the right battery. He then insisted that they take the battery without charge.

The odds that management can live with the decisions made by employees are raised considerably through efforts to communicate the mission of the organization and to forge a common bond among all its members. An organization in which the message of "who we are" has been effectively ingrained virtually guarantees that every member of an organization thrust into similar situations will make similar decisions.

A LEADER'S GUIDE TO ENCOURAGING INITIATIVE IN OTHERS

Although Warren Bennis and Burt Nanus do not hold up Admiral Hyman Rickover, founder of America's nuclear navy, as a role model, they do quote him as saying, "Good ideas are not adopted automatically. They must be driven into practice with courageous patience." A company rarely succeeds in inculcating initiative overnight. There are, however, things that an organization can do to make initiative at every level commonplace: Make initiative a core value, structure for it, and recognize and channel creativity.

The essential first step in making initiative a core value is to verbalize its importance. Prior to World War II, an army manual had this to say about the topic:

But the leader who smothers initiative within his unit, through distrust of the abilities of his subordinates or through a well-meaning but nevertheless vicious desire to see that everything is done exactly right—the leader who does these things in time of peace and during training at any time—is denying to those under him what is perhaps the chief tradition of American troops in battle, the tradition of estimating the situation with

speed and acting accordingly whether or not there are orders
from higher authorities to cover the situation. It has been initiative that has marked our most successful units in our wars of
the past. It has been a lack of initiative (often, it is true, due to
briefness of training) that has brought about most of the mistakes American commanders have made in past wars. But as a
whole, the American soldier, both officer and enlisted man, has
taken pride in his ability to act and to act successfully in the
face of any circumstances, no matter how confused, that war
might bring.

No one reading this statement could be in any doubt about how important initiative is in the American military. A final bit of Marine Corps
exhortation on the topic of initiative as a core value contains a call to
action applicable to any organization bent on continual improvement
and faced with the ever-changing demands of customers:

> Initiative, the willingness to act on one's own judgment, is a
> prerequisite for boldness. These traits carried to excess can
> lead to rashness, but we must realize that errors by junior lead-
> ers stemming from overboldness are a necessary part of learn-
> ing. We should deal with such errors leniently; there must be
> no "zero defects" mentality. Not only must we not stifle bold-
> ness or initiative, we must continue to encourage both traits *in
> spite of mistakes.* On the other hand, we should deal severely
> with errors of inaction or timidity. We will not accept lack of
> orders as justification for inaction; it is each Marine's *duty* to
> take initiative as the situation demands.

As with self-development, it is not enough to recognize the merits
of the concept of initiative without a concrete plan for achieving the
goal. In an organization that embraces empowerment as a central
tenet—assuming the working definition of empowerment to be authority equal to responsibility—initiative can be practiced either by individuals or by groups. For the most part, the Quality Revolution met the
challenge of structuring for initiative through widespread use of suggestion systems, quality teams, and self-directing work teams, all of
which were recognized and rewarded for enterprise and resourcefulness.

Encouraging initiative in others was at the heart of the Clinical Process Improvement plan shepherded into existence by Dr. Mike Dean, former head of the Pediatric Intensive Care Unit (PICU) at Primary Children's Medical Center, a 232-bed pediatric tertiary care hospital in Salt Lake City, Utah. In the fall of 1991, Dean, who has since moved on to become interim medical director of the hospital, took part in the Advanced Training Course in Clinical Process Improvement developed by Intermountain Health Care and got religion. Dean saw that Continuous Quality Improvement (CQI) could be used to save money and improve patient care in PICU, but he knew that it was not possible to realize his vision single-handedly. Only through the success of the nursing staff could a CQI program succeed. He set about providing a budget, structure, and training.

Katy Welkie, the nursing director of the PICU, was Dean's first convert. Dean arranged for Welkie to attend the Advanced Training Course and the two of them sent a proposal to the CEO and CFOs suggesting CQI be funded from cost savings resulting from changes in PICU procedures. They also proposed a unique arrangement to create a discretionary development account: 20 percent of annual savings (minus CQI expenses) would be returned to PICU. The finance department agreed.

The next step was to create a position to coordinate and oversee CQI teams, provide data analysis, and do the cost analysis required for the "kickback" part of the proposal. Mary Price was hired for the position, which was at risk until savings could be calculated. Price was given access to a computer and the programs necessary to analyze the data. Dean acted as her tutor for the software.

With the help of the hospital Quality Management coordinator, the trio developed one-and-a-half to two-day workshops and held them at a nearby resort. To the delight of the nursing staff, the hospital picked up the tab for two nights at the Snowbird Ski and Summer Resort for spouses and immediate family, and each employee received $50 a day for dinner. Sessions were held during off-duty hours, and the cost to the hospital was negligible.

The training curriculum consisted of a series of team-building exercises, an outline of the basic concepts of CQI, and "real" projects. Large groups were divided into smaller groups, given a problem, and asked to write a mission statement and use CQI problem-identification techniques. The team could request information and the faculty created data, using a portable computer. Assuming that the team asked for the right data, it was able to use the charts and graphs to suggest improvements and realize the mission statement. Later, other functional groups, such as the "rehab" department, heard about the course and arranged to take it.

Dean was personally involved in every one of the training sessions, teaching and providing personal examples and experiences. The message "you can make a difference" was impressed upon attendees, and Dean communicated the expectation that anyone who attended a training session would lead or be involved in a CQI team.

Dean's initiative in putting together a CQI process for PICU paid off. In 1993–1994, the first full year, the unit turned in $120,000 in savings, and PICU received back approximately $15,000 for its unrestricted account, which was used for such things as employee recognition. Some of the projects had dramatic financial impact: Between June 1993 and September 1995 a change in the placement of bedside feeding tubes resulted in approximately $203,000 in savings; using Critical Paths on a group of simple postoperative heart patients reduced patient charges by over 30 percent. Other projects with harder-to-document financial savings also improved patient care: Skin care awareness resulted in fewer decubitus ulcers. What is noteworthy is that all the projects were led by PICU nurses or nurse practitioners.

Developing initiative in others takes more than commitment to an idea, it takes careful planning. Paul Malone III in *Love 'Em and Lead 'Em* offers a list of "specific questions to ponder and answer" which amount to a planning primer:

- How do you plan to keep your subordinates informed about the mission, goals and objectives of the organization?
- How do you plan to keep your subordinates informed of "what's hot," the current top priority activities of the organization?
- What standards do you plan to set for the organization? How do you plan to let your subordinates know of your expectations of them?
- What are your policies regarding the recognition of outstanding performance? Conversely, how do you plan to deal with sub-standard performance?

- How do you plan to provide for "downward communications"—keeping subordinates informed of events that affect their working lives?
- How do you plan to provide for "upward communications"—keeping yourself informed of what's going on, to include the "bad news"? Do you plan to wander around a lot and discuss things informally or will you use the chain of command exclusively?
- How and to what degree do you plan to involve subordinates in the decision making process? Do you plan to ask subordinates for their ideas? How?
- What steps do you plan to take to maintain and enhance subordinate morale, loyalty, motivation, and productivity?
- To what degree are you committed to developing your subordinates and helping them to grow? How do you plan to do this?
- To what degree are you available to assist subordinates in the resolution of their personal problems?
- How do you plan to deal with change, conflict, and crises that affect the organization?

It is possible to encourage initiative in others; it is also possible to discourage it. A Marine Corps manual provides a list of phrases that have a chilling effect in either a military or civilian setting. It cautions readers:

Beware of killing initiative and motivation by using some of the stock phrases you see below. Glance over the list, then promise yourself never to use such killer phrases on yourself or on your [people]:

- Why should we lead the way?
- Let someone else try it.
- We already have too much to worry about.
- I heard they tried it over at . . .
- It's not our responsibility.
- We will have to look into it.
- Let's study it.
- This is the wrong time of year.

- Someday there may be a need for this.
- Is this new?
- If it's "his" idea, I don't like it.
- The boss doesn't like that type of thing.
- How do you know it is better?
- Research says . . .
- Show the research to prove it.
- They tried it at battalion.
- It's change for change sake.
- The problem isn't important enough to bother with.
- Leave it alone and it will go away.
- Yes, it is annoying, but you'll get used to it.
- It is too complex for anyone to even solve, so why try?
- What problem?
- Impossible.
- If we try this, it will upset the SOP [standard operating procedure].
- If the idea has any value, it would have been suggested before.
- It will require too much training—it's too complicated to adopt.
- It will be hard to get concurrence for this.
- It will be hard to enforce.
- It is not considered a good management practice.
- How do we know it will work?

MORE IDEAS FOR MAKING INITIATIVE COMMONPLACE

The most uncomfortable part of encouraging initiative is that it invites activity outside well-established norms. At the Paul Revere Insurance Group during the third year of their Quality Has Value process, a team consisting of a dozen administrative workers decided to revise a form that they believed required useless information in some areas and failed to call for vital information in others. The co-captains were two young female high school graduates who had agreed to share the position because neither felt up to the task alone. When the team decided that the next step was to have the form checked for legal implications, the two were reluctant to approach a company lawyer. Their team members talked them through it and sent them on their way.

Without the quality process, the revamped form might have been put in the traditional pipeline for approval: from supervisor to manager to director to second vice president to vice president for operations to the head of the legal department to a lawyer to the lawyer's "I'll get to it" box (normally located to the left of the "In" box) and, eventually, back again. Although they were scared to death, the co-captains approached a lawyer and asked him to read things over. He assured them there were no problems, gave them his name in case anyone had any further questions, and they returned triumphant—mission accomplished.

Too many individuals at all levels identify unorthodox procedures with rocking the boat. It is costly and dangerous to label individuals as troublemakers when in fact they are displaying initiative or ingenuity in proposing solutions. Creative talent is too precious to waste. Squashing even one person's innovative impulses might well discourage others from ever speaking up, and at that point, the organization loses countless new and exciting ideas. Employees at all levels must feel certain that their ideas and their initiative are not only acceptable, not only sought and welcomed, but imperative. They must believe that "It is better to ask forgiveness than permission," and that their seniors want them to act accordingly.

The organization's role is to identify creativity and to support and channel it. When a mistake occurs, subordinates cannot be abandoned in the name of "letting them learn the hard way": Adopting a hands-off policy is akin to laziness or an abdication of responsibility. When mistakes are made—and they will be—the leader's role is to insure that the errors are not ultimately damaging, to make certain that lessons were in fact learned, and to further the subordinates' development as leaders in their own right.

A rough analogy might be that of a parent watching a child's first attempts at walking—a wildly innovative act for the youngster, requiring an astonishing degree of initiative. The first time the child falls, the parents could, in theory, decide that it was obvious that their offspring was never going to learn to walk, and that baby might hurt himself or herself (or damage some expensive knickknack) with the next tumble. Having made that decision, the child could be picked up and lugged about for as long as the parents' strength held out. But to do so would be absurd. It would be better all around to help the little one back up, hide the bric-a-brac, guard against head-splitting falls as much as possible, and be prepared to cheer.

How to cope with and benefit from the "inventive energies of junior leaders" is the subject of a list of recommendations in a Marine Corps manual:

1. Stop the detailed supervision of tasks assigned to subordinates. Substitute a technique of review and conduct all review in a way that stimulates initiative,

2. Treat all mistakes that are not malicious as exactly what they are—valuable experience. Correct the mistakes, but exploit the experience gained in a way that builds initiative and confidence,

3. Train to practice initiative and teach it as an indispensable characteristic of leadership,

4. Declare war on "nit-pickers." If a letter conveys the desired meaning, don't waste time and kill initiative by polishing it into what, in only one opinion, is a literary gem.

Creativity can result from looking at something ordinary in an extraordinary way—from the garage sale that advertised itself as offering "Jackie O's Other Stuff" in the wake of Sotheby's auction to a major corporate initiative. In May 1996, Kodak rolled out Advantix, a new way to take pictures using cartridge film that allows the photographer to choose between three formats when shooting or processing film—and to switch back and forth between formats on a single roll. Better still, each frame carries with it lighting and focus information so that it can be developed under ideal conditions. In addition to prints and the cartridge, the customer receives back a proof sheet with numbered photos in miniature from the developer.

One portion of the Kodak effort was directed by Joe Byrnes, who worked with a team of five direct reports as an internal consultant tasked with delivering custom software for the film manufacturing site. His team took a radically different approach and used tools and development technology outside the status quo. Although Kodak questioned every step, Byrnes prevailed and the result was a low-cost, easy-to-use system. The internal customer was so pleased that Byrnes won Kodak's Stock Option Award, established in 1995 by CEO George Fisher, who arrived from Baldrige-winner Motorola with the goal of giving recognition a higher profile at Kodak.

Spotting creativity is itself an art. While initiative requires creativity, it is rarely totally off the wall. An army manual makes this distinction: "It is an utterly vital matter for every leader to develop initiative among his subordinates. . . . there is a difference between genuine initiative and undue license." A Marine Corps manual gives some guidelines for spotting "highly creative people," based on characteristics that tend to be fairly common:

> . . . [F]irst, there is a tendency for them to gain a reputation for having wild and silly ideas; second, their work is considered by their high productivity of "off the beaten track" ideas; and, third, their work is characterized by humor and playfulness. The three characteristics which emerge here would appear to be of considerable importance to the leader in assisting his highly creative people to adjust without sacrificing their creativity.

The manual goes on to list sixteen traits of creative people (which could also be used as a baseline for identifying personal strengths and weaknesses):

1. They are not easily stereotyped.
2. Are well-above average in intelligence.
3. Express themselves well verbally.
4. Have unusual capacity to record and retain, and have readily available the experience of their life history.
5. Creative people are discerning and observant in a different fashion; they are alert, capable of concentrating rapidly and shifting if appropriate; they are fluent in scanning thoughts and producing those thoughts that serve the problem they undertake; they have a wide-range of information at their command.

6. Intelligence alone will not tend to produce creativity. Creativity is the relevant absence of repression and suppression as mechanisms for the control of impulse and imagery. Repression operates against creativity, regardless of how intelligent a person may be.

7. They are given to expression rather than suppression or repression; therefore, they have fuller access to their own experiences, both conscious and unconscious.

8. Openness to experience is one of the most striking characteristics of a highly-creative person.

9. Highly-creative people have a closer identification of traits or characteristics in themselves than noncreative people. They are more open to feelings and emotions.

10. Everyone perceives and judges, but the creative person tends to prefer perceiving to judging. "Where a judging person emphasizes the control and regulation of experience, the perceptive creative person is inclined to be more interested and curious, more open and receptive, seeking to experience life to the full."

11. Artists in general show a preference for feeling; scientists and engineers a preference for thinking. Architects are somewhere between the two groups.

12. A highly-creative person is genuinely independent.

13. Creative people are relatively uninterested in policing their own impulses and images or those of others.

14. Creative people have preference for complexity, and their delight is in the challenging and the unfinished.

15. Creative people almost always display a good sense of humor.

16. Creative people tend to be more self-sufficient, more self-assertive, more introverted, but bold and more resourceful and self-accepting than the average person.

By making initiative a core value and structuring for it, creative people are given greater latitude in implementing their ideas to everyone's benefit without arousing undue anxiety in those around them. Anyone can learn to live with the bustle and complexity that initiative and creativity engender.

It may take some adjustment on the leader's part. Take the case of Baron von Steuben, the Prussian soldier who came to train troops at Valley Forge during the Revolutionary War. It would be an understatement to say that initiative was not a core value in the military tradition of Prussia's fighting forces, and von Steuben had no intention of structuring for it when he came to the colonies. To his credit, however, he recognized that there were characteristics about the soon-to-be-American soldiers that distinguished them from the professionals that he had been used to: asking why something was necessary, wanting to do things "my way," and insisting on being treated with respect. In short, they displayed all the elements that create initiative. He modified his approach, carefully combining European military discipline with explanations of the hows and whys of his orders. By embracing the culture and traditions of the ragtag army he had come to train, Baron von Steuben inspired a willingness to risk everything and created an effective fighting force that changed history.

6

STAYING THE COURSE: CHARACTER, VIRTUE, ETHICS

B ecoming an effective leader requires making two entirely different decisions: What do you want to do, and who do you want to be? Applying initiative to the first question results in acquiring new skills; applying it to the second can result in becoming a different person. Because it requires profound introspection, character development is the single most difficult issue in leadership. It is one thing to admit that you are "lousy with numbers" and take a math course, and quite another to recognize that you are dishonest or cowardly and make appropriate changes; but the results make the discomfort worthwhile. As English author Thomas Carlyle said, "Make yourself an honest man, and then you may be sure there is one less rascal in the world."

Encompassing both the rational and emotional components of leadership, the United States Coast Guard Academy has defined "good character" as "moral action demonstrated in all circumstances. It is the result of reasoned and willful coordination between heart and mind." Character is not, of course, enough by itself. As noted in Chapter 2, the Coast Guard establishes "Four C's" as guideposts on the way to becoming a successful leader: character, competence, commitment, and community. These four are identified as a "natural outgrowth" of the stated Coast Guard core values of honor, respect, and devotion to duty. While not every individual will wish to copy these core values or the "Four C's" verbatim, every individual and organization benefits from a conscious determination of, and statement of, exactly who they are and who they wish to be.

Without a moral compass, leadership deteriorates—sometimes to an alarming degree. Men and women whose motivation and goals are genuinely detrimental to the common good, but who are willing to use their ability to convince others to follow them, do an astonishing amount of damage. On the macro-level, they are easy to identify: Adolf Hitler falls into this category. On the micro-level, anyone who creates an environment that either allows or condones unethical behavior on the part of subordinates qualifies for the sobriquet "bad leader." Such leadership goes beyond incompetence: It is evil.

The view that employees of an organization deserve a surrounding structure that reflects ethical values is not a new one, as pointed out in a Coast Guard paper prepared for a conference on leadership at the United States Naval Academy at Annapolis:

> According to Aristotle, governments and other social institutions should be set up so that it is both possible and sensible for people to be honest, loyal, compassionate, fair, etc. It is unwise to create and perpetuate work environments that make ethically responsible behavior into acts of moral courage. . . . organizations need to be places where ordinary life is not a daily moral struggle.

Being a leader in the true sense of the word requires more than being able to accumulate followers: It means being able to lead them somewhere worthwhile. In short, character counts. Personal values and philosophy count. And the ability to love counts. Any individual aspiring to a leadership role must consciously choose moral and ethical standards, looking both internally at his or her beliefs, values, attitudes, and behavior and externally at how he or she is perceived by others. "Establishing a philosophy" does not mean that every leader, or would-be leader, is expected to become a modern-day Socrates, but it does mean deciding who you are, what you value, what your priorities are, what you will stand for and what you will not—and making sure that everyone knows what those decisions are.

Sometimes the more difficult a situation is, the simpler an ethical code can be. Vice Admiral James B. Stockdale, USN, after spending eight years as a POW in North Vietnam, said that he had, in the course of his imprisonment, boiled his values down to one unbreakable rule:

"You are your brother's keeper." When specifically asked, "What kept you going? What was your highest value?", his answer was, "The man next door." Adherence to that value drove his behavior throughout his confinement in Hanoi.

VIRTUE IN THE TWENTY-FIRST CENTURY

Traditionally, moral and ethical issues have been addressed through legal, religious, and social institutions. During the last century, all three have undergone transformations. Society has lost much of its shorthand for conveying "truth," as diversity and multiculturalism have redefined what is desirable in the body politic. Formerly sacrosanct institutions have come under scrutiny and revision: Even Mom and apple pie are controversial in some quarters. Values can, in fact, change as circumstances and understanding of them change. What seemed of great importance to an individual or group in one age may seem silly with the passage of time and additional information.

When looking for common values today, individuals must not only assess their own beliefs and goals, they must define themselves to others, and they must seek an understanding of those others based on fact rather than conjecture. To show how assumptions about common knowledge and common beliefs no longer hold up, consider the following passage from an article by Chaplain Robert Phillips, the former Senior Chaplain at the Coast Guard Academy. The reader should keep in mind that cadets at the Academy are among America's best and brightest. They are at the Academy not as the result of political appointments, but through a series of competitive exams and interviews. These young people have chosen to go through an extremely difficult course of study in order to serve their country. They are patriotic, idealistic, bright, committed, and focused.

> . . . [T]he military must take a serious look at its assumptions about the moral and ethical standards of those it commissions or recruits . . . the influence of organized religion as a conduit

for shared social and human values has waned. On my first day teaching a Morals and Ethics class at the U.S. Coast Guard Academy, I gave the 24 cadets in class a quiz to determine what formal knowledge they brought to the course. The last question asked the cadets to name as many of the Ten Commandments as they could. As the commandments are one of the foundations for ethical reflection in Western civilization, it seemed like an appropriate question. I figured that even if they had seen the Cecil B. De Mille movie, they should be good for a couple.

I was wrong. One cadet knew eight commandments. Seven knew between four and six commandments. Eight knew between one and three. Eight cadets—one third of the class— could not with confidence name a *single* commandment. They had heard there was such a list but were unable to say with certainty that any particular behavior was part of it. . . .

The institution must face the reality of incoming officers and enlisted personnel whose allegiance to and even awareness of long-standing traditional ethical values are shaky.

Leaders contemplating how to create an appropriate environment for subordinates or how to formulate plans for training others to lead face the problem of having to find or build areas of agreement in ethics, values, character, and behavior. *Leaders and followers must hold some things in common.*

Every group of humans with any sense of togetherness has a set of values, regardless of whether or not those values have ever been formally articulated. Values are, at their core, those ideas and ideals that organizations hold precious and that the people of an organization believe accurately describe who they are. Shared values give people a reason to gather together and establish sufficient cohesion for them to be recognized as an entity. These values could be as lofty and mighty as those that provoke an armed revolution and lead to the formation of a new nation—or as straightforward as providing day care for the children of employees.

A vision expresses organizational values in that it is the result of picturing what could happen to the present organization after an extended application of those values. It is a public extrapolation of those values and must be consistent with the leader's personal philosophy. As President Ronald Reagan once observed, "To grasp and hold a vision, that is the very essence of successful leadership—not only on the movie set where I learned it, but everywhere."

A vision seeks to inspire. It taps into what people believe they can be and want to be—and what they are willing to endure in the effort to become. It connotes action. At its best, it is more than simply an incremental step away from the present. To truly inspire, there must be a leap of faith imbedded in a vision—a hop of hope won't cut it. Only faith coupled with self-confidence can solidify a vision and inspire leaders and followers for the work ahead.

Every group is unique, every vision is unique, every leader is unique. Visionary leaders are not interchangeable commodities. Vastly popular leaders of two nations, for instance, could not swap places and expect to be as effective in their new countries as they were in their original ones. Imagine Queen Victoria in the Oval Office or Abraham Lincoln at Buckingham Palace. If a leader's vision does not hold promise for people, if potential followers do not perceive the vision as one they believe is possible and one that reflects their own values, the new "leader" will be rejected—no matter what technical skills the leader possesses. A manager can coerce his or her juniors to a certain level of performance. A leader, however, inspires juniors to accomplish much more than rule makers ever envision.

To be judged as a leader, a person must be seen as embodying either the as-we-are values of an organization or, even better, the as-we-want-to-be vision. The leader must know and understand the behaviors, attitudes, values, and ethics of the individuals who make up the organization. As appropriate, she or he must influence others through example, by teaching, and through moral suasion.

There is no single way to do this, but consistency is one key to evaluating its success. In a Tom Peters–inspired U.S. Naval Postgraduate School thesis on "Excellence in the Surface Navy" Commander Gregg G. Gullickson and Lieutenant Commander Richard D. Chenette came to this conclusion:

Values associated with and styles for dealing with subordinates, superiors, and peers tended to be consistent among the various levels of the chain of command on each of these ships. That is not to say that all of these ships had similar values or leadership styles, they did not: but on any given ship in this group, values and leadership style tended to be consistent and similar. However, what seemed important to these crews was not the attention given a specific value or set of values, but the fact that the leaders of these ships were value driven when dealing with people and their actions tended to be consistent and in harmony with their emphasized values. The captains were not viewed as being capricious, and they did not allow their officers and senior enlisted to be so. People knew where the leaders were coming from and they appreciated the sense of stability that resulted.

That "sense of stability" is important—very few people actually like surprises unless it's dinner for two or tickets to a ball game. Juniors at all levels feel the need to know more about their seniors than just their names—and if seniors don't make an effort to define themselves, those juniors fill in the blanks with whatever image fits the information available. Once individuals decide who their bosses are and what they can be counted on to do or not do, then they can decide whether to stay or to go. Further, if they decide to stay, the individuals can settle on a level of commitment, depending in large part on how closely the boss's perceived values and vision match their own.

Fortunately, there are some things that Americans still agree are worth striving for. It is instructive to compare the chapter titles in William J. Bennett's enormously popular *The Book of Virtues* with the list of fourteen leadership traits from the military cited in Chapter 4. The degree of overlap is encouraging. Responsibility, courage, and loyalty appear on both lists. Self-discipline and self-knowledge, work and initiative, perseverance and endurance, honesty and integrity run parallel. Compassion and friendship are civilian versions of one of the eleven leadership principles: Know your Marines and look out for their welfare. Tact, justice, and unselfishness are also acts of compassion and friendship. Neither list is definitive, but either is an excellent basis for principle-based leadership. The only virtue missing from both lists is the one that underpins every relationship between moral leaders and subordinates: love.

Fourteen Leadership Traits	The Book of Virtues Chapter Titles
Integrity	Self-Discipline
Knowledge	Compassion
Courage	Responsibility
Decisiveness	Friendship
Dependability	Work
Initiative	Courage
Tact	Perseverance
Justice	Honesty
Enthusiasm	Loyalty
Bearing	Faith
Endurance	
Unselfishness	
Loyalty	
Judgment	

LOVE AND LEADERSHIP

Asserting that leadership is not solely rational raises isolated arguments; stating specifically that effective leadership embraces emotional elements causes a greater number of people to fidget, but will generally be accepted. All but a few people, however, will be uneasy talking about the relationship between leaders and led as something closely akin to (if not a subset of) love. Yet there is no other word, no other concept, that explains the bond forged when leadership is at its best.

Military leadership theorist Major C. A. Bach stopped short of using the word love when he wrote in 1917, "[B]y doing all these things [i.e., practicing leadership] you are breathing life into what would be otherwise a mere machine. You are creating a soul in your organisation that will make the mass respond to you as though it were one man. And that is *esprit.*" An invitation to love is embedded in the quote: What better expression of love is there than to create life—and how can life be sustained without love?

The military is more comfortable using the word love than most civilian organizations, perhaps because it faces life-threatening situations. The biblical passage John 15:13 reflects this connection: "Greater love hath no man than this, that a man lay down his life for his friends." In *The Leadership Challenge,* James Kouzes and Barry Posner reported that love was crucial to leadership:

> We once asked U.S. Army Major General John H. Stanford to tell us how he would go about developing leaders, whether at Santa Clara University, in the military, or in private business. He replied, "When anyone asks me that question I tell them I have the secret to success in life. The secret to success is stay in love. Staying in love gives you the fire to really ignite other people, to see inside other people, to have a greater desire to get things done than other people. A person who is not in love doesn't really feel the kind of excitement that helps them to get ahead and lead others and to achieve. I don't know any other fire, any other thing in life that is more exhilarating and is more positive a feeling than love is."
>
> "Staying in love" is not the answer we expected to get, at least not when we began our study of leadership bests. But after numerous interviews and case analyses, we noted *love* was a word that many leaders used freely when talking about their own motivations to lead. The word *encouragement* has its root in the Latin word *cor,* meaning "heart." When leaders encourage others, through recognition and celebration, they inspire them with courage—with heart. When we encourage others, we give them heart. And when we give heart to others, we give love.

The overwhelming majority of the people interviewed by Kouzes and Posner were civilians, but the conclusion was the same: Love is an integral component of leadership.

In the Marine Corps, new recruits are encouraged to love each other and the Corps, not to hate the enemy—and this is done for quite practical reasons. Hatred is close to fear on the emotional scale, enough so that Marines going into battle with hatred as their primary driving force are vulnerable. Love is a stronger emotion; love is the reason Marines stay a little bit longer to help other Marines. Belief in mutual love—and the simple fact that Marines don't leave their dead on a battlefield—will keep Marines in place . . . perhaps long enough to turn the tide. As with everything else, the preaching and practice of love has a pragmatic undertone.

Allowing love to become part of one's approach to leadership is not without risk. In his book, *Servant Leadership,* Robert Greenleaf states, "Love is an undefinable term, and its manifestations are both subtle and infinite." He adds that love has only one "absolute condition: unlimited liability! As soon as one's liability for another is qualified to any degree, love is diminished by that much." In *Leadership Is an Art,* Max De Pree touched on love when discusing an employee's "right to a covenantal relationship":

> True covenants, however, are risky because they require us to be abandoned to the talents and skills of others, and therefore to be vulnerable. The same risks as one has when falling in love. If you wonder whether this whole idea has a place in corporate life, please ask your nearest poet or philosopher.

When people choose to become leaders, they forfeit a portion of their privacy, for if they are to excel they have to make themselves known to others. Leaders set the example in ethics and values and structure. It is not fair to ask for a subordinate's commitment without letting that person know what to expect from the relationship. Technical knowledge and competence are surely important, but without moral character and reciprocal commitment—displayed in everything from a well-articulated and well-publicized philosophy to a willingness to risk emotional ties—long-term effective leadership is impossible.

In their paper "Excellence in the Surface Navy," Gullickson and Chenette wrote of the importance of caring in gaining commitment:

> One commodore stated he had concluded that excellent leaders were "tuned to people and their needs," and they were "in frequency and in harmony with the ship." The commodore implied that caring for people and being in touch with them were means needed to gain commitment of individual sailors to the goals of their command.

Love freely given and understood is most often returned in full. Subordinates sense character and commitment along with competence on the part of leaders, and the results are advantageous both to the organization and to the leader. Quite simply, neither will let the other fail, neither will allow the other to be put at risk unnecessarily—either on a battlefield or on a production floor. Two examples from the Civil War and one from the Crimean War underscore this point.

Colonel Robert Gould Shaw was pretty much a forgotten character in American Civil War history until the movie *Glory* reminded people of his actions and accomplishments as the white commander of an all-black regiment in the Union army. One of the members of his regiment, Corporal James H. Gooding, wrote a series of letters to the *New Bedford Mercury*. These letters were printed as a running commentary on the progress of the war and, in particular, the role of the 54th Massachusetts Volunteer Infantry Regiment. After the "glorious failure" of the attack by the regiment on the Confederate Fort Wagner (the battle that cost Colonel Shaw his life), Corporal Gooding's letter contained the following testimony to the relationship Shaw had with his men:

> One poor fellow, struck no doubt by the Colonel's determined bearing, exclaimed as he was passing him, "Colonel, I will stay by you till I die," and he kept his word; he has never been seen since. For one so young, Colonel Shaw showed a well-trained mind, and an ability of governing men not possessed by many older and more experienced men. In him, the regiment has lost one of its best and most devoted friends. *Requiescat in pace.*

Another story in Alice Trulock's biography of General Joshua Lawrence Chamberlain demonstrates both the intensity and the tenderness of the relationship possible between leader and led:

> His men knew him to be oblivious to danger while he performed what he insisted was his duty, but when some case shot exploded pieces of iron that fell in fragments around him, some of his sergeants could stand it no longer. Rushing into the open, they seized him bodily and carried him to the shelter of the

works, risking their lives and possible discipline for such insubordinate action, but demonstrating their affection for him in a way that could not be doubted, only pardoned.

A separate story explicitly uses the word love:

> One man later told him that not only had he been popular with both officers and men in the brigade, but that they, "loved you as a father and you in return loved them like your children and treated them as equals and was not afraid to lead them." They were "not afraid to follow you or go wherever you ordered them to go, having implicit confidence in your judgment and ability as a commander."

Love does not have to involve death-defying acts; a sense of community and a conscious decision to sacrifice personal comfort for the benefit of others is also love. Florence Nightingale was an example of both. During Britain's involvement in the Crimean War in the mid-nineteenth century, Nightingale risked her life to establish a hospital for British troops in Scutari, on the shore opposite Istanbul. Despite falling ill herself, she oversaw the nursing staff, raised funds, and engaged in nursing:

> "She had an utter disregard of contagion," wrote the Reverend Sidney Godolphin Osborne. "The more awful any particular case, especially if it was a dying man, the more certainly might her slight form be seen bending over him, administering to his ease and seldom quitting his side until death released him."

Nor did her efforts to reduce deaths in the military due to filth, disease, and wounds end with the war. Over the next fifty years, despite frail health, she engaged in contentious debate with the War Office and the Home Office and pushed through recommendation after recommendation. Her cost accounting system for the army medical services was still in use at the beginning of World War II, eighty years later. When she died in 1910, her coffin was carried by six sergeants of the British army.

So it is with corporations. When followers and leaders are bound together by something more powerful than intellectual assent, they stay longer and try harder for each other. Love is returned in full.

ETHICAL BEHAVIOR IN PRACTICE

The military has long known that for an organization to function at peak efficiency, there must not only be common values, but these common values must be integrated into everyday activities. The Coast Guard Academy has identified four steps for developing their code of values; an individual could adapt this same approach to define and deploy his or her own personal ethical code:

1. Identify and codify organizational values
2. Promulgating, Explaining, and Demonstrating the Codified Core Values
3. Hold cadets accountable for evidencing character induced behavior in a supportive environment that is consistent with the espoused values
4. Assessing character development from individual and organizational perspectives

The cadets are expected to be active participants in the constant dissemination, as well as assessment, of the organizational values and philosophy. Acknowledgment or agreement on the part of subordinates is not accepted as enough; results are called for. The leader (or an individual) can be sure that his or her philosophy is having an impact only by observing the actions of those who are functioning in the same environment.

The Coast Guard also makes a distinction between external and internal motivation and accountability:

Behavior based on "external" control is effective only in the presence of an outside mechanism (i.e., when "getting caught" is reasonably probable). Behavior that is subject to an "internal locus of control" does not require an external instrumentality for compliance. This is the domain of "character."

Self-reinforcement refers to a process in which individuals enhance and maintain *their own behavior* by rewarding themselves with rewards that they control whenever they attain self-prescribed standards. . . .

As in the case of intellect, we normally don't recognize someone as having character unless it has been "tested." We say someone is "smart" only if we have seen one or more occasions in which the person has demonstrated "smartness." It is not a dimension that can be evaluated in the absence of observed behavior. Similarly, character must also be tested so that one can find evidence of the demonstration of "moral action."

External controls lead to situational ethics; internal controls lead to responsible behavior. In a democracy, both external and internal controls are necessary. There will be times when internal decisions are subject to review by others. The Coast Guard refers to "the-front-page-of-*The-New-York-Times* test"; *Leading Marines (FMFM 1-0)*, states more completely, "If you are prepared to talk about your actions, or lack thereof, in front of a national audience, made up of all your seniors, peers, subordinates, and friends who share the same professional values, and whose opinions you value, then your behavior was, or is, probably ethical in nature."

The actions of FedEx employee Alice Soliwoda provide as dramatic an example of ethical behavior as anyone is likely to find. On January 27, 1996, she was asked to trace medicine for a brain tumor cancer patient who was visiting with her mother-in-law. The patient had taken her last dose in the morning and expected delivery of new medication by FedEx by 10:30 to alleviate her pain. Soliwoda picked up the trace when the original agent left work at the end of her shift. No scans appeared to give the location of the original shipment, so she requested the shipper to contact a local pharmacy to arrange for a prescription to give the patient enough medication to hold her through until Monday when her shipment would arrive.

At this point, Soliwoda was doing a superb job. But the story doesn't end there. In talking with the patient and her mother-in-law during the day, Soliwoda found out that they were without transportation and did not have funds to pay for the prescription, which cost more than $100. After leaving work, Soliwoda took it upon herself to go to the pharmacy, pay for the prescription, and deliver it to the two women. When she returned to work on Monday, she requested that a thank-you letter be sent *to the pharmacist* for his help. FedEx awarded her a Golden Falcon Pin for outstanding dedication to customer service.

A Marine Corps manual lays out several definitions in the process of helping individuals and groups articulate a moral philosophy. A code of ethics is an individual's or group's statement of beliefs as to what is right and what is wrong. Values are an individual's or group's basic ideas about the worth or importance of people, concepts, or things. Attitudes are an individual's or group's feelings toward someone or something, and are usually expressed or demonstrated in likes and dislikes. Attitudes are not as deeply held as values, although they could be values in the making. Behavior is a person's or group's outward manifestations of either attitudes or values. The manual continues with a description of how these concepts interrelate:

> Three attributes which must be developed for a Marine to become professional are technical competence, values, and ethical conduct. . . . Values, in general, are those things that are important to you. . . . To develop professional values and attitudes you simply resolve to let nothing be more important to you than the welfare of your Marines, the accomplishment of your mission, and your personal integrity. . . . Your personal integrity is based on your code of ethics—your sense of right or wrong. . . . If, on the other hand, you desire to improve yourself (a value), you work to improve your knowledge and ability (technical competence), and you use methods which are fair and honest (ethical conduct), you are on your way to being a professional.

Knowing yourself is only half the puzzle; the rest is conveying that knowledge to others. In "Excellence in the Surface Navy," Gullickson and Chenette emphasize the importance of a personal philosophy and suggest ways in which to communicate that philosophy to every member of the crew:

> One point that was repeatedly emphasized during our interviews was that commanding officers of the best ships arrive on board with a "command philosophy" or a "game plan" of leadership and management for achieving excellence. . . . No one command philosophy was thought to be the best. But it was clear that the captain should have a plan to lead and manage his ship and that he should be working continuously at implementing it. A commodore, for example, felt it was important that the captain have and promulgate his command philosophy both in writing and at frequent meetings with all levels of the chain of command. He suggested that the captain discuss elements of his philosophy with department heads at formal weekly meetings and with division officers and chiefs every other week. Having a philosophy was a starting point on the road to excellence, and getting this philosophy to every member of the crew was the next step.

In *The Leadership Challenge,* Kouzes and Posner cite Tom Melohn, the "head sweeper"—that's what it says on his resume—and co-owner, president, and CEO of a San Leandro, California, manufacturing company, on how important it is to match actions and beliefs:

> "Another action that reinforces our belief in the importance of our employees is called caring. Simply stated," says Melohn, "at NATD [North American Tool and Die] we care about our people. We care a great deal. Not just as employees, but as human beings, as friends. And we try to help them in any way we can." From sending flowers, to buying doughnuts, to loaning company trucks, to monthly "Super Person" awards, Melohn shows how much he cares.
>
> "The only way to achieve these goals, we decided, was to create an atmosphere of complete trust between us, the owners, and all our employees." But Melohn adds "one admonition:

you've got to really mean it when you say you want such an atmosphere. You have to truly believe it. Then you've got to work at improving relations every day in every situation. Otherwise, your employees will sense the hypocrisy, and all will be for naught."

There is, of course, no one philosophy that can be adopted universally. The person in charge of an organization of any size can be consistently hardheaded or consistently softhearted and turn out a passing job of handling the outfit. If, however, that person appears arbitrary, shifting his or her pattern—if she or he is so inconsistent that subordinates feel insecure in their relationships to her or him—failure is all but inevitable.

Each leader exercises his or her power in a unique manner, and to the extent that he or she is able to convey that uniqueness, believability ceases to be an issue. The concept of fairness, however, plays a large part in implementing a leadership philosophy, particularly in the United States where the national sense of fair play is rather highly developed. If a leader or would-be leader is not seen to be absolutely fair in everything both adverse (extra duties, extra loads, etc.) and beneficial (praise, benefits of any sort), subordinates rapidly lose respect for him or her.

One of the masters in American business at making sure not only that he has a fair, consistent philosophy, but that everyone within his organization knows what it is, is Fred Smith, founder and CEO of FedEx. His program of daily communication—using, among other means, his own television network—not only serves to distribute news about the company, it also lets all of his employees know that he values them as business partners. Alice Soliwoda's generous decisions noted above reflect Smith's corporate philosophy.

A key feature of FedEx and the relationship among employees at all levels is their Guaranteed Fair Treatment program. If an employee at any level feels aggrieved by an action taken by his or her organizational senior, the employee can request time to speak to his boss's boss in order to get a "fair hearing." If that discussion does not resolve the issue to the employee's satisfaction, she or he can climb the corporate ladder and get a meeting with his boss's boss's boss—all the way up to Smith if need be. In point of fact, Smith reverses earlier decisions in 10 percent or fewer of the Guaranteed Fair Treatment cases that reach him, but the employee has been given every possible opportunity to plead his or her case.

Guaranteed Fair Treatment is a powerful and valuable tool for achieving Fred Smith's leadership philosophy. It conveys his sincere belief that individuals have merit and that each should be treated as a distinct, important member of the team. And he is willing to spend time and money to back up that belief. While Guaranteed Fair Treatment is a pioneering effort in corporate America, it wasn't completely original with Smith, a former Marine Corps officer. Like all truly successful business leaders, Smith doesn't care where a good idea comes from—only that it is a good idea. In the navy and in the marines, the procedure is called Request Mast—a name that harks back to the days when a junior member of the crew would upon request end up talking with the captain next to the main mast of the ship. The steps followed at FedEx are virtually identical to those defined by the navy and the marines.

PUBLISH OR PERISH

In addition to behavior, a written statement of policy can go a long way toward keeping an organization honest. Does the leader's or organization's philosophy actually need to be written down and published? Strictly speaking, no. In theory, if a leader is consistent, every one of his or her subordinates should have a clear picture of what the leader's philosophy is, and the organization will act accordingly. On the other hand, if a leader fails to make his or her philosophy regarding the work environment explicit, a philosophy will be assumed. The leader's choice is not whether to have an environment, it is whether he or she will define it or let it be established by default. Either way, subordinates act on what they believe to be true.

In practice, it might be of great value to a leader to ask subordinates to write out what they believe her or his philosophy of leadership to be. Such a request could bring either ugly surprises or wonderfully valuable lessons—perhaps both—and would doubtlessly motivate leaders to spell out their philosophy completely. The Quality Revolution made explicit what was only implicit before: Publishing a mission statement, or a vision statement, or a statement of corporate ethics *and following through* can bring success, whether measured by the bottom line or some other criterion. When employees and customers share a common vision of an organization, there are fewer misunderstandings and greater customer satisfaction.

Humans benefit from clarity, from a conscious effort to come to a mutual agreement on what is important. Whether done on a large scale or a small one, the statement should always be considered a work in progress. As the world occupied by the individuals involved changes, as people leave or join the organization, as customers require new goods and services, as opportunities present themselves, the statement of "Who we are and who we want to be" must be open to review. It is a living document, not an archival treasure. Even the Constitution of the United States has amendments.

The goal of a code of ethics or a statement of core values is to define reality for the organization: What is the actual world in which the organization must live and how will it be dealt with? While traditionally associated with specialized fields (e.g., medical or legal ethics), giving folks a structure that they know is common to everyone is an asset for any organization. Once the organization's philosophy is known, it is reasonable to expect action consistent with that philosophy, even if there are no precise written rules for a particular case. One of the many benefits of a well-defined and well-publicized statement of organizational values or leadership philosophy is that when an emergency happens at 3:00 A.M. in the farthest reaches of the organization, a capital-L leader need not be personally involved. The small-l leader on the scene will know the "right" thing to do. Trust can reasonably replace vigilance. Without a written document as a touchstone, on the other hand, it is all too easy to find that high ideals perish in the hurly-burly of events.

The "Code of Ethics" quoted below is from a Marine Corps manual. It assumes leadership at every level of the organization, and it is focused quite clearly on the primary mission of the Marine Corps and its life-and-death implications. In so doing, the code leaves to the individual the application of ethics in day-to-day operations. A code of this level of detail and intensity is, of course, no more meaningful than the "Here—sign this" ethics pledge common in many large firms. (Ironically, these forms tend to show up most frequently in firms who do business with the Department of Defense.) Just because there happens to be a statement of the rules of conduct for a particular profession hanging on a wall somewhere does not guarantee that any, or even a significant percentage of, the members of that profession know what that statement is, much less practice it daily. Unless there is a vigorous attempt not only to promulgate the written word, but to hold the organization's members accountable, it is irrelevant:

- I am a member of a profession which exists solely to serve American society. I therefore at all times place the interests of my country, my profession, my unit, and my mission above personal and career ambitions or loyalty to any individual.
- I am a member of a profession which is unique in the scope and severity of the consequences of incompetence in its practice. I therefore strive single-mindedly to achieve the highest degree of proficiency achievable in the practice of my professional arts.
- I am a member of a profession which possesses the legitimate capacity for the systematic application of force to accomplish its mission. I therefore, while attaining the highest degree of proficiency achievable in the practice of my profession, will never glorify the use of violence or use excessive force, and will at all times maintain a high regard for the value of human life and dignity.
- I am a member of a profession in which decisive individual initiative is often necessary for success. I therefore do not allow conformity to precedent, procedure, or regulation to prevent the exercise of individual judgment when necessary and always accept responsibility for decisions I have made.
- I am a member of a profession in which unified corporate effort is necessary for the achievement of objectives. I therefore at all times esteem above my own interests the welfare and dignity of individuals under my command and my fellow professionals.
- I am a member of a profession in which all members are responsible for the actions of each individual within the profession. I therefore do not tolerate unethical conduct on the part of my fellows.

The Marine Corps "Code of Ethics" models the three essential characteristics for usefulness: It is brief, clear, and believable. The fact that it is impossible to write a totally comprehensive set of rules, a code that specifically covers every possible case, means that an organization's code of ethics can focus on establishing a moral summary on which to base expected/acceptable behavior. Anyone who thinks that short, to-the-point statements of principles are ineffective might recall that the Gettysburg Address is less than 300 words and the Declaration of Independence fits on less than three pages of a standard-size textbook. More than a pious hope, both became lodestars for a vibrant democracy.

Once again, it is impossible to understate the importance of consistency, the foundation for clarity and believability. The Coast Guard has this to say on the topic:

A second, and equally crucial, part of the process [after identifying and articulating values] is examining our "statement of values" for consistency and conflict. Cadets will be quick to notice that value A can only be honored at the expense of value B (e.g., truth versus loyalty), and ask "Which is more important?" While "both" may be the politically satisfying answer, it is useless to the cadet struggling with "doing the right thing." We should not be surprised to get cheating, for example, if we place demonstration of *knowledge* **ahead of** demonstration of *character*.

Where there is a potential conflict between values, and it is almost sure to exist, we should try first to resolve the conflict and, failing that, prioritize. To walk away from this toughest of all value issues is to fail our Corps of new officers.

Establishing a code of ethics for an organization needs to be done carefully. It cannot end with a bureaucratic form that everyone knows is driven by the legal department's desire to be able to cast individuals adrift if something goes awry. A statement of a company's values, the establishment of an ethical compass, needs to be thrashed out, agreed upon, and understood by people with a realistic view of the organization, past, present, and future.

Any statement of ethics must be vigorously introduced early in the training of both current and future leaders—and must continue to be integrated throughout the organization. The newest Marine Corps training manual, *Leading Marines (FMFM 1-0)*, has quite a bit to say on the topic:

> These standards and the others contained in the appendices are learned by all Marines at entry-level training. They provide points of departure and a yardstick from which Marines can determine their own leadership abilities and assist their subordinates. They are generally self-explanatory, and are always best discussed through the use of action-centered examples. Because they are simple concepts, they can be used to build a "short list" of actions and techniques that will assist leaders everywhere. They are straightforward and very basic, and that is their value. Although they do not guarantee success, just as the principles of war are used to help us think about warfighting, these tangible elements help us think about leadership. These standards and ideals—from ethos to traits to principles to our core values—are recognized as essentials of good leadership. But they are only so many words unless Marine leaders breathe life into them. They do that through personal example.

Never underestimate how important it is to keep ethics center stage as a topic of discussion, both in formal training and in informal discussions. Formal discussions can be in the nature of either integrated portions of leadership training courses or facilitator-led conversations among "assigned" personnel at all levels. On the informal side, senior leaders might make a specific point of initiating discussions of organizational values with a predetermined number of subordinates each month. A valuable source of input for any statement of corporate values is customers. Soliciting their comments and introducing them into the conversation can act as a reality check.

The goals for all these discussions, formal or informal, are twofold: to reinforce belief in and understanding of the organizational values and to seek out ideas that might possibly force a reassessment of the current statement. Multiple conversations are necessary because different people can—and will—interpret written statements in different ways at different times. A goal of "respect," for instance, is a worthy one, but how does that translate into everyday activities for a particular individual?

Consciously defining and articulating the values of an organization can be the catalyst for reconciling individual and corporate values. For folks who previously never took time to actually think through their personal beliefs and simply drifted along "comfortably enough," this can bring about tremendous growth. For people who have value conflicts, casually or purposefully acting in ways that are at cross-purposes with the organization's values, questionable acts will be pushed into the spotlight.

But in every situation, actions speak louder than words. When fire destroyed Malden Mills Industries Inc., in Methuen, Massachusetts, in December 1995, the 1,400 employees found out that one of life's greatest blessings is to work for a moral organization. Aaron Feuerstein, president of the company, responded immediately, saying that his first priority was to help his employees. "My father, who was a very observant Jew, taught me, and I still remember his quotation, which was, 'In those circumstances where there is a moral vacuum, do everything within your power to be a man.' And that's what he instructed his children to do. And that's what I'm trying to do." He promised to rebuild. In the meantime, he continued workers' wages for thirty days and health insurance for ninety days. One month later, 65 percent of the work force was back at their jobs, and the company extended pay for another thirty days for those who were still out of work. Within two months, 80 percent of the employees were back at work.

Local and national businesses responded with offers of help and money: Bank of Boston, Raytheon, and L.L. Bean each gave $50,000; Patagonia donated $30,000. The employees' union contributed $100,000. Even competitors got into the act. Roger Milliken, CEO of Milliken & Company, a Baldrige Award winner in 1989, responded personally. Since Milliken & Company had once suffered a devastating fire, Milliken offered his company's expertise to answer any questions Feuerstein might have about getting the business up and running. He also told Feuerstein to have Malden Mills' managers call him directly so that he could hook them up with the right people.

To thank those who came to their aid, Feuerstein took out a full-page ad in *USA Today*. The ad contained an admittedly partial list of those who had helped with money, food, gifts, and other assistance.

Community fire departments from thirty surrounding communities were named, as were dozens of individuals, *Sports Illustrated*, and Timothy School. In total, the list had over 240 entries. It read in part: "On Monday, December 11, we experienced an industrial fire. On Tuesday, we experienced the fire of human compassion."

Phone calls to the company produced the information that the company had no formal written philosophy or mission statement. So strong has Feuerstein's influence on his company been, however, that the switchboard operator sounded surprised when questioned about how the mill articulated its corporate values. Her response was eloquent: "We just always knew."

7

RELATING TO OTHERS: COMMUNICATIONS, MOTIVATION, COUNSELING

Truthfulness and tact go a long way toward assuring effective communications. Great oratorical and writing skills are rare; being honest and being empathetic must not be. Both subordinates and leaders need to examine how they currently use words and how well they listen. Often how well a person relates to others depends not so much on being able to get across his or her own message as it does on hearing what others have to say.

Leader and *communicator* are not synonymous terms; it is possible to be a powerful communicator and not be a leader. It is also possible for someone to reach a position of power and still be communications impaired. The relevance of the ability to communicate to leadership, however, is summed up in one sentence in a Marine Corps manual: "Communicating is the essence of leadership, because no leader is effective unless he can communicate." General George S. Patton is quoted as having said that a leader must "talk with the troops." His choice of words is precise. He did not say "talk *to* the troops"; he said, "talk *with* the troops." General Patton understood that sending a message is only one component of communications.

There are two primary threads running throughout the topic of communications. First, it is certainly possible to communicate too little, but it is virtually impossible to communicate too much. Patton also

129

said, "In the long run, it is what we do not say that will destroy us." The second main theme is that a variety of methods of communications must be used—with physical presence being high on every list. Leaders do not get out of their offices and walk around the area a lot because it is good exercise; they do it because it is the best way not only to transmit information, but to receive information. A one-way flow of ideas and announcements does not constitute a communications process.

This chapter looks at how to improve communications from several standpoints. Students who are looking for a short writing or speaking course will have to look elsewhere. The emphasis here is on analyzing what makes communications work in the philosophical sense, not the technical. Without the ability to influence behavior, any communication loses its meaning. Leaders can use the information in this chapter to develop plans for fostering motivation and for counseling. While counseling is rarely discussed as a form of communications, it is precisely that. On this topic, technical details are provided. Communications, motivation, and counseling are all things leaders will want to have in their tool kit.

PRACTICAL ASPECTS
OF INFORMATION FLOW

Communication—both in terms of what information is passed on to subordinates and how well it is done—has an enormous impact on the workplace. In the words of General Thomas D. White, former Air Force Chief of Staff, "Information is the essential link between wise leadership and purposeful action." Whether disseminating information throughout the entire organization or talking with one person, the fact is that sharing information is vital.

The need for improved top-to-bottom information flow has been dramatically increased by the growth of the service sector in the U.S. economy. Besides having an impact on the quality of what gets to the market, employees affect paying customers with increasing frequency and potency. When the majority of the employees of an organization were safely cooped up in large buildings making things, their attitude, their morale, and their apparent willingness to be an ambassador for the company was less obviously important.

This is no longer true. A much larger percentage of employees now have direct contact with external customers, even in manufacturing firms. Some companies enclose their telephone number and the picture of the person who makes their product in the packaging and invite customers to call if they have questions. And, too, the importance of the treatment of internal customers is now recognized and summarized in the statement, "External service never exceeds internal service."

For more organizations every day, the "real world"—as defined by where their competitors and customers are located—has expanded to include much more of the whole world. Virtually no one is the "only act in town" any more or, if they are and they abuse either their employees or their customers, their local monopolies are shortlived.

Workers want to consider themselves part of a team effort. In an Ernst & Young survey of 250 workers from Fortune 1000 companies conducted in late 1995 and reported in *USA Today,* 86 percent of the workers agreed with the statement, "Employees will be more motivated if they know their job helps the company make money." People who know where they fit in, and how what they do contributes to the bottom line, work harder. So important has this idea of sharing financial information become that it has acquired its own term: *open-book management.*

Being stingy with information in the belief that knowledge is power and exclusive knowledge is extraordinary power is contrary to the basic notion of leadership. Withholding information deepens the gulf between those in power and their subordinates. On the flip side, for an organization to empower its employees (e.g., giving nonmanagement employees in a manufacturing plant the authority to stop an assembly line) makes no sense without also sharing all appropriate financial and organizational implications. It invites decisions that are well-intended, but fact-free and potentially disastrous.

Not surprisingly, the idea of sharing information and insuring that every member of the organization knows how he or she contributes to the organization's bottom line is not limited to the civilian world. "Excellence in the Surface Navy" by Commander Gregg G. Gullickson and Lieutenant Commander Richard D. Chenette (mentioned in the previous chapter) confirms this point:

> These captains went to great lengths to keep their crews informed of how the ship fit into the big picture, why it was

going from point alpha to point bravo, the impact the ship's actions would have on the fleet, the Navy, and the nation. Even the mundane tasks were explained as to the importance they had with regard to the ship being battle ready and able to carry out its mission. The crews appreciated the explanations of how what they were doing contributed to the whole of what the ship was doing.

The 1995 Ernst & Young survey also illuminated what information was shared and how:

- Seventy-two percent of those surveyed said that at least half of the employees knew the trend of the company's stock price.
- Sixty percent felt that only "some or few" of the employees knew what it cost to provide the company's service or product.
- Methods that senior management of the same companies say they are using to get financial information to their employees included:

    Newsletters—91%
    Meetings—82%
    E-mail—66%
    Word-of-mouth—64%
    Videotapes—43%
    Voice mail—43%
    Video conferencing—25%

Employees feel that sharing financial information would lead to better performance; senior executives feel they've put a great deal of effort into doing so. The numbers demonstrate room for improvement.

Looking at the list of means used to communicate, there is an interesting blend of verbal and nonverbal methods. There is also a blend of passive and active communications—those that require a response from the listener and those that do not. There is, however, no means for assessing reception cited anywhere in the survey.

This failure to look at reception is not unique in the civilian community. "Excellence in the Surface Navy" also points to a variety of ways to use multiple forms of communications without following up on reception:

Excellent ships have excellent communications, and they don't assume that all that needs to be done to communicate effectively is to put the word out at officers' call and in the plan of the day. The key to excellent communications is the captain. He keeps the crew informed by using the ship's public announcing system, holding periodic meetings such as captain's call with the crew, and most importantly by talking to individuals one-on-one during his daily tours of the ship.

Despite the emphasis on disseminating information, what counts is what is being heard, not how advanced or how numerous the means of transmission are.

Using a variety of means of transmission, however, is absolutely critical: different people hear things different ways. A Marine Corps manual defines three categories of communication: verbal, nonverbal, and symbolic. One of the keys to credibility is insuring that all the messages sent are consistent. Quality observer Keith Taylor cautions would-be leaders to make sure that "your hips and lips are going the same direction." It may well be that verbal communications, while of primary importance in one-on-one situations, slips to third place in importance as an organization grows in numbers. Sam Walton didn't have to talk with everyone at each Wal-Mart he visited; just the news that he had been there—in the building, somewhere—had great impact. Tom Peters maintains that, "They watch your feet, not your lips," no matter what size organization you run.

Conscious or not, accurate or inaccurate, communication of ideas, information, and news happens continually in all sorts of ways. Every technological breakthrough makes it all the more inevitable that information will be shared—with or without senior management's consent. A major factor in the fall of the USSR and in the continual turmoil in China is that communications-transfer technology finally overwhelmed the central government's ability to keep citizens in the dark. The threat of atomic weapons may have stopped the spread of international Communism, but it was the fax machine that brought down the Berlin Wall. It is systems such as the Internet that are loosening ideological monopolies in dictatorships today. A corporate head cannot stop the spread of information; a leader insures that what is being heard is as accurate a reflection of the truth as possible.

LISTEN DOWN AND SPEAK UP

One Marine Corps manual divided the common barriers to communications into two categories: physical and psychological. Physical factors include distance, size of the group, and noise/distractions; psychological ones include differences in background and experience, poor listening habits, closed minds, or know-it-all attitudes. The techniques to improve communications recommended by the same source are straightforward: Reduce distance physically or by use of an electronic device, limit the number of discussions going on in the group and control the discussions, eliminate or attempt to reduce any noise or distractions, try to see things from others' point of view, don't let your mind wander, and be willing to listen to new points of view.

Assumed in this is an ability to guide a discussion, one of the tools of the leadership trade. Even if a leader is naturally shy, he or she must be able to create an environment in which communication takes place. The accurate dissemination of information depends in part on this ability. As one Marine Corps manual puts it:

The success or failure of a guided discussion depends on the leader. The responsibility of the leader is to eliminate any negative conditions and to create a relaxed atmosphere where trust, acceptance, respect, and positive characteristics necessary to facilitate group learning and sharing become a reality.

Under the best of circumstances, there can still be another significant barrier to communications: subordinates who come to discussions unwilling or unable to participate. Part of a leader's responsibility is to help subordinates develop their own communications skills.

It may be useful to think of communications in a reversal of traditional patterns. The normal sequence is for people at each level of the hierarchy to listen up and to proclaim down. Everyone—military or civilian—tends to be taught from their first day in any organization or corporation to pay attention to those people further up the hierarchy. (This even happens in families. Who hasn't been admonished to "Mind your older brother"?) The implied belief is that each layer knows everything that is known by all lower layers, and that the only legitimate source of greater knowledge for any individual is someone at a senior level.

Think of newly promoted leaders, specifically of ones who find it difficult to listen. It is possible that they may have attained their hierarchical position in large part because of an ability to broadcast, to present ideas to superiors. If these fast-trackers have been listening at all, they have been listening to their superiors, looking for information to put themselves "in the know." Most of them are willing to concede that their boss has something to teach them—after all, he or she occupies the chair the corporate aspirants covet.

The best advice for these neophytes (and, in fact, for all leaders) is to "listen down." Rationally, virtually everyone concedes that there is knowledge at the lower rungs of the corporate ladder, knowledge that is unknown at higher levels, both about how something might best be accomplished and about who the best people are to accomplish it. Emotionally, however, things are not so clear cut. For someone to ask for information from a person lower on the corporate ladder is to admit that he or she lacks something. Only the truly self-confident can do that, but then only the self-confident can be leaders.

Listening down is a particularly effective leadership technique because it recognizes that each individual is the expert at his or her own job. Seniors must routinely and consciously listen down so that they can benefit from the knowledge held by their juniors. It isn't enough to wander around; a leader also needs to stop and learn. If the organization is to flourish, all helpful information must be made generally available. Even Ed Wood, winner of the Golden Turkey Award as the worst Hollywood movie producer ever, knew this much. In the wonderfully horrible film *Glen or Glenda,* the narrator's monologue at one point drones out, "Even the employer needs advice now and then."

The flip side of this is that subordinates must have something to say. The weight of responsibility is with the leadership position, but communication is a shared obligation. What the seniors can do to aid juniors is to model the behavior they expect in return. Initiate conversations. Ask questions. Share information. Don't make a visit from the boss such an unusual occasion that subordinates go comatose from surprise. Seniors can also help subordinates develop clarity by suggesting that they take a class in logic, or join Toastmasters, or prepare a presentation.

Joe Posk, an internal consultant for a power company, recalls the difficulty his organization had when they decided to build their own coal ship as a cost-cutting measure. The 700-foot ship carrying 40,000 tons of coal docked about twice a month. There were back injuries virtually every time. Worse, there had been a couple of near fatalities. More than a dozen management teams, committees, and individuals—including MIT-trained engineers—studied the problem without finding a solution before Posk was asked to conduct a meeting consisting of the top executives of the power company and the top executives of the shipping company. He objected, asking what they thought they knew about docking a ship. Although he ended up chairing the meeting, it, too, failed to produce a solution.

Posk then suggested an alternate approach: a meeting with dock workers. When the six workers came in, their de facto leader (a gentleman who stood about 6-foot-four, weighing about 300 pounds) walked up to Joe's desk, pounded on it and proclaimed, "You're management. You're the problem. You guys bought those heavy lines [ropes] to save money. You're going to get us killed." "Heavy lines" became the first entry on the list of possible causes. Using problem-solving procedures, supplemented with data gathered by the dock workers and Posk's midnight visit to the docks (by invitation) to witness a docking, the problem was solved. The lines were involved, but they were not the culprit: The design of the cable tie-downs on the dock was faulty. Lines tossed from the ship to the dock could hang up on the tie-downs, necessitating a hurried effort to dislodge them while the huge ship continued to move. The team designed a modification to the tie-downs that made it possible for lines to move over them without getting caught. That was in 1986. There has not been one injury since.

Another technique to improve communications is to verify that reception of a message matches transmission. Transmission is what someone thinks she or he is saying; it is the message he or she intends to send and is usually pretty sure has been sent. Reception is what is actually heard. In truth, transmission is of relatively minor importance; reception is paramount. People react to what they hear, and it may not be at all what was intended.

Consider the following set of data presented in a conversation with an executive of a National Basketball Association team about one of the players the team had under contract. The executive told the listener that a player who was seven feet tall had failed to make the 275-pound weight called for in his contract and was fined $100,000. The six-foot-two male listener, whose personal weight has ranged as high as 225 pounds and who has been a longtime fan of professional basketball, agreed that the "lazy fat-body" deserved the fine. When this same man retold the story to a five-foot-six, 125-pound woman (admittedly not a sports fan), she was appropriately impressed by the size of the fine. But then she asked what the team expected the player to do to get his weight *up* to 275 pounds!

The woman heard all the same words, but since she did not have the same background as the man telling the story, she pictured the miscreant player as underweight rather than overweight. The transmission and reception between the NBA executive and the longtime fan had been trouble free, but the message sent and the message received between the fan and the nonfan were completely out of step.

By talking *with* people rather than *to* them, by inviting questions and comments, it is possible to quickly assess whether transmission and reception match. The basketball fan was able to quickly amend his story so that the woman understood the true situation; leaders, too, can quickly refine their wording if feedback is sought.

MAKING (AND TAKING) OPPORTUNITIES TO COMMUNICATE

It is surely obvious that communications are ongoing. And informal communications are often more potent than formal ones. A Vietnam veteran tells a story that illustrates the point, even while admitting that the lesson involved came as a revelation to him at the time:

> I was the commanding officer of a 225-man artillery unit in Vietnam. One of my most important senior enlisted men was Gunnery Sergeant Chapman, who as Communications Chief was in charge of an enormous array of radio and wire communications gear that was absolutely vital to the operation of the

unit. Chapman was a technical wizard; he seemed to know everything about the field of communications and could fix anything.

One day, the Regimental Communications Officer announced to me that he was going to have to take Gunny Chapman from my unit, that his expertise was needed at the higher level. In his place I was to get Gunny Chavez, who was currently serving in an administrative billet with no leadership responsibilities. The Communications Officer assured me that Chavez was a "good man" while admitting that he was nowhere near the technical expert that Chapman was. I did some ineffectual grumbling and accepted Chavez.

After a couple of weeks, it occurred to me that there was indeed a very important difference between Chapman and Chavez, but it wasn't what I had expected. Whenever there had been a problem before, Chapman had personally fixed it. Now, when a young corporal reported a problem, Chavez asked him how he thought it should be fixed and worked with him to figure it out. The junior enlisted were responding enthusiastically to Chavez, and equipment that used to wait until Gunny Chapman got around to it was being fixed by the person closest to the problem.

That afternoon I happened to walk past where Gunny Chavez was sitting, taking a break and having a cup of coffee. For no specific reason, I stopped and said, "Oh, by the way, Gunny. You probably know I wasn't real happy about getting you in place of Gunny Chapman. Well, I just want you to know that if I were offered the chance today to trade back, I wouldn't do it." And I walked on. Didn't give it any thought.

Several months later, after a transfer to a neighboring unit, three or four of the senior enlisted men from my old artillery outfit gathered me up and took me to their club for several rounds of beer to celebrate my last night in Vietnam. During the evening, Gunny Chavez turned to me and said, "Do you know why I like you, sir?" I replied that I didn't.

"It was that time when you stopped and told me you wouldn't trade me back for Chapman even if you could. I was sitting there feeling pretty sorry for myself and generally being pretty miserable when you said that. I'll tell you what, Captain, I'd follow you to hell."

Until that moment, I had no idea what impact I had had on Gunnery Sergeant Chavez. I could have very easily missed that moment—or screwed it up.

Never assume when it comes to communications. Make relating to people a conscious act. It is dangerous, for instance, for the leader of a relatively small group of people, whether a subset of a larger organization or a complete corporate entity, to think, "We're small and we see each other every day so I know our communications are good." One need only look at current divorce rates and the number of times that "inability to communicate" is listed as a contributing factor to understand the need to communicate deliberately, to assume nothing.

As a practical exercise in communications, an individual could keep a three-by-five-inch index card next to the telephone and make a notation whenever he or she says "thank you" to anyone. Advanced students of leadership will also take note whenever criticism is voiced to any employee. At the end of each day or week, a glance at the three-by-five card would give an indication of exactly how well this kind of opportunity to connect with others has been utilized. Goals might be set, for instance, that the number of entries on the "thank you" side of the ledger should reach a certain number each week, or that the number of entries on the "thank you" side of the ledger should be a particular multiple (twice? five times?) of the number of entries on the complaint side. It would also be possible to check to see if particular people or units receive all the thanks, while another person or unit receives a disproportionate percentage of the criticism. From that information can come an action plan.

One of things that hinders leaders and subordinates in their efforts to communicate is multitudinous layers of hierarchy between the sender and recipient of a message. An organization may benefit from having a way around the normal bureaucracy, a path available to be used when the need for speed and accuracy outweighs other considerations. General Patton advised, "Keep a quick line of communications."

A 100 percent quality effort provides just such a communications channel. If every member of an organization is, for instance, on a quality team, an organization can function as a three-layer group without touching the official job/title structure. There is the company president, the team leaders (about 10% of the whole), and the entire work force. At the Paul Revere Insurance Group in the mid-to-late 1980s, President Aubrey K. Reid Jr. rarely made use of this communications option—usually once or twice a year. People recognized the importance of the occasion when Reid sent a message to all employees via the team leaders, and team leaders knew they had access to the top when occasion demanded.

CREATING A CLIMATE OF MOTIVATION

Two of the most important forms of communications employed by a leader are motivation and counseling. They both require a considerable investment of self, and a leader's success can make the difference between barely adequate results and truly superlative performance. Motivation, enthusiasm, and the willingness to contribute more than the mandatory minimum are voluntary—a point that can never be forgotten by a leader at any level. A leader can, and must, construct environments and situations that make it likely that others will sign on with enthusiasm for the task at hand. But the hard fact is that motivation is essentially subjective and based on perceived satisfaction of needs.

After stating that "The establishment of a 'climate of motivation' is the single most important aspect of the development of a well-disciplined, highly proficient unit," a Marine Corps manual explains the point in this way:

> "You've got to motivate your troops," says the senior leader to subordinate leaders. Wrong! The leader does not motivate. The misconception that the leader motivates is probably the one most common in our profession today. Rather, motivation is individual and self-serving. It is a process that occurs internally within each individual based on individual human needs.
>
> Since the strengths and priority of needs vary with each individual, motivation also varies with each individual. Individuals motivate themselves. The leader's job is to create a climate in which subordinates understand that they may attain

their personal goals by behaving in ways which are congruent with the unit's accomplishment of mission. . . .

The climate of motivation is created through efforts by the leader to balance the expectations of the individual and the Marine Corps. The degree to which each party is successful directly relates to the effectiveness of the unit. This establishment of a climate of motivation leads to high-quality performance which results in mission accomplishment.

A study of motivational psychologist Abraham Maslow's Hierarchy of Needs can be invaluable in helping leaders analyze what one consultant calls the "WIFM factor": What's in it for me? The Maslow hierarchy states that every human has the same basic needs and strives to fill these needs in a generally sequential manner. Beginning with physiological needs, the hierarchy continues through several phases: safety and security, belongingness and love, autonomy and self-esteem, and self-actualization. Too often leaders forget or ignore that people instinctively act in their own self-interest. Knowing where an individual is in the hierarchy can help a leader decide how to help subordinates understand how they may reach their personal goals by meeting organizational goals.

Consider the rush to reengineer in the early 1990s: While most companies concentrated on downsizing, a wiser few promised to preserve jobs and directed their reorganization efforts at capturing market share. Care to guess which efforts had employee support? It's difficult to exercise initiative (autonomy and self-esteem) or act as part of a team (belongingness and love), when your job is under siege (safety and security). Meeting basic needs enables a person to operate further up the hierarchy. John Mellecker's definition brings the relationship between Maslow's Hierarchy and superior leadership sharply into focus: "Leadership is the creation of an environment in which others are able to self-actualize in the process of completing the job."

The leader, of course, needs to understand his or her people in order to create a climate of motivation that works for everyone. For the small-l leader with relatively few followers, this means getting to know people as individuals in order to have a positive impact. Good leaders identify personal needs, characteristics, values, and goals—or needs, characteristics, values, and goals shared by a majority of followers.

As a person climbs the promotion ladder and more and more people are affected by his or her decisions, it becomes impossible to know everybody to the same degree. In these cases, the leader can get to know the women and men who are most directly impacted by any decisions—and to devise methods for getting an accurate reading of the needs and capabilities of subordinates who are beyond daily contact. That "reading" should be confirmed (and updated regularly) through frequent communications with a sampling of that latter group.

The key to motivation, as in so much else in leadership, is combining the emotional and rational. When the football coach at half time "motivates his players," he is inviting them to add the element of emotion to the skills and talents already developed through weeks and months of preparation and training. Neither can stand alone, and a large boost of one can go only so far in replacing the other. Even the most motivated high school football team in the country wouldn't have a chance against the Dallas Cowboys.

A leader's personal credibility also impacts how successful she or he is in this endeavor. Credibility is based on past performance. If a leader has disregarded subordinates' needs, hoarded information, or promised actions without coming through, subordinates respond by doing as little as possible. A Marine Corps manual provides a list of examples of personal leadership actions that are likely to meet subordinates' needs and contribute to a climate of motivation:

1. Assign subordinates to useful jobs and tasks.
2. Provide subordinates with necessary guidance and assistance. Avoid oversupervision.
3. Show appreciation for the individual's job.
4. Provide recognition for outstanding performance.
5. Encourage innovation.
6. Avoid humiliation and group embarrassment.
7. Challenge subordinates in accordance with their capabilities. Generally they will live up to the leader's expectations.

It is imperative to note that recognition—in all its forms—plays a central role as a piece of the puzzle. When people understand that their efforts and contributions have been noticed and are appreciated, it adds to the climate of motivation needed to insure continued top performance.

The army also has a list (what else?) of "Fourteen Principles of

Motivation" that a leader can incorporate into his or her personal behavior:

1. Make the needs of the individuals in your unit coincide with unit tasks and missions.
2. Reward individual and team behavior that supports unit tasks and missions.
3. Counsel or punish soldiers who behave in a way that is counter to unit tasks, missions, and standards.
4. Set the example in all things.
5. Develop morale and esprit in your unit.
6. Give your subordinates tough problems, and challenge them to wrestle with them.
7. Have your subordinates participate in the planning of upcoming events.
8. Alleviate the cause of the personal concerns of your soldiers so that soldiers can concentrate on their jobs.
9. Ensure your soldiers are properly cared for and have the tools they need to succeed.
10. Keep your soldiers informed about missions and standards.
11. Use positive peer pressure to work for you and the unit.
12. Avoid using statistics as a major method of evaluating units and motivating subordinates.
13. Make the jobs of your subordinates as challenging, exciting, and meaningful as possible.
14. Do not tolerate any form of prejudicial talk or behavior in your unit.

At the corporate level, developing and publishing a vision statement or statement of philosophy helps to build and sustain a climate of motivation—so long as corporate actions and statements lend credence to the values espoused. No one understood this better than L. A. (Pat) Hyland, who led Hughes Aircraft Company between 1954 and 1980. In his book *Call Me Pat,* he talked about money and recognition and motivation and concluded, "To be on a bonus plan in any degree, no matter how small, is a mark of prestige that is valued at all times." But he didn't see money as a primary motivator and provided a list of things of importance to employees:

- Adequate working quarters—nothing fancy, but suitable and to a degree which gives expression to the personality of each.
- Association with and stimulation by those with whom they work.
- Respect for and from their supervisor and co-workers.
- Knowledge that they are masters of their own destiny to the extent that they have the delegations they need to do the job at hand. If problems arise, knowledge that they can expect intelligent help and not criticism.
- Recognition of the need for and implementation of continuing education.
- Recognition for achievement and for leadership qualities.

Nordstrom is an organization that works to provide an environment in which employees can self-actualize. Employee compensation is based on commissions and profit-sharing; the store is famous for giving salespeople the freedom to do whatever it takes to make the customer happy (as long as it is legal); decision making is pushed down to the sales floor and there is only one primary rule: Use your good judgment in all situations. The company is structured to support employees in this highly competitive environment, according to Robert Spector and Patrick D. McCarthy in their book *The Nordstrom Way:*

> Nordstrom is informally organized as an "inverted pyramid," with the top positions occupied by the customers and the salespeople, and the bottom position filled by the co-chairmen. Every tier of the pyramid supports the sales staff.

Nordstrom goes to great lengths to make the salespeople's job easier. A sample of their selling and buying policies illustrates the point:

> Salespeople are free to sell merchandise to their customers in any department throughout the store. This promotes continuity in the relationship between the salesperson and the customer.
> Buying at Nordstrom is decentralized, which means that buyers in each region are given the freedom to acquire merchandise that reflects local lifestyles and tastes.

Empowerment for getting the right merchandise in the store begins not in the buying office, but on the floor—at the point of the sale. Nordstrom encourages entrepreneurial salespeople to provide input to their manager and buyer on fashion direction, styles, quantities, sizes, and colors.

Full inventories are a measure of customer service. To make it easier for employees to make sales, Nordstrom stocks a wide and deep range of sizes, so that there is something for virtually everyone.

Creating a climate of motivation is hard work. It takes more than inspiration; it takes planning and persistence. A climate of motivation is more than merely saying exciting things or making attractive promises about the better life that awaits those who succeed. The leader is responsible for seeing that the mechanics, the procedures, to make possible whatever she or he has promised are in place, and that her or his own personal behavior reinforces those procedures. Leaders who rely on inspiration alone actually demotivate employees when they fail to create an environment that supports their goals.

PERSONALLY INFLUENCING OTHERS

According to a lesson plan expressly written to teach newly commissioned Marine Corps officers about counseling, counseling is a facet of communication closely affiliated with motivation:

> Counseling is that part of leadership which ensures, by mutual understanding, that the efforts of leaders and their Marines are continuously directed toward increased unit readiness and effective individual performance.

Effective counseling is said to give the leader "a chance to strengthen your unit—one individual at a time."

Traditionally, juniors do not counsel, but there are times when the same techniques used in counseling can go a long way toward improving communication between two peers or between a junior and a senior.

What will be missing in these exchanges is the element of control implicit in a senior/junior relationship. Think back to the example in Chapter 5 in which the secretary requested a meeting with her boss. She was setting up a counseling session.

The counseling being proposed and discussed here is not in the sense of psychiatric therapy, but rather something more akin to a lot of listening, demonstrating concern and common sense, and focusing simultaneously on the accomplishment of the mission and the needs of the individual. Counseling in this sense may well include referring (and urging) an individual to seek professional help for emotional problems; it may even include giving someone a hard push toward acceptance of appropriate professional help. For the most part, however, counseling is something with simpler overtones:

> Counseling is the process of listening and communicating advice, instruction, or judgment, with the intent of influencing a person's attitude or behavior. . . . No matter how or where you perform counseling, it is an essential part of good leadership.

Of course, whenever a leader counsels a subordinate, the leader must make sure that he or she immediately follows up with any action promised during the session (e.g., getting a question about salary resolved or scheduling a meeting with an appropriate specialist). Being a good listener and being empathetic are important, but results are what build the leader's reputation as someone who can be turned to.

Three types of counseling sessions are identified: initial, follow-on, and event-related. The Marine Corps recommends an initial counseling session within thirty days of the beginning of a new senior/junior relationship, and it expects this session to lay the groundwork for a future partnership. The senior person in the discussion takes the opportunity to explain her or his goals and expectations for the organization and explore how those goals and expectations relate to that particular junior and his or her aspirations. Together, they establish goals for the junior to meet before their next formal meeting.

For the most part, a follow-on counseling session is recommended ninety days after the initial session, with sessions every six months thereafter. Counseling sessions for very junior folks are recommended every thirty days until both are comfortable with the junior's progress.

In short, staying in touch with subordinates is a time-consuming process.

Follow-on counseling sessions are scheduled and carried out for the purpose of monitoring the individual's progress, resolving any problems, and planning targets for the next period of time. These meetings serve to identify possible trouble areas and insure that information continues to flow both top to bottom and bottom to top.

The follow-on meeting is also considered to be a "formal" counseling session, while any event-related counseling session is labeled as "informal." The major difference between a formal and an informal counseling session is that the formal session is scheduled in advance and both participants are expected to spend some time preparing for it.

There are at least three indications that an event-related or as-appropriate counseling session is called for. The first of these is solicited or called-for help, in which case it is up to the leader to listen and to offer all possible assistance. Perhaps more often than not, the subordinate tells one or more other employees that he or she is having problems—and one of them lets the leader know. The leader at that point initiates a discussion.

The second indicator of the need for counseling is a sudden change in attitude or behavior. Even if not yet appearing to affect job performance, this is a signal that a counseling session may be called for. The leader must exercise an element of judgment about if and when to initiate a session.

The most obvious indicator that counseling is appropriate is a drop in performance. The exact cause(s) of the drop may be any of a wide range of possibilities with the only sure thing being that there is no particular reason to believe that things will get better without intervention. The leader again initiates a conversation with the intent of solving the problem, not criticizing the employee. There is a distinction between "performance counseling" and "performance evaluation." The former is focused on future behavior; the latter, on past lapses.

Dr. W. Edwards Deming liked to cause a stir by advocating the elimination of written evaluation forms. If, indeed, the only time an individual ever hears how he or she is doing is during a formal annual report focused on the past, such evaluation has little effect on future performance and is a waste of everyone's time. Written evaluations are beneficial only if they are one component of a complete counseling program, if they summarize a series of conversations over a period of time, and if the subordinate knows what standards he or she was being measured against. Those standards must be objective: It is grossly unfair to set rules such as "just be at least as good as George and you'll get along fine here."

Counseling sessions are most likely to be successful if certain conditions and techniques are present. Subordinates can also use the following information to help make a counseling session more productive from their point of view. The USMC Counseling Program taught at The Basic School breaks the counseling sessions into five sections. The details are presented in an outline (arguably not the most readable form of prose):

A. Preparation
   1. Review the junior's current performance.
   2. Define counseling objectives.
   3. Give the junior advance notice; request self-evaluation and improvement plan.
   4. Select appropriate location.
   5. Plan how to conduct session.
      a. Directive, non-directive, or collaborative counseling
      b. Agenda
B. Opening
   1. Set the junior at ease.
   2. Review counseling objectives.
C. Main body
   1. Review progress against targets.
   2. Involve the junior in the process.
   3. Elicit targets and plan for improvement; provide input and guidance.
D. Closing
   1. Summarize strengths, improvement needs, targets, and plan for improvement.
   2. Ensure common understanding; gain commitment.
E. Follow-up
   1. Document the session.
   2. Monitor performance.

The first section of the outline, "Preparation," raises a question about the differences among directive, nondirective, and collaborative counseling. Directive can be, but is not necessarily, a "chewing out." The counselor identifies what the problem is and dictates a solution. There is very little, if any, input from the person being counseled. Nondirective counseling is used when the counselor really has no clue what the problem is, or when the counselor wants the individual to identify the problem and come up with a solution on his or her own. Generally, this is going to take more time than the other two approaches. Collaborative is a combination of the directive and nondirective approaches and is the most common and most effective technique. It allows input from both sides, but gives the counselor the opportunity to guide the conversation.

Elsewhere, the Marine Corps presents a counseling session in a slightly different way. Since this jam-packed outline is about as digestible as C-rations or, in current jargon, MREs (Meals Ready to Eat), it appears in Appendix C, and its contents are served up paraphrased below, seasoned with comments from the *USMC User's Guide to Counseling.*

A counseling session is divided into six parts, each requiring the counselor to master different techniques: active listening, questioning, giving feedback, problem solving, setting targets, and planning for improvement. Active listening requires being aware of obstacles to communication—such as lack of concentration, interruptions, lack of fresh air, facing an unshaded window, sitting behind a desk—and remedying them as much as possible. The *User's Guide* suggests establishing rapport at the start of the session with a cup of coffee and a few minutes of general conversation. It also points out that both parties must know why they are holding the session.

Active listening, according to the *User's Guide,* involves not only hearing what the junior says, but also interpreting what it means. There are a variety of techniques suggested in the outline: listening not only for facts, but also for generalizations; distinguishing between facts and opinions; and watching for changes in the subordinate's volume, tone, and rate of speech. Observing what the junior does physically is also recommended.

During the questioning portion of the session, counselors are advised to vary the type of questions they ask so that feedback to subordinates can be based on the most accurate information possible. Questions are divided into four categories: closed-ended, open-ended, probing, and interpretive. According to the *User's Guide*, closed-ended questions can be answered by *yes* or *no*; an open-ended question requires a fuller response. The first is useful for getting out the facts; the second establishes rapport. Probing questions are used to generate additional information; interpretive questions are used to clarify or amplify what the junior has said. The guide offers two more suggestions: echo questions and confirming questions. An example of the first is, "And you got no response?" A confirming question is used to gain commitment, such as "So, you're now ready to take the test?"

Counselors need to combine a variety of techniques with an awareness of human nature to make feedback effective. Use positive reinforcement and focus on events—not on the person. Align individual goals with organizational goals to create a climate of motivation. Probe for silent agreement and allow the person being counseled to vent emotions. The counselor is responsible for seeing that the feedback stage does not degenerate into argument. Truly useful feedback depends on several elements: It deals with things that can be changed, it is timely, and it is given to satisfy the individual's needs. In addition, the counselor has to be willing for the individual to respond.

Since the whole point of having a counseling session is to solve a problem, most of the outline is devoted to how to define a problem and tailor corrective action to the deficiency. Four primary questions are suggested: What is happening that shouldn't happen? What is not happening that should happen? Is there something about the individual preventing performance? Is there something outside the individual's control impeding performance? If the individual is part of the problem, it is necessary to find out whether he or she has the ability, knowledge, and skills to do the job, or whether the problem is one of attitude. Perhaps the individual does not know his or her performance is not meeting expectations—perhaps the individual does not care. It is important to distinguish between the two.

The *User's Guide* adds one question: Is the senior part of the problem? There are a series of questions for the senior to consider, among which are the following: Has the senior made the junior's targets clear? Has the senior failed to praise the junior when performance has been up to expectations? Is the senior (or others) making conflicting or competing demands on the junior's time? Does the junior have the authority and resources necessary to do the job?

Tailoring corrective action to the deficiency depends on defining the problem accurately. If knowledge is the problem, provide information; if it's skill, provide guidance and feedback; if it's attitude, employ nondirective counseling. When there are obstacles outside the individual's control, they almost always exist because the senior is part of the problem. Once a deficiency has been defined, obstacles can be removed or targets adjusted. Part of tailoring an effective solution is to evaluate the impact of several solutions. What are the likely consequences of each? Which is the most practical? What resources are required? What are the likely benefits? What is required in the way of support and follow through? Which is the least complex to implement?

The next two steps are to set targets and plan for improvement. The targets must include yardsticks for measuring performance and identifying problems, as well as motivational and planning tools. Effective performance targets have the following characteristics: They are stated as a result or outcome; they are measurable, realistic, challenging, and limited in number; and they are revised when circumstances change. They are also mandatory. Any plan for improvement should be developed jointly between the counselor and the person being counseled and then used to track progress and identify future problems.

Buried in the outline is the assumption that counseling is not punitive. Military writer Major C. A. Bach observed that there are cases when unpleasant corrective action is unavoidable. Here, too, the leader's judgment makes the difference in how productive the results are:

Fairness is another element without which leadership can neither be built up nor maintained. There must first be that fairness which treats all men justly. I do not say alike, for you cannot treat all men alike—that would be assuming that all men are cut from the same piece; that there is no such thing as individuality or a personal equation.

You cannot treat all men alike; a punishment that would be dismissed by one man with a shrug of the shoulders is mental anguish for another. A company commander, who for a given offence [sic] has a standard punishment that applies to all is either too indolent or too stupid to study the personality of his men. In his case justice is certainly blind.

Study your men as carefully as a surgeon studies a difficult case. And when you are sure of your diagnosis, apply the remedy. And remember that you apply the remedy to effect a cure, not merely to see the victim squirm. It may be necessary to cut deep, but when you are satisfied as to your diagnosis don't be divided from your purpose by any false sympathy for the patient.

8

MAKING IT WORK

" Anyone could lead perfect people, if there were any," said Robert Greenleaf, author of *Servant Leadership*. Since there aren't, it's a waste of time trying to create them. It is even a bigger waste of time trying to change people to be like you. Meeting people where they are, however, is no easy matter; and it is even more difficult to get people to do what you want. While communications, counseling, and motivation are valuable in bringing individual and organizational goals into alignment, accomplishing those goals requires something more. This chapter puts three additional leadership tools at your disposal.

The first tool is a choice of leadership styles. Every interaction between a leader and follower can be categorized as either authoritarian, participative, or delegative. This chapter looks at these very different leadership styles and sets guidelines to help leaders decide when to use each.

Next, the topic of teamwork is covered. While the concept is not complex, molding a successful team is. As one Marine Corps manual puts it, "Winning teams do not just happen, they are created by hard work and leadership." This section is divided between team-building techniques and a review of the underlying philosophy of teamwork: trust and mutual accountability.

The third topic in this chapter is discipline. Between leaders and followers, within teams, and among individuals, discipline is imperative. Like counseling in the last chapter, the concept goes far beyond the merely punitive. Discipline is the controlled behavior resulting from training and instruction. The ancient Greek scripture, *Apocrypha*, Malachi 6:17, links it to the best that leadership has to offer: "For the very true beginning of her [wisdom] is the desire of discipline; and the care of discipline is love."

AUTHORITARIAN, PARTICIPATIVE, AND DELEGATIVE LEADERSHIP

The United States Army's 1983 version of *Military Leadership (FM 22-100)* defines leadership style as being "the manner and approach of providing direction, implementing plans and orders, and motivating others," and goes on to define three basic types. The first is admittedly the military stereotype: authoritarian. "That's an order. Do it!" seems incomplete to most people without adding the phrase "Or heads will roll!" The manual confronts the stereotype and debunks it:

> A leader is using the *authoritarian leadership style* when he tells his subordinates what he wants done, and how he wants it done, without getting their advice or ideas. This style is clearly appropriate in many military situations. Sometimes people think a leader is using the authoritarian style when he yells, uses demeaning language, and leads by threats and abuse of power. This is not the authoritarian style. It is simply an abusive, unprofessional style of leadership.

While there are times when an authoritarian choice is warranted, effective leaders use authoritarian leadership sparingly. All three of the following conditions must be met:

- You have all of the information to solve the problem.
- You are short on time.
- Your subordinates are motivated.

The final point is not to be glossed over. People are unlikely to be motivated unless leaders have spent hours building a bond between them. According to this army manual, the judicious use of both participative and delegative leadership styles does just that:

When using the *participative leadership style,* the leader involves one or more participants in determining what to do and how to do it. In this style, however, the leader maintains final decision-making authority. He simply gets advice from one or more subordinates and then makes the decision. This style is appropriate for many leadership situations. Do not ever think that getting good advice from a subordinate or using a subordinate's good plan or good idea is a sign of weakness on your part. It is a sign of strength that your subordinates will respect. On the other hand, you are responsible for the quality of your plans and decisions. If you believe your plan or your idea is better than those offered by your subordinates, you must do what you believe is right, regardless of pressure from subordinates to do otherwise.

This second, participative leadership style is frequently the most comfortable for both leader and led. It is suitable when the leader has part of the information necessary to solve the problem or accomplish the mission, and certain key subordinates and other people have additional information. After consultation with appropriate personnel, the leader makes a decision. He or she does not forfeit either authority or responsibility, nor is a vote called for.

The third leadership style, this manual continues, is the most difficult for many leaders because it requires the greatest degree of trust:

When using the *delegative leadership style,* the leader delegates decision-making authority to a subordinate or group of subordinates. He is still responsible, however, for the results of his subordinates' decisions. This style is also appropriate for many situations.

What makes this option so difficult is that authority is delegated while the leader retains responsibility for the successful completion of the task. True, the subordinate has to answer to the leader, but the leader bears full responsibility in the eyes of his or her superior. This process has been characterized as saying to someone, "Here's my career. Go play with it for a while." On the other hand, the subordinate is also taking a risk. A senior may second-guess a solution, lay off the responsibility when things go wrong, or take credit when things go right. It's all about trust.

An Air Force training manual expounds on the subject of delegative leadership:

> Delegation is a leadership skill which involves the development of an understanding between a leader and follower about how they'll share authority and responsibility for accomplishing their portion of the mission. . . . Delegation is hard work and is a slippery skill to master. Delegation calls for planning ahead, coordinating activities, establishing goals, clearly drawing lines of authority and responsibility, and having the fortitude to give tasks to subordinates and trust in their ability to carry them out.

The army manual uses an example to spell out when this style might be warranted:

> The delegative style is appropriate when certain key subordinates are able to analyze a problem or situation and to determine what needs to be done and how to do it. You cannot do everything. You must set priorities and delegate certain tasks to subordinates.
>
> There will be times when a subordinate is better able than you to accomplish a certain task. For example, a new lieutenant on his third day as platoon leader might receive a task to plan individual training for the next month. The platoon leader simply does not yet have the required knowledge or experience. The platoon sergeant has both. He knows the strengths and weaknesses of the platoon and how to plan and conduct individual training. The platoon leader, therefore, could delegate the task by saying, "Platoon Sergeant, I trust your judgment. You determine what to do and how to do it. I will approve your plan."
>
> Let us change the above example. The platoon leader has been in his job for several weeks and has observed some weaknesses in the way the individual training has been planned and conducted. He might then decide to use a participative style to

plan the next month's individual training. To do this, he holds a leadership and training seminar. . . . He gets meaningful input from key troops, squad leaders, and the platoon sergeant. He considers this input and then makes a decision. His subordinates will appreciate his listening to their concerns. If they are a part of the planning process, they will be more motivated to carry out the plan.

It is also possible to use a mix of styles in handling a particular situation. A squad leader can call a meeting of his squad. He can then say, "I have decided that we will go to the field in 3 weeks for 3 days of challenging training. During the next hour I want your ideas on what training we should do and how we should plan it and conduct it." When he tells the squad they are going to the field, he is being authoritarian. When he says he wants their ideas on how to plan and conduct the training, he is being participative. Thirty minutes later he may be delegating tasks to certain people.

Choosing a leadership style requires analyzing both the people and the forces in play in any given situation. Determining who has the information and ability—both to illuminate the problem and to carry out the solution—helps a leader determine which style to use.

Chapter 7 on communications provided options for exchange of information that parallel the different styles of leadership. A one-way lecture/announcement—whether in person or over a loudspeaker or any other form of electronics—is akin to authoritarian leadership; a meeting in which questions and answers are welcomed and responses are given can be compared to participative leadership; and the goals set in a counseling session are the equivalent of delegative leadership. As with leadership styles, there is no one communications style that is always apropos—but successful leaders use the authoritarian option sparingly.

Participative and delegative skills are valuable under even the most trying conditions. While most leaders instinctively take charge in an emergency, the use of authoritarian leadership is not always desirable—even when there is a pressing interest in getting things right the first time. Consider the following example.

On February 24, 1989, a cargo door blew off United Airlines Flight 811 shortly after takeoff from Hawaii on its way to New Zealand. Nine people were killed in the explosion, but the plane managed to return to Hawaii with no further loss of life.

In the course of extensive interviews following the incident, the pilot, Captain David M. Cronin, repeatedly credited the fact that both he and his crew had been through "command leadership resource management" training as the major factor in their ability to fly the crippled aircraft safely. At a time when authoritarian leadership would have been the norm, Cronin and his crew knew there were other alternatives.

The thirty-five-year United veteran explained that the training stressed the delegation of duties within the cockpit and the importance of having crew members question their captain's actions and offer suggestions. By combining technical expertise with leadership training, the crew was able to overcome a situation that an after-the-fact computer analysis concluded was hopeless.

Cronin described how several times during the twenty-four-minute emergency he took time to discuss things with the other professionals in the cockpit. "In the old days the other crew members didn't speak or do a thing until the captain told them to. Those days are now over," said Cronin.

Early in the emergency, the copilot, Gregory S. Slader, hesitated to follow normal procedure that called for extending the wing flaps to slow the descent of the airplane. He checked first with Cronin, who told him to hold off. Slader agreed. The flight engineer contributed by using an emergency procedures manual to extrapolate the proper landing speed for a plane with two disabled engines and a flap problem (a situation not covered in the "how-to-solve" manual). Closer to landing, Cronin accepted Slader's recommendation to extend the wing flaps beyond the point that he, Cronin, thought appropriate—and the copilot proved to be right. Flight attendants later told investigators that it was one of the smoothest landings they had ever experienced.

THE MIDDLE MANAGEMENT DILEMMA

The fact that there are different styles of leadership carries perhaps the greatest significance for mid-level leaders or middle managers. Followers do not have the opportunity to practice authoritarian leadership. CEOs can get away with being petty dictators. Middle managers, on the other hand, contact significant numbers of seniors, peers, and juniors on a continual basis. Here's where getting a mix of leadership styles right is critical.

Everyone in an organization, but especially middle managers, should take to heart the advice of former Chief Master Sergeant of the Air Force Robert D. Gaylor (the senior enlisted person in the Air Force). In a manual designed to teach leadership to, among others, Air Force ROTC cadets, he was quoted as saying, "Sure, everyone wants to be an effective leader, whether it be in the Air Force or in the community. You can and will be if you identify your strengths, capitalize on them, and consciously strive to reduce and minimize the times you apply your style inappropriately."

The word "inappropriately" suggests a value judgment, and what is appropriate in the workplace has changed dramatically for many people. It became fashionable in the early 1990s for senior executives to proclaim that they had "turned the pyramid upside down"—and there were a few organizations, such as Nordstrom, that actually did it. What this meant was that the old organizational model of a pyramid with the boss at the top and nonmanagement employees spread across the bottom was inverted. Instead, the point of the pyramid (the boss) was now at the bottom, holding up and supporting the rest of the company with frontline employees at the top being supported not only by the boss, but by everybody else. The objective was to create a progressive, responsive company.

Note whose position did not change. Despite the orientation of the pyramid, the group of employees commonly called "middle managers" were still in the middle, providing a buffer between top and bottom, while simultaneously holding top and bottom together. The pressures remained enormous, as did the responsibilities.

One of the primary roles of middle managers is to see that the organization fulfills the newly hired worker's expectations and, at the same time, to see that the newcomer fulfills the corporation's expectations. Middle managers also have a unique role as the keeper of the corporate memory. They are often the ones who have been with the organization long enough to know "how things are done," to include the fragments that aren't written down. A pre–World War II army manual, making reference to the role of the military's middle managers, notes, "To some commanders this may be an irritating state of affairs—to have as an assistant a staff officer or noncom [a sergeant or petty officer] who is always right. Other commanders, the true leaders, thank God that they are lucky enough to have such assistance."

The relationship between senior management and middle management goes a long way toward defining how well the organization functions and, in particular, how the organization is perceived by external and internal customers. Disrespect for middle management brings an organization grinding to a halt. In the book *Leadership Secrets of Attila the Hun* by Wess Roberts, Attila is quoted as saying, "Always pay proper courtesy to your subordinate leaders. Should you fail to accord them respect, so will their subordinates."

There are several ways to pay proper courtesy to middle managers. The first is to actively recognize their role and its impact. Capital-L leaders get the boat headed in the right direction, but unless they encourage middle managers to practice small-l leadership, there is virtually no hope of reaching port. In *Training for Leadership,* British author John Adair advises senior managers to leave middle managers to do their own job:

In the "middle management" area one would expect more emphasis upon the functions of leadership, such as *delegating* and *coordinating,* which become especially important when one is dealing with subordinates who are themselves leaders of groups.

The second way to show proper courtesy is to provide adequate training. In most civilian organizations, the path to the presidency—even though it is realistically out of reach from the outset—is the *only* path. The military has an advantage in this regard because it has a corps of professional middle managers—men and women whose formal career goal is to attain a senior enlisted position. With the understanding that "middle manager" is a career goal, not a place to get stuck, it is possible to build training courses centered on the unique challenges of middle management without a stigma being attached. Where a civilian working for Corporation XYZ for three years might be put off by being sent to a class on how to be an effective mid-level leader, a young enlisted man or woman feels no such constraint.

Leadership training for middle managers, for senior executives, and for new employees differs not in kind, but in emphasis. Middle managers must excel as "interpreters." They must be able to accurately hear what senior managers say and accurately restate directives so that the work load is appropriately divided and goals met. At the same time, they must be able to accurately hear what juniors have to say and carry those messages and information back up the chain of command. An organization helps by using the same concepts and vocabulary at all levels, but it's still a tough role. "Being a middle manager" and "being caught in the middle" are often synonymous.

Managers who are trained as coaches, mentors, cheerleaders, and resources are able to utilize participative and delegative leadership styles to the advantage of the organization. No matter which way the pyramid is turned, the fact remains that the people with whom the frontline and nonmanagement employees have the most contact are middle managers. They make or break the morale of an organization according to a Marine Corps manual:

> Morale is the fine line relationship between the SNCO [staff noncommissioned officer, the middle level leader] and his Marine. If the relationship results in recognition and confirms each Marine's importance and value to the unit, morale will be strong. Every Marine knows most of what happens to him is not determined by the Corps or by his commanding general, but by the leaders with whom he is in daily contact. Thus, morale is the most important factor in motivating a Marine's performance, influencing his attitudes and satisfying his needs. Members of units with high morale usually have SNCO's who take a personal interest in them.

Civilians at the working end of the corporate ladder also know that what happens to them is usually determined by middle managers: No matter how "hands on" the boss may be, he or she cannot match the personal impact of a middle manager.

LEADERSHIP AND TEAMS

The leadership role as described in *The Leadership Challenge* by James Kouzes and Barry Posner looks a lot like the middle-management leader as described above. It also looks a lot like team leadership:

Exemplary leaders enlist the support and assistance of all those who must make the project work. They involve, in some way, those who must live with the results, and they make it possible for others to do good work. They encourage collaboration, build teams, and empower others. *They enable others to act.* In 91 percent of the cases we analyzed, leaders proudly discussed how teamwork and collaboration were essential. Additionally, our data on others' perceptions of leaders indicate that this is the most significant of all the five practices [see Appendix B for the other four]. . . . They feel empowered, and when people feel empowered, they are more likely to use their energies to produce extraordinary results.

Ideally, every leader in an organization creates and maintains the atmosphere that makes it possible for teams to function. Just as the air one breathes helps to define the quality of life, the leadership environment in which an organization's members operate determines the quality of life in the organization. Joel Marvil, president and CEO of Ames Rubber Corporation in Hamburg, New Jersey, describes his role as the leader of the approximately 500 Ames "Teammates," a designation chosen by popular vote sometime after Ames made the commitment to become a quality company (in part at the urging of its major customer, Xerox):

We know we are in a race without a finish, and Ames is committed to getting better. We are proud of what we have accomplished. We have absolutely the best people in the world here and if we can create an environment to allow them to perform to the best of their ability, we will be the best company in the world.

The vitality underlying the statement produces extraordinary teamwork—even after office hours. When senior management discovered to their astonishment that 65 of their 445 employees were functionally illiterate, they put the Teammates designation to the test. Marvil and Ames Rubber Corporation called for volunteers from among the work force to learn to be reading instructors. The company funded the training, and then had Teammates teach Teammates. The literacy problem was seen as a family problem and solved as a family problem. Marvil really believes that he has "the best people in the world," so he treats them accordingly—and they react in kind. A 1993 Baldrige Award winner, Ames is a very, very successful and profitable company.

Being a member of a team is a challenge. It requires forfeiting a degree of privacy and self-determination that most individuals find uncomfortable to one degree or another. People who opt out of social opportunities by declaring "I'm really not a joiner" are unlikely to be thrilled at a team assignment. Other people resist giving themselves over to unselfish participation even when it is in their own best interest. Think of what happens with athletic teams. Only on rare occasions does the group of players with the most talent on paper become the champion in any sport or league. Time and again—in fiction and in fact—the team with the best "chemistry" wears championship rings.

Leaders minimize resistance to teams if they understand a bit about psychology. David Keirsey's and Marilyn Bates's work *Please Understand Me* provides tips on conflict resolution through respect for individual personalities. They set up four dichotomies for understanding why people respond differently to the same situation:

- Extroverting or Introverting: Where do you focus attention? How do you get energized?
- Sensing or Intuiting: How do you find out about things? How do you perceive your world?
- Thinking or Feeling: How do you interpret what you find out? How do you make decisions?
- Judging or Perceiving: How do you create your work and life style?

Group dynamics depend in large part on how individuals in the group answer these questions. As either a member or a leader of a group, it helps not only to know the styles of the members, but also to know your own style.

Balance between the individual and the group is essential. As one Marine Corps manual puts it, "Every Marine must be able to perform his individual job and must know how to keep the unit operating at peak efficiency." Stephen Covey echoed the same theme when he stated, "In effect, once we become relatively independent, our chal-

lenge is to become effectively interdependent with others."
Functioning as a member of a team is an essential activity for both followers and leaders, but it may well mean tempering individual inclina-
tions. But while teamwork calls for cooperation, it does not call for
capitulation. Keep General George S. Patton's observation in mind:
"No one is thinking if everyone is thinking alike."

Being willing to become a member of a team means being willing
to enter into a covenantal relationship. And the experience is liberating,
according to Max De Pree's *Leadership Is an Art:*

> Covenantal relationships, on the other hand, induce freedom,
> not paralysis. A covenantal relationship rests on shared
> commitment to ideas, to issues, to values, to goals, and to man-
> agement processes. Words such as love, warmth, personal
> chemistry are certainly pertinent. Covenantal relationships are
> open to influence. They fill deep needs and they enable work to
> have meaning and to be fulfilling. Covenantal relationships re-
> flect unity and grace and poise. They are an expression of the
> sacred nature of relationships.

A Marine Corps manual concludes that effective teams are based
on effective relations between people:

> Effective personal relations in an organization can be satisfac-
> tory only when there is complete understanding and respect be-
> tween the individuals. "Effective personal relations" means
> that people can work together to accomplish a mission.
> Commonly referred to as teamwork, it can be characterized by
> Marines having confidence in themselves and their leaders.
> This confidence comes from an understanding and respect be-
> tween you, the leader, and your juniors—respect which must
> be fostered and reinforced continuously.

Adair proposes information and communication as a critical first
step in creating group motivation:

> This is a key function, for unless the team members know what
> the task is, they cannot participate very fully. Moreover, a

leader must "relate the group emotionally to the task"; he must explain if possible, not only *what* is to be done, but *why* it is necessary and important; how it fits into the wider pattern of the main plan. In other words, although the task does not arise in the group, but is given to it from above, the leader must ensure as far as possible that it becomes *their* task.

One of the challenges facing an organization is to establish teams within the larger context of the overall "team": teams that strive to excel in their own right without becoming overly competitive. When one team's victory is another team's loss, it hurts the organization:

> One important responsibility is training Marines as a team and developing that team's loyalty. While developing a strong team loyalty, you must not do so at the expense of the other teams within your unit.

It won't be easy. Europeans often comment on the degree of competitiveness evident in so many segments of life in the United States: sports at all levels, business, social events. Designating a number one is almost a national obsession. But that also creates a crowd of individuals or groups eager to wrest the crown from the current champion. It takes a first-class balancing act to call forth energy, creativity, and commitment without setting one internal team against another.

A team at the Devereux Center in Massachusetts furnishes a classic example of team building. After Devereux decided to assign everyone on the payroll to standing teams, the housekeeping department organized themselves into the "Environmental Service Peons." It doesn't take a genius to see the team name as a red flag. Mary Imbornone, Director of Training and Continuous Improvement, knew that the team had an additional problem: Team leader Karen Thompson had been with the organization less than six months and the other housekeepers were definitely not pleased with her promotion.

Thompson forged a team through leadership. First, she attended a Devereux class on team leadership and continuous improvement; then, she engaged the nine team members in writing performance standards. None of the housekeepers had previously received training in how to do their jobs, and standards had been maintained by frequent inspection. Thompson decided that it was much more productive to ask the team "How do we clean a bathroom?" than to double-check it. Before long, the team began to view their jobs as a challenge and they started benchmarking themselves against other institutions with a reputation for cleanliness. When someone heard about another facility with pristine conditions, all ten housekeepers would pile into a Devereux van to pay a visit, using the travel time to discuss chemicals, costs, equipment, procedures, and so on. Inspections became a thing of the past. The team had so much fun and took such pride in their work that they changed their name to "The Clean Team."

Recognition can either encourage or discourage teams. The Clean Team keeps a scrapbook of all their complimentary letters and awards—originally they posted them on the wall, but they ran out of room—and in 1995, the team was picked as Devereux's Continuous Improvement Team of the Year. Thompson was named Supervisor of the Year. Thompson herself goes out of her way to show team members that they are appreciated. When she heard one of them say, "Sure would be nice if we could have a meeting in the big conference room like the big people," she immediately arranged for them to have all future meetings scheduled for the conference room. And she made sure that coffee and bagels were served.

Ongoing recognition pays substantial dividends by keeping everyone engaged. When the only effort at recognition is a once-a-year gathering with canonization of a designated few, the president of the organization may as well say, "This team is a winner. The rest of you are losers." The same applies for individuals. If recognition is an annual event and is limited to a small number of people, the message is, "Sally and Nguyen and Chris and Fred are special people. You aren't." Even in sports, that most obviously competitive of endeavors, virtually every league at the high school, college, and professional level has end-of-the-season awards—but they also have weekly and monthly awards. It may be true that a particularly gifted athlete is a shoo-in for Player of the Year, but that doesn't mean that one weekend someone else can't have the best game of his or her life and be celebrated for the effort.

In the workplace, the equivalent is saying thank you to both teams and individuals both at year's end and whenever they have met or exceeded some predetermined standard. The standard may be objective (the team has implemented ten ideas) or subjective (the employee has "gone the extra mile" to delight a customer); the important thing is that recognition given to one team or person does not preclude extending recognition to another team or person when appropriate. And that saying thank you is a vigorous, ongoing effort.

Devereux has fun taking recognition seriously. In addition to an annual awards ceremony, the entire leadership team (consisting of the executive director and all the other directors) show their appreciation for improvement on a quarterly basis by holding a design-your-own-sundae bash with the directors serving up ice cream and toppings. In fact, Devereux celebrates success at every opportunity—with chocolate playing a major role. Such an approach requires a noticeable investment of time and energy on the part of leaders, both at the senior and the middle levels. But only when every team functions without the fear that another team will beat them out of something they deserve does the larger team reap the full benefit from the talents of its employees.

DISCIPLINE—THE RIGHT WAY

As one Marine Corps manual hastens to point out when beginning its discussion of discipline, "In Latin, to discipline means to learn or to teach." The manual goes on to state, "This climate of discipline is a function of morale, esprit de corps, and open communication channels so that the Marine can communicate upward and receive accurate communications from above."

When Gary Hodges took over as General Manager of the Line Creek Mine (part of Manalta Coal Ltd.) in Sparwood, British Columbia, he found discipline was lax. Employees often failed to show up for work. The situation was so serious that the then-current attendance record was handicapping the company's effort to capture international markets. Hodges talked with the union and people at all levels, explaining how and why good attendance was important to future growth and job security. With input from both management and non-management people, an attendance control program was devised that made people accountable for their behavior. Attendance improved dramatically in just one year (1991–92), and the discipline and commitment that spread throughout the organization proved to be invaluable when a subsequent quality effort was initiated.

If people assume that exercising discipline means imitating the dictator of their choice, progress and improvement halt abruptly. Even Attila the Hun understood the true purpose and meaning of discipline (or, at least, he did when his leadership secrets were spelled out by Professor Roberts):

> Discipline is not suppression. It is the teaching of correct ways expected of Huns. . . . Without discipline, Huns cannot behave with common action. . . . Discipline does not mean a loss of individuality. . . . Morale results from pride in being a Hun. Discipline brings about morale.

The glue that makes both teams and individual efforts work is discipline, as Major C. A. Bach observed:

> Consideration, courtesy, and respect from officers towards enlisted men are not incompatible with discipline. They are parts of discipline. Without initiative and discipline no man can expect to lead.

Baron von Steuben brought discipline to the American troops in Valley Forge, but he also brought freedom—long term and short term. A complete definition of discipline found in a Marine Corps manual illuminates just how much the term incorporates:

> Discipline is the individual or group attitude that insures prompt obedience to orders and starting of proper actions in the absence of orders. Discipline is an internal attitude that motivates men to conform to the informal and formal requirements of their leaders and the service. It is a state of mind that produces a readiness for willing and intelligent obedience and for proper conduct. Discipline insures stability under stress; it is prerequisite for predictable performance.

In short, discipline is absolutely necessary to the functioning of any organization, but it works only if it is understood and correctly applied.

In the pre–World War II army manual cited in Chapter 1, there is a chapter entitled "Discipline—But Not Through Fear" that begins with the following quote:

Since our Government is founded on the fostering of individualism, "discipline" is a word repellent to the American ear. In no other country have the citizens received less hammering from the top. Therefore, if discipline is conceived of as a cowed, fearful, and blind submission to the will of the superior, the men of our nation should be less amenable to discipline than the soldiers of almost any other nation on earth. . . .

[T]he more [one] leads rather than drives, the less application of any force whatever becomes necessary. . . . There is no special objection to discipline itself, for its necessity is recognized. But restrictions that appear unnecessary, that seem to have been imposed under the assumption that they might be aids to discipline, have usually the opposite effect and may arouse resentment and indiscipline through the thought that such requirements represent an arbitrary and harsh exercise of power. The martinet antagonizes those on whose support he must rely.

Discipline is founded upon two things—training and morale. . . . Military discipline is popularly misunderstood to be a state created and maintained by force. A discipline of force, which tries to compel adjustment rather than to prevent maladjustment, arouses reaction and opposition. . . .

True discipline, accordingly, is the result of volition and is gained through building willingness, enthusiasm, and cooperation—never through fear of punishment. It exists not only while men are under the eyes of their superiors but while they are off duty, because they *want* to do the things a soldier should do. This discipline is voluntary; it is based on knowledge, reason, sense of duty, and idealism.

If a leader has built up such a state of mind in his troops that they give him their utmost in trust and support, the force of public opinion has almost entirely supplanted official compulsion. He rules them not through unlimited and arbitrary power but through having developed in his men a cheerful and willing obedience that wants to respond—that *wants* to carry his orders out—a spirit of mutual helpfulness and confidence in which all ranks, moreover, desire to take much of the burden from their superiors. The unit becomes regarded by its members as a co-operative and mutual military business in the success of which every man is personally interested as a shareholder.

Inescapably, the word discipline is associated with corrective action in most people's minds; but punishment is what happens when discipline fails. When something does call for corrective, or even punitive, action, a Marine Corps manual recommends "fair and impartial punishment. Pampering people or abusing them will not get them to perform consistently well." And sometimes mistakes in punishment occur. When they do, an army manual gives the following guidance:

Here it should be said that under stress few leaders will not, at one time or another, jump on a subordinate unjustly. Realization of such a mistake usually follows quickly. Just as quickly then should follow an acknowledgement on the part of the leader that he was wrong. There should never be the slightest hesitancy in his so doing. If he has spoken sharply in the presence of others to one of his men, then he should speak as openly and plainly in acknowledging his own haste. Such words as, "I was quite wrong; you were right," are human words and readily taken as such, and they promptly restore morale. There is no need of over-doing, of laboring the point abjectly, and once the apology is made the leader may well go on directly with other details of the matter as he now sees them.

A Marine Corps manual concludes its section on discipline with a summary that holds true for any organization:

. . . [M]ental and physical abuses are often conducted under the guise of enforcing discipline. Marines resent and object to any infringement on their right or dignity. The Marine Corps has the right to expect disciplined responses from its Marines, and the Marines, in turn, have the right to expect consideration for their individuality and self-respect from the Corps.

Consideration for individuality and self-respect is the right of every employee at every level in every organization. Without it, there will be no discipline.

AN EXAMPLE OF DISCIPLINE: DRIVING TO SUCCEED

To illustrate the difference between an organization in which discipline prevails and one where it does not, consider two separate scenarios in which the goal is to get ten cars through an intersection. In the first scenario, the traffic light is red, Chris is the driver of car number 10, and the nine drivers in front of Chris are strangers to one another. The light turns green. Car number 2 makes sure that car number 1 is in motion before shifting into gear; one-by-one, movement ripples back to Chris, biding time at the rear. In the second scenario, the traffic light is red, Fran is the driver in car number 10, but there is a major difference in the skills of the other nine drivers: all of them have been trained to drive in convoy. When the light turns green, Fran's line moves forward as a unit.

Think of Chris as being in a line of managers and Fran as being in a line of leaders. Car number 1 in the management line may get through the intersection at the same time that car number 1 in the leadership line does, but after that the advantage clearly goes to the leaders. Fran will get to the intersection noticeably sooner than Chris, and interim progress will be smooth and continuous. It isn't the length of the chain that determines how quickly movement takes place, as much as it is the discipline of the people in the chain. Being in Fran's line is not without risk, however. Although all the drivers are trained and proficient, and they all understand the green light in the same way, there could be trouble if one driver fails to act responsibly.

Corporations face a dilemma. "Slow and sure" may seem like the safest way to proceed; but in today's business environment, speed is a significant factor. Trust, discipline, and leadership at every level promote speed; they also leave the organization open to minor fender-benders. On the other hand, companies unable to function as a cohesive unit chew up irreplaceable time: Nothing concrete happens at any level until managers see action at the next higher level. When there is a new policy, boss number 2 waits to see if boss number 1 is really serious (or is this like the last several "great ideas" that have died on the vine?). If boss number 2 decides to move, boss number 3 will give the idea serious consideration—and so on down to boss number 10, waiting cautiously at the end of the line. The advantage for a manager-driven company is that there may be fewer collisions; the disadvantage is that the organization may never get where it wants to go. In today's economy, it may come to a halt altogether.

While not every organization reaches the degree of mutual devotion embodied in the Three Musketeers' cry of "One for all, all for one," combining leadership, trust, and training allows people to act in a coherent, disciplined fashion while moving toward a common goal.

9

MEASUREMENTS AND LEADERSHIP

Management has been defined as a subset of leadership. Think of a large circle with a smaller circle in the middle. Leadership is the outer circle, management is the inner circle. Measurement is an even smaller circle within the other two—a bull's-eye. Measurement is rooted in experience and neither leadership nor management can accomplish anything without it. While most people think of measurement as a way to quantify (length, width, depth, mass), you don't always need a yardstick. Measurement is also a way to qualify. Awareness of what is going on around you is the heart of measurement; anything that serves as a basis for evaluation or comparison falls into this category. Conversations are rife with measurement: "This fish tastes funny." "Did you hear that Pat bought a bigger car?" "Sure had a lot of snow this winter." "That's the cutest dog I've ever seen."

Leaders have a variety of measurement techniques at their disposal and this chapter reviews some of the most common. Sometimes, however, the difficulty is not so much in deciding *how* to measure as it is in deciding *what* to measure. It is possible to take even the most subjective material and convert information about it into numbers. The question is, do those numbers have meaning? Does it really do any good to count the smiles a receptionist flashes a guest? Or to rank the beauty of the last five sunsets? Accumulating data for data's sake gives measurement a bad name. There are only two legitimate uses of measurement: (1) to gather information to use as a source of ideas, and (2) to check to see if there has been progress. When progress falls short, take that information and refer back to number 1.

Measurement is also a powerful communications tool between

173

leader and led. It lets everyone know what is expected; better still, it gives them a way to talk about it. When subordinates are doing well, measurement sets the basis for recognition. Although subordinates may already know they have met or exceeded standards, hearing from their superiors that they know it too is very important. When performance is falling short, refer back to number 1 in the previous paragraph. Using measurement as a source of new ideas is an important part of performance counseling.

There are two common measurement traps. One is to use information intended to track progress to punish people—rather than to improve performance. The consequences are deadly. Subordinates get even. The next time around, they fudge the data, making it impossible to get an accurate picture of what is going on. Measurement also goes astray when leaders draw illogical conclusions from it. During the Vietnam War, the United States and South Vietnam dropped leaflets offering everything from food to money to immunity from prosecution to any North Vietnamese or Viet Cong soldier who voluntarily surrendered. When defectors started arriving, a State Department official proposed (in all seriousness) that dividing the number of pamphlets dropped by the number of defectors would yield information on how many pamphlets were necessary to end the war.

The most counterproductive claim in measurement is, "You can't measure what I do." It's a good bet that if a boss responded, "Well then, we'll cut your wages in half and see if that seems about right," the person addressed would find some parameters to measure. Measurement interprets the world. It is a way of expressing goals, relationships, and results. The bulk of this chapter is devoted to a case study from the field of education, showing how one organization met the challenge. Anything can be measured—even leadership. The chapter concludes with information on how the Marine Corps does just that.

TOOLS OF THE TRADE

If growth is to be more than a random process, it needs to be supported by a system of measurement to identify when time and energy are dissipated on unproductive practices and to evaluate possible solutions.

To that end, a variety of both objective and subjective measurements need to be taken, used, updated, and taken again. Information can be presented in a number of ways: numerical, visual, textual. The sampling presented below runs the gamut, but the goal is always the same: to provide information for decision making. Traditionally, these tools are thought of in an organizational context, but some of them can be equally valuable in identifying and achieving personal goals.

Surveys

Perhaps the most accessible and easiest measurement technique, surveys can be either written or verbal, and can be directed at groups either inside or outside the organization. Surveys need not be formal or complex. "The thing that keeps me from doing my job right the first time is:" is an excellent (although potentially explosive) survey even though it consists of only one question. Surveys that lead to improvement follow several guidelines: They are repeated on a regular basis, data are communicated to the appropriate people, data are used to seek improvement, and results of actions taken are then communicated. The worst thing an organization can do is to take a survey without being prepared to respond if the "wrong" answer pops up. Surveys raise expectations; inaction breeds cynicism. This is equally true with personal surveys. Using a personal survey to create a self-development plan and failing to follow through can create ugly emotional fallout.

Benchmarking

Comparing something to an ideal can lead to improvement. People do it all the time. Every time someone steps on a bathroom scale, he or she is benchmarking against some standard for health or beauty. Organizations use benchmarking to identify best practices as a source of ideas.

Statistical Process Control (SPC)

There is something off-putting about this term. It seems to suggest perspiring brows and pocket calculators. Rest assured: SPC is far simpler than the name implies. As one consultant put it, "If you have to take a square root, you've gone too far."

SPC charts variability in a process. It uses a variety of control charts for conveying information, but a basic chart might be generated like this: Suppose an assembly line produces plastic bottles. If a bottle is taken off the line every twenty minutes, there is likely to be some variation between samples—one might be a smidgen too elongated, another too squat. When a line on a graph represents the ideal bottle, the elongated bottle is represented by a dot above the line, the squat one by a dot below it. Over time, a pattern emerges. If a line connecting the dots continues to rise or fall, it signals that the machine requires adjustment. If most of the dots cluster close to the line "within tolerance," the machine can continue to run—even if it produces a very odd bottle once in a while. Random occurrences are not considered a cause for alarm.

Pareto Analysis

Also called the 80-20 rule, the Pareto Principle states that 80 percent of problems come from 20 percent of causes. In other words, identify the causes of your biggest problems, tackle them first, and 80 percent of your problems disappear.

Value Analysis

One of the important tools for analyzing business processes, value analysis starts with identifying a goal. It looks first at current behavior to decide how much it contributes to accomplishing the goal, and then brainstorms for behavior that might be more productive. The result is a list of recommended changes. In order to clarify the situation, value analysis enlists a grammatical device: Everything must be expressed in one verb and one noun. The relationship between goal and recommendations is presented in a diagram. While it is unusual to use this technique in a personal setting, it is not impossible. A value analysis diagram for achieving personal leadership goals might look something like this:

Value Analysis "Wiring Diagram" for Leadership

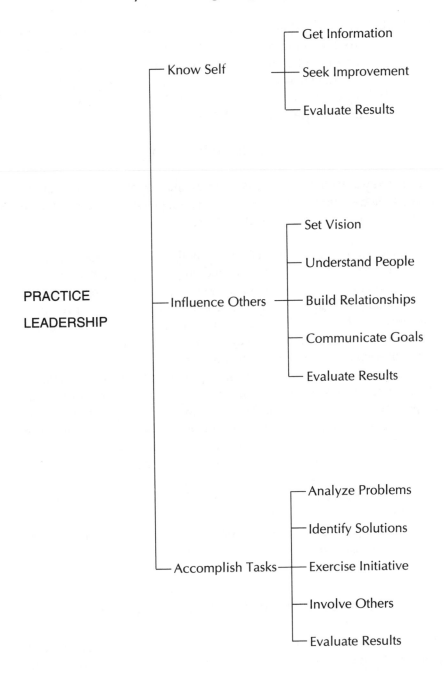

Blueprinting

Much like a computer flowchart, the sequential representation of operations in a process can uncover serious anomalies and flat-out weaknesses. Blueprinting identifies every element in a current process and presents the relationships between the elements in a diagram showing where decisions occur or actions are taken. Both information and resources can then be directed at weak links.

Fishbone Diagram

The Ishikawa Method is a visual representation of cause and effect using a diagramming technique that looks suspiciously like a fishbone (see Figure 9.1). It is pretty much self-explanatory.

There are other less formal, but equally accurate, techniques for gathering information. Observation and conversation are two of them. People tend to dismiss observation as too subjective and unreliable, but it can stand with the best of them. Astute leaders work at developing their powers of observation. As a youth, General Joshua Chamberlain learned to tell trees apart with his eyes closed, simply by listening to the different sounds the wind made rustling through their leaves.

Whether struggling to design a new product or service, gain market share, or restructure a company, measurement makes it possible to anticipate pitfalls prior to action. The alternative is to expend tremendous effort in correction after a glitch has already occurred. The importance of prevention isn't news. Folk adages have long endorsed it: "An ounce of prevention is worth a pound of cure," "Look before you leap," "A stitch in time saves nine." The problem is that too many people downplay the importance of prevention, claiming a time crunch or a need to act with boldness. For a leader, there is a difference between boldness and rashness. That difference is informed judgment: a judgment based solidly on measurement.

A CASE STUDY IN MEASUREMENT

While it is not unusual to find case studies abounding in graphs and tables in business books, it is rare to find a case study in which data

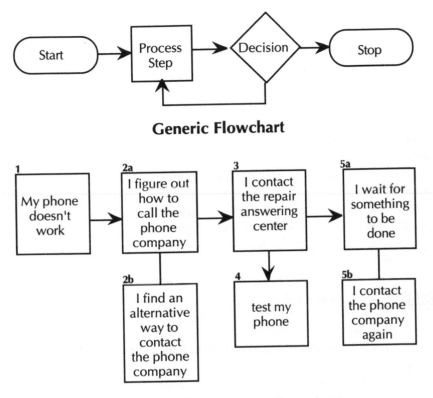

Generic Flowchart

Section of a "Service Blueprint"

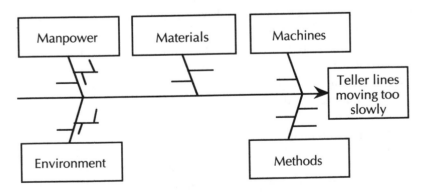

Fishbone Diagram

Figure 9.1.

are presented almost solely in words. Nevertheless, measurement is measurement when it is used as a source of ideas and as a standard for accountability whether the data are expressed visually, numerically, or textually. At least in the beginning, small-l leaders are likely to use words more frequently than charts; a self-improvement plan is a prime example. The following case study is particularly interesting both because it is textual and because it is in the you-can't-measure-what-I-do setting of education—a setting that everyone has been part of.

When you enter the South Grafton Elementary School in Central Massachusetts, one of the first things you see is a twenty-five-foot-long mural. In the center is the school's mission statement, surrounded by cut-out figures of children (one figure for every student) and houses and buses; signs identify neighborhoods; and the background is colored in with roads and trees. The building hums with the energy of 390 pre-kindergarten to third-grade students. Admittedly, it is in some ways an atypical school, located in a small rural town with a new, thoughtfully designed physical plant. Its greatest blessing, however, is the people who put together its "School Improvement Plan": teachers, administrators, children, parents, and members of the community.

This is no ordinary plan. It begins with the Mission Statement and the Statement of Philosophy (see page 181) and then finds a way to translate both into action. There are five Goals, each supported by Objectives, an Action Plan Index, Expected Outcomes, Assessment Index, Budget, Participants, and Involvement of Teachers, Parents, and Community. The plan grew out of two surveys: one of teachers, parents, and selected members of the community, and the other of students. Survey results are bound together with the plan. On page three, the plan quotes a philosophy of measurement from two authors/educators, John Goodland and Robert Anderson:

There is a past, a present and a future to be taken into account in school improvement. Unless educators know where they have been, they cannot judge the relevance of where they are going. Unless they know where they are, they cannot properly appraise the skills required to get where they want to be.

MISSION STATEMENT

We are an early childhood school and serve as the foundation for lifelong learning. Our mission is to facilitate the growth and guide the development of each child's self-esteem, sense of competence, and positive attitude toward learning. Above all, our knowledge of the development of young children provides the framework for our school's beliefs and practices, bringing our early childhood mission to life.

STATEMENT OF PHILOSOPHY

South Grafton Elementary School is a community deeply committed to fostering the highest academic and personal standards. The students, staff, and parents work together as a family to promote a child-centered learning environment. Our school is a safe, comfortable place where children learn and grow, build self-esteem and show respect for others.

We believe in children and welcome the wealth of treasures each child has to offer. We love learning. We are proud of what we do and stand prepared to continually improve it. These ideals are shared in the hope that children will realize they are the most important part of our school family and that they are loved.

Our philosophy is supported by these guiding principles:

We are committed to providing our children with a command of the basic skills, an introduction to the arts and sciences, the opportunity to think critically, to communicate clearly, and to work cooperatively.

We acknowledge that children have varying learning styles and our educational programs recognize these differences.

We encourage risk taking in an effort to allow children to use their creativity to expand all their capabilities.

We believe that the responsibility and accountability for our children's education lies with teachers, students and parents.

We see our school as a place whose walls extend beyond the school grounds, incorporating the knowledge and experience of community members to enhance the relevance of our children's education.

Our school philosophy defines who we are and affirms a commitment to continually strive to be our best. We believe in ourselves, our children, and our school.

The thirteen-page plan is too long to quote in full, but the five goals, the assessment indices, and other selected information are provided below:

Goal #1: To continue the implementation of our school's mission statement.
Action Plan Index [one of three points]: The restructuring of the library/media area to an information technology center will continue. A listening center for children will be established with tape/CD stories and matching books. A book publishing center staffed by parent volunteers will be established. Additional resources will be added to the Teacher Resource Room.
Assessment Index: Observations by Principal, Council, parents and faculty will determine to what degree this goal and supporting objectives are being achieved. Mid-year and end of year assessments will take place annually.

Goal #2: To reach a common understanding of how young children learn through the continued education of staff, parents, and community.
Expected Outcomes [one of three points]: Professional staff will offer parent/community workshops in at least two areas each year.
Assessment Index: Observation by Principal, Council, faculty, parents, community, and written evaluation following workshops, forums, etc. will be used to determine to what degree this goal has been achieved.

Goal #3: To provide a playground that is developmentally appropriate for all children at South Grafton School.
Objectives [one of four points]: The school's PTG [Parent-Teacher Group] will direct a series of fund raising efforts for the purpose of planning, constructing and/or purchasing new playground equipment.
Assessment Index: Observations by Principal, faculty, support staff, Council and PTG members will help determine the degree of playground renovations subject to both a fund-raising plan and phase in plan of the installation of new equipment and materials.

Goal #4: To improve communications between school and home/ community.

Action Plan Index [two of seven points]: The Principal will encourage classroom teachers and their children to publish newsletters/newspapers to inform parents of classroom happenings [on the same equipment the students use to publish their own stories]. A videotape of our school facility, daily happenings, and some special events will be made for sharing with parents who are new to the school.

Assessment Index: The *doing* of this goal will require the active participation of the Principal, teaching staff, and PTG. Outcomes of efforts in all aspects of communication need to be discussed at faculty, PTG, and Council meetings as to timing, content, and effectiveness of delivery.

Goal #5: To guide and direct children toward standards of acceptable behavior within our school community.

Expected Outcomes [one of three points]: Expectations for acceptable behavior will be consistent throughout the school.

Assessment Index: Discussions at faculty, PTG, and Council meetings will monitor progress towards meeting objectives. The Principal will be more visible in cafeteria and playground areas to monitor efforts.

The School Improvement Plan also includes a list of three goals set the previous year, along with specific outcomes achieved in pursuit of those goals. The final two entries in the booklet are results of surveys conducted with parents, community, staff, and students. The introduction to this section contains the following information:

> The survey statement receiving the *most* positive response (99%) was: "South Grafton Elementary School offers an open, supportive and enjoyable atmosphere." The survey statement receiving the *least* positive response (73%) was: "The maintenance and equipment of the playground are appropriate for the children."

The latter response was the basis for the third goal noted above. What is impressive is the degree to which the children were involved in every step of the improvement plan. Under Goal #3, one of the entries in the Action Plan Index was a direct result of a survey response from the children. When they were asked, "How can we make our playground a safer and more fun place?", the runaway top response was "Pick up trash." The action plan enlists them in fulfilling that goal and provides a way for them to do it: "Through education, children will be more responsible for the prevention of litter on the playground. To help in this effort there will be two additional barrels for trash."

Because this is pre-kindergarten through third-grade, the students' survey was conducted by class, rather than by individual, with teachers asking the questions. The answers reflect areas of class consensus. For instance, when classes were asked, "What three things would you like to learn at your school?", the top vote getters were Math, Reading, and Computers. When asked, "Name the three best things about your school," the leading answers were (in order of popularity) teachers, recess/snack, principal, cooperate with each other, it's fun and nice, computers, library, P.E., and friends. It's enough to make you want to take up the profession.

Goals, relationships, results: The South Grafton Elementary School met the challenge of measurement in the field of education. The principal, Anthony Cipro, credits the Griffin Center for Human Development for their assistance and ideas, but Cipro is obviously the guiding hand. Teachers, staff, parents, and students made possible the clearly stated assessments of the school's past, present, and future needs and possibilities, but without the impact of Cipro's personal leadership the effort would be greatly diminished.

MEASURING LEADERSHIP

Leadership is too complex a topic to be brushed aside with "I know it when I see it." That isn't enough for education and it isn't enough for leadership. A more sophisticated analysis is necessary. Those who seek influence with others are measured by potential followers, and they measure themselves against rivals and predecessors. The results can be expressed in a number of ways.

One raw assessment of effective leadership is yielded by an examination of how a leader spends his or her time. Time is, after all, the most valuable asset that someone in a position of authority has to invest. How much time a leader spends talking and working and being with "real people" impacts the leader, the follower, and the organization. No leader grows in isolation. No leader retains credibility if her or his statements don't ring true—and her or his statements cannot possibly have any authenticity if she or he is working entirely with second- or third-hand information. The presumption is that when leaders spend time with their followers, the impact will be positive. The only time the old adage "Familiarity breeds contempt" is valid is when the leader is contemptible.

Another way to get a reading of the capabilities of a leader is to look at his or her followers' actions and accomplishments. Think back to John Mellecker's definition of leadership:

> Leadership is the creation of an environment in which others are able to self-actualize in the process of completing the job.

Unfulfilled and ineffective followers are symptoms of poor leadership. Military theorist Major C. A. Bach did not hesitate to say,

> Remember what I tell you. Your company will be a reflection of yourself. If you have a rotten company it will be because you are a rotten captain.

If how a leader spends time and what followers accomplish are primary ways to judge leadership, the leadership of Cavalier Maintenance Service in Washington, D.C., would appear to be in good hands. Kevin Rohan, the company's president, spends fifty percent of his workday going from building to building to talk with and to say thank you to his people. To gain the hours necessary for this effort, he has about twenty of his employees at various levels work out the business plan for the organization, rather than do it himself. The company receives many letters of appreciation over the course of the year, a sampling of which are below:

Dear Mr. Gonzales,

Words will never be enough to express the deep and sincere thanks to you for finding and returning my jewelry. There were many sentimental things in the case—things that never could have been replaced. . . .

Dear Mr. Rohan:

Our firm is a tenant at the above address which is maintained by your firm and specifically by Mr. Galicia. We wish to commend Mr. Galicia, not only for performing his job in an exemplary manner, but also for his recent role in adverting a major loss for us at the hands of burglars.

Mr. Galicia after cleaning our office and while he was in the lobby of the building noticed a suspicious individual carrying what he recognized as a box which he had seen in our office. The individual was leaving the lobby through the rear doors, and Mr. Galicia challenged him. Even though the individual hurriedly left, it was later discovered that he had other items from our office in the elevator. . . . Without a doubt, Mr. Galicia's intervention prevented what would have been a major loss for us, not only in the value of the goods which would have been stolen, but also in the vital databases which are part of the computers.

Memorandum for Cavalier Maintenance Services, Inc.

Subject: Letter of Appreciation

This memorandum is to express our personal thanks and appreciation to Aracelis Perdomo for her superb efforts in keeping the Dewey Building clean and attractive!

Cavalier Maintenance Service has been providing cleaning services to our building for several years and it is time to recognize the excellence and diligence of Ara during this past year. The professionalism and dedication demonstrated by Ara during the long and difficult winter were impressive. Without any hesitation or prompting, and always with a cheerful disposition, she vacuumed, mopped, and kept the Dewey Building extremely clean under some very adverse conditions.

Her efforts, dedication and commitment demonstrated during the last year are praiseworthy. She is energetic, diligent, calm and a great representative for Cavalier!

Dear Mr. Rohan:
The purpose of this letter is to call your favorable attention to Mr. Miguel Reyes. . . .
In the execution of his assigned tasks, Mr. Reyes noticed that an indentification/proximity access card had somehow ended up in a trash can. Mr. Reyes retrieved the card, determined to whom it was assigned, and placed it on that person's desk together with a note of explanation. Mr. Reyes' efforts enabled [us] to avoid the administrative burden and costs associated with cancelling the existing card and issuing a replacement. . . .

Employees at Cavalier are eager to help. One of the employees came up with an idea to smooth over the language barrier for those employees who are new to the United States. On the back of every employee badge is printed in English, "My English is not every good although I am trying to learn. For now, please let me go and get my supervisor who does speak English."

Marine Corps manuals identify four "Indicators of Leadership" when looking at the behavior of followers: morale, esprit de corps, discipline, and proficiency. The first three are soft measures, requiring interpretation from data gathered through observation, conversation, and surveys. Taken together, these indicators can provide an accurate measure of the skill and effectiveness of either a capital-L or a small-l leader.

Morale is considered "the most important leadership indicator because the other indicators are affected by [it]." As defined by the Marine Corps, morale and discipline are closely related:

Successful handling of men implies the application of the qualities of intelligent leadership. The goal of leadership is the instant, cheerful, and willing obedience and cooperation of subordinates. Thus, true discipline is concerned with the desires, the mental states, of individuals and groups. "Mental state" falls naturally under the label *morale*.

Leadership and morale are not synonymous; yet they are as inseparable as the component parts of an electrical circuit. Morale is like the current—the powerful electromotive force— and leadership is like the conductor that guides and transmits that force to the motor. Hence the state or quality of morale produced is directly proportional to the quality of the conductor or leader.

Because morale is an individual attitude, there are only three ways a leader can measure it: "by close observation of his Marines in their daily activities, by inspections, and by talking with them." Inspections, in this instance, take on a counseling function, much like that in Chapter 7. Criteria is provided well in advance, and the objective is to assess progress, not to catch and punish. Inspections can force people in charge to think through best practices and contrast them with what has become the "way we do things around here."

Morale can also be measured in such things as turnover and absenteeism rates. Winners of the United States Malcolm Baldrige National Quality Award have consistently lower rates of both when compared to other companies in their own industries. The same practices that produce quality produce high morale, and the pull the company has on employees is measurable. One early Baldrige finalist reported that in the first five years of its quality efforts, over 100 people left the company and came back—even when it meant a cut in pay. While most had left for salary increases and "lateral shifts," interviews indicated that they came back for quite a different reason: No one wanted to listen to their ideas in their new company. They learned that work was more meaningful when they were treated as contributing adults.

A Tom Peters–inspired thesis by Major Jerry A. Simonsen, Captain Herbert L. Frandsen, and Captain David A. Hoopengardner also drew a connection between subordinates' behavior and leadership. "Excellence in the Combat Arms" concluded the following about army units:

> Yet statistics are used in varying degrees in all the divisions we visited. We learned that good statistics probably don't make you excellent; but bad ones might keep you out of the running.

Barracks larcenies, AWOLs, blotters, and USR (Unit Status Report) were the most often mentioned indicators. These measures cannot be used in isolation. . . . They are corroborating evidence that must be interpreted.

Esprit de corps is the second factor in evaluating leadership. One manual stated, "Esprit de corps depends on the satisfaction the members get from belonging to a unit, their attitudes toward other members of the unit, and confidence in their leaders." It has also been described as "the personality of the unit":

> Esprit, of course, means spirit—vivacity, ardor, enthusiasm—and pertains alike to the individual and the group. Esprit de corps applies to a unit as a whole. It is a mental state that represents the sum total of all forces that make for cohesion, for sticking together, for organized willing endeavor. It is enthusiastic support, by and of the group, along with a jealous regard for the integrity and performance of the group. It is the sense of strength and pride that comes from feeling one's self a part of a distinguished and efficient organization of splendid traditions.

Examiners for the Baldrige Award report that they can often tell from the moment they walk into an organization whether or not the company is a viable competitor for the award. There is something exciting in the air, something special going on. While less than an exact measurement, this awareness has been proven time after time. In an organization that counts good leadership and high quality among its characteristics, people like each other, people know that their ideas will be listened to, and there is a palpable sense of energy.

In "Excellence in the Combat Arms," several generals confirmed the value of observation when assessing esprit de corps:

> While they look for evidence of technical and tactical competence, we were convinced that in the final analysis, "It's something in the eyes of the soldiers" that tells them whether the unit can fight and win.

Neither the Baldrige examiners nor the army generals accepted their first impressions as final evaluations of esprit de corps; both confirmed them through observation, conversation, and surveys.

Discipline, the third indicator of leadership, was discussed at length in the previous chapter. The same tools—observation, conversation, surveys—are available to assess a number of factors: attention to details, devotion to duty, relations among individuals, proper senior-subordinate relationships, promptness in responding to orders, adherence to the chain of command, and willingness to perform without supervision. A Marine Corps manual spells out the stark contrast between a well-disciplined unit and one with poor discipline:

In a well-disciplined unit, Marines will work together without regard to personal differences or attitudes because they realize the mission must be accomplished as quickly and efficiently as possible—which requires teamwork. Poor discipline, on the other hand, can result in little regard for mission accomplishment, little concern for working with other Marines, and everyone waiting to be told what to do rather than taking initiative on their own.

The fourth leadership indicator is proficiency: the ability of the individuals and organization to successfully accomplish the mission. One Marine manual states that high proficiency (i.e., the apparent ability to carry out any assignment) is the best indicator of leadership among the four measures. Proficiency is subject to "hard" measurement and is what businesses measure most.

One such measurement is the bottom line. The proof is in the pudding. Good leadership is not only about helping people grow and become more satisfied with who they are and what they are doing, it is also about making or offering an excellent product or service. When personal and corporate goals coincide, there is a measurable impact on the bottom line. Looking at the bottom line in isolation is not a definitive measurement of leadership—much else goes into determining a company's position in the marketplace—but it is valid as part of an assessment effort. The longer an organization maintains a strong bottom line, the more likely it is that the organization's leaders understand and practice sound leadership principles.

10

PASSING THE TORCH

This book opened with the premise that personal and corporate success in the twenty-first century depend on the ability to recognize and develop leadership in others. This requires a high degree of personal commitment. One Marine Corps manual summarizes it nicely:

> You can argue whether great leaders are born or made, and whether leadership can be taught; however, no one would disagree that good leaders can be developed. And you are in the position to make good leaders. You must set and enforce high standards in all things which you try to do. You must set the example and have the moral courage to guide, correct, and listen to your juniors. You must provide the atmosphere and working environment for your subordinates so that, like you, they can learn to be good leaders. You must develop those who will succeed you as a leader.

Another significant way to show personal commitment is to actually teach leadership. Teaching leadership implies some version of formal instruction during which the transfer of information takes place. Unlike golf, which according to actor Leslie Nielson can be taught, but not learned, leadership can be both learned and taught. In contrast, developing leaders almost exclusively refers to a more personal, less theoretical experience—with the understanding that the line between the two is not absolutely clear. Mentoring takes the form of both developing and teaching others.

This responsibility to teach and develop leadership begins at the top. The Marine Corps provides a set of guidelines for commanders that (with a little judicious editing) could fit any organization:

1. A Marine's initial instruction introduces him to the Marine Corps' philosophy of leadership.
2. All Marines, both officer and enlisted, participate in leadership training. The lance corporal fire team leader has the same responsibility to develop leadership in his Marines as the squad leader or platoon commander.
3. Leadership training is conducted throughout the year.
4. Leaders have a great deal of flexibility in accomplishing leadership training.

This chapter sets out the minimum requirements for classroom training to be successful: a curriculum with something to say and a teacher with platform expertise. While the first is obvious in most people's minds, the second often receives too little consideration. Mentoring is also part of this chapter. An organization thrives when there are not only leaders at every level, but also teachers at every level. Mentoring is an opportunity for everyone to take part in teaching outside of the classroom.

The ability to teach is a valuable skill every leader must develop, one that confers benefits on both students and teacher. Teaching calls for transferring information to others, but it also calls for something else: the ability to articulate things that a person "just knows." The result for the teacher is personal growth. French moralist Joseph Joubert had it right when he said, "To teach is to learn twice."

LOOKING FOR AN IDEAL CURRICULUM

The first consideration in teaching is finding a curriculum with something to say. This presents a problem when looking for a leadership curriculum because, according to leadership gurus Warren Bennis and Burt Nanus, very little leadership training goes on in the MBA factories:

The gap between management education and the reality of leadership at the workplace is disturbing, to say the least, and probably explains why the public seems to hold such a distorted (and negative) image of American business life. . . . What's needed is not management education but leadership education. . . . The world is far more fascinatingly complex than the straight linear thinking that dominates so much of what passes for management education.

Outside the academic community, leadership courses have a disturbing tendency to be taught by former management instructors who appear to write leadership courses by making a few vocabulary changes to old management material. And many seminars suffer from the additional flaw of presenting leadership in isolation. This is a fatal flaw, according to British author John Adair:

> . . . leadership training could be called a symbiotic activity, i.e., it flourishes best alongside other forms of training. When isolated and made the centre of educational programmes it often shows signs of malnutrition.

There are, however, curricula that have met the challenge of teaching leadership effectively. The United States Coast Guard Academy is one; its "Leadership Outcomes" are provided in Chapter 2. Perhaps the best civilian example is the University of Richmond's Jepson School of Leadership. Jepson is unique in that it offers an undergraduate degree in leadership based on completion of a four-year program, concentrated mainly in the junior and senior years. The "Curriculum Goals" for graduates reads like a summary of leadership benchmarks:

- Serve effectively in formal and informal leadership roles in a range of settings
- Help others exercise leadership and hold other leaders accountable
- Develop cooperation and teamwork while inspiring commitment and trust
- Combine knowledge with judgment and imagination to creatively solve problems with others
- Apply the modes of inquiry and knowledge bases of many disciplines to the study and practice of leadership
- Think critically about leadership knowledge and practice

- Exercise moral judgment, imagination, and courage in the practice of leadership
- Imagine worthwhile visions of the future and inspire others to join in bringing about change when desirable or necessary
- Continue their development as leaders by self-directed learning

To support the pursuit of these goals, Jepson has a set of "Integrated Curricular Themes," including communication, critical thinking, values and imagination, and social and individual differences. All classes combine theory with practice. Moreover, students are required to complete a course in service learning (community service) and an internship in a governmental, corporate, or nonprofit setting.

From the student's point of view, an ideal corporate curriculum also offers more than rote memorization and exams. It provides opportunities to practice. An eight-hour course spread over four days is likely to have better results than one eight-hour session precisely because it gives students an opportunity to try out classroom material between sessions.

It is also important to meet students at their level of understanding. Beware of presenting leadership as a *fait accompli*—which is what courses based on personalities tend to do. Trying to learn leadership by studying Golda Meir is akin to trying to learn construction by looking at pictures of skyscrapers. While it is inspiring to be aware that such buildings exist, it is more helpful in the beginning stages to know how to pour a concrete foundation.

When corporations build or buy their own leadership training, it would be wise to keep both the Coast Guard's and Jepson's goals firmly in mind. At the same time, training programs must be personalized. It may be that an early step in the process of choosing or developing a leadership curriculum is to formalize what exactly the leadership philosophy of the organization is. This could be done through a series of meetings in which management and nonmanagement personnel are asked to discuss their own leadership abilities and beliefs. Feedback from these sessions could be used as a basis for writing a statement of philosophy to be incorporated into the overall curriculum. In any event, senior executives must become personally involved in defining and establishing leadership training. Leadership is too vital to the lifeblood of an organization to be left to chance—or to an inexperienced or undirected training department.

The reality is that no one training curriculum is going to work for all organizations. Training must match experience inside the company: Curriculum material must reflect the organization's own philosophy, habits, and opportunities. Most organizations will end up with a curriculum that combines a training vendor's products with the specific needs, history, culture, and vision of the future of the organization. What brings that vision to life is superior teaching.

LOOKING FOR AN IDEAL INSTRUCTOR

Author George Bernard Shaw once said of the teaching profession, "He who can, does. He who cannot, teaches." It's a clever comment, but it's also dead wrong. The best teacher is someone who is competent at what he or she is teaching—especially in leadership.

The act of teaching is in itself a way to extend leadership capabilities. Leadership skills have a limited shelf life. When knowledge and understanding, rational and emotional capabilities, and acquired and innate characteristics are not regularly augmented by new thought and experience, they go stale. More simply put: Grow or die. Everyone can name a young woman or young man who attracted followers like a magnet in high school and who subsequently sank from sight.

Teaching acts as a catalyst for personal growth. If an individual has never thought through the unique blend that accounts for his or her own leadership successes, teaching requires just that. If an individual has never stopped to consider why a particular approach seemed to work well with one person and not with another, mastering a new theory—like Maslow's Hierarchy of Needs—can bring it into focus. These activities serve to improve the instructor's own leadership practices.

Teaching leadership requires stamina and tenacity, courage and curiosity. Paul Malone III in *Love 'Em and Lead 'Em* likens it to being an explorer:

Leadership is tough to teach because the body of available knowledge is inconsistent and incomplete. Every practitioner must, to a degree, be his/her own "pioneer" exploring unknowns for him/herself.

There are a number of important characteristics a leader can bring to teaching. The first two are openness to experience and an ability to draw conclusions from that experience. "Excellence in the Surface Navy" by Commander Gregg G. Gullickson and Lieutenant Commander Richard D. Chenette gives a wonderful example of both characteristics in a warrant officer (W4), one of the mid-level ranks in the Navy:

> Talking to a W4 bosun on one of the ships we visited, we heard that relatively late in his professional life he learned the importance and power of recognizing good performance. Whereas in the past he might not have recognized a job well done because he thought everyone was expected to perform well, he now took the time to give recognition. He said that his change of views regarding recognition resulted from his realizing how good he felt in his last job when he was commended for doing well. This happened a lot in his previous job (getting commended and feeling good because of it), and he said that it spurred him on to even better performance. He now saw it as his duty to recognize his subordinates' good performance.

Any leader-in-training can use his or her own feelings as a guide to both self-development and to what he or she teaches others. As with the bosun, if something consistently makes him or her feel good, it may work with others. "The Golden Rule" is, indeed, grounded in reality. Treating people like you want to be treated is an excellent approach when contemplating action.

A third characteristic a leader must demonstrate is the ability to teach. Teachers are both born and made. Some people seem to teach as easily as breathing; others are gasping for air. And good leaders are not automatically good teachers. The ability to teach and the ability to lead are interconnected, but not synonymous. Witness the number of top-flight athletes who, by inspiring loyalty and setting an example for teammates, were hailed as "team leaders" during their playing days, then went on to become lousy coaches. How well a leader is able to teach depends in large part on how much he or she has been relying on natural talent/charisma and how much has been a result of conscious choice. There are also techniques that can be mastered.

It is not fair to ask people—anywhere in the corporate hierarchy—to teach without being sure that they have teaching skills. No matter how good the material, it's impossible to get the message across without proficiency as a presenter. Consider the case of Vice Admiral James B. Stockdale, USN, an acknowledged leader, a brilliant thinker, a gifted author, and an interesting one-on-one conversationalist with a great deal to say. He is, however, a horrible public speaker—which doomed the way he was perceived by the public during his bid for the vice presidency of the United States in 1992.

The military solves this problem by sending personnel to instructor training classes in conjunction with instructor billets (or job positions). As an example, one military officer during a twenty-year career was required to take three separate courses in how to teach: Prior to teaching artillery, he attended a week of classes, followed by sixty hours of rehearsal time (during which other instructors rated performance as either satisfactory or unsatisfactory); an ROTC billet was preceded by a two-week class on teaching techniques; and a portion of the ten-week curriculum for Public Affairs officers was devoted to teaching. His experience was not atypical.

Teaching leadership demands more than the ability to deliver a riveting lecture. It may be pedagogically sound to teach math to beginners by saying "Two plus two equals four" without asking "Do you think that's the best answer?", but anyone who teaches leadership that way falls short. Leadership necessitates probing questions from the very beginning.

One of the topics that require in-depth discussion is the emotional aspect of leadership. It is not logical to assume that it is possible to teach someone to summon up the "correct" emotional response for a particular situation. That is simply not how humans operate. It is, however, possible to teach someone that it is all right to *have* an emotional response, even the "wrong" one. There is a difference between action and reaction; people do act counter to their first impulse. When faced with downsizing, for instance, the natural instinct may be to avoid the topic entirely. A wise leader will tackle the issue head-on.

Teaching executives to be honest and tactful with their people is not simply a matter of reading tales of how other executives handled a similar situation and exhorting everyone to go forth and do likewise. Students need to be invited (or prodded) into discussing what they believe their own behavior would be—or should be—under similar conditions. This gives people tacit permission to act as complete human beings when in a leadership role.

Good teaching is as much an act of will as good leadership is and here, too, there is a tool kit: curriculum development, pacing of material, use of audiovisual materials, classroom control, voice, and posture. Think of teaching as theater: an interesting script, attractive sets, and good acting. Sometimes it is possible to get by on style alone. Presenting sound leadership theory in a compelling manner can put a theory at a student's disposal—even if the teacher has difficulty putting that theory into practice himself or herself.

While it is possible to be a good teacher without being a good leader, á la George Bernard Shaw, ideally no one who is not a leader would be assigned to teach the subject in a classroom; nor would anyone who did not genuinely want to teach be asked to do so. Teachers who want to teach do so with enthusiasm and enthusiasm is contagious. There are, however, special reasons for asking senior executives to teach, whether they volunteer or not: The organization benefits when executives get to hear from and about their juniors and juniors get to know them. This gain outweighs any reluctance an executive might feel about taking a turn in the classroom—as long as executives are prepared for the role in advance.

MENTORING: TEACH AND TRUST

Traditionally, mentoring is any one-on-one relationship in which a less experienced person benefits from advice from someone more experienced. Mentoring conveys benefits to both the mentor and the mentee. It is just as possible for a junior secretary with computer expertise to mentor a senior secretary without it, as it is for a senior vice president to mentor a junior executive on strategic planning. Anyone can be a mentor.

Bob Knezovich, manager of quality management at Armstrong Building Products Operations, winner of a Baldrige Award in 1995, points with pride to the company's practice of sharing information to leverage expertise. The goal is to create experts by having individuals learn, do, and teach, so that the company doesn't always have to rely on one person for advice. Whenever anyone at any level develops a specialty, Armstrong BPO makes sure that everyone in the organization knows about it.

W. Melvin Truett, manufacturing manager at the Marietta, Pennsylvania, plant, was a winner of the Armstrong President's Award in 1995. Throughout his career, Truett acquired skills and knowledge that have made him a Boardmill expert. In 1995, improvements under his leadership generated direct cost and freight savings in excess of $1,000,000. He frequently shares information and best practices with his peers at other plants. Don Geib, an energy technician at the same plant, has become the company's recognized authority on combustion technology and Boardmill dryer operations, saving time and money in the process. Winner of a 1991 President's Award, Geib spent time at plants in Team Valley (England), St. Helens (Oregon), Pensacola (Florida), Mobile (Alabama), Macon (Georgia), Hoogezand (Netherlands), Muenster (Germany), and Pontarlier (France), in the three years prior to his award. His contributions to the St. Helens plant start-up effort were significant. All this was in addition to fulfilling his job at Marietta.

Another winner of the President's Award in 1995, Terry Farrell is a production operator at Team Valley near Newcastle. Farrell is also the senior shop steward (union president) and he has led the plant and the union in driving improvements into the workplace, teaching union members why change is necessary and how to take advantage of it. His work was key in simplifying the traditional rule books and instituting the first gain sharing in Armstrong BPO's European operations. The Team Valley plant is now considered the benchmark for the whole company in such areas as low scrap (the lowest worldwide), low claims, and process performance. According to the award citation, "He has given up his own time to preach his philosophies and principles for driving a successful business to other internal and external organizations (i.e., Pensacola, Mobile, Macon, Beaver Falls [Pennsylvania], and the Confederation of British Industry). In addition, he finished the year by giving the benefit of his experience to the Marietta Fabrication Redesign group."

Mentoring is not quite a classroom situation and not quite a learn-from-experience one. It includes instruction, but it also includes action. When the mentoring relationship is between a senior and a junior, it provides an excellent opportunity for the senior to explain why it is important for the junior to grab the initiative and practice appropriate authority—and then to encourage him or her to do so. It is one thing to know *what* behavior is expected, but quite another to understand *why* it is necessary. A mentoring relationship can explore the relationship between authority, responsibility, and accountability, and provide a safe way to practice initiative under a watchful, but friendly eye.

Opportunities to mentor exist everywhere. It is especially important for senior leaders to step in and help in the leadership development of juniors as the situation permits—the more, the merrier. In fact, no aspiring leader should be the sole responsibility of one leader/mentor, if for no other reason than that it is an advantage to learn from a variety of personalities. And seniority is no guarantee of competence. Willingness to mentor is effective only when it is accompanied by the ability to articulate sound theoretical principles and create a setting free of distractions in which juniors can engage in discussion. A junior with several senior mentors is more likely to be exposed to leaders who meet this criteria.

The basis of any mentoring relationship is mutual trust. It is even more essential in a mentoring situation than in a classroom setting because of the personal nature of the exchange. The senior sets the tone, whether he or she is acting as mentor or mentee. The junior is always the one potentially at risk. Consider the following from "Excellence in the Combat Arms" by Major Jerry A. Simonsen, Captain Herbert L. Frandsen, and Captain David A. Hoopengardner:

> . . . [E]xcellent units allow mistakes. The battalion commander is not keeping a notebook on every officer writing down mistakes. Instead, as one officer told us, "The fact that we do more than what's required, and the fact that we can try new things

without having our heads chopped off, makes us good." One battalion commander related another story: "The hardest thing I had to overcome when I assumed command was getting my officers to talk to me. With my predecessor, they were afraid to say something wrong because of the repercussions. I want them to talk to me so that I can hear their ideas. I'm not out to roll heads because they don't know something."

Overcoming wariness and uncertainty is the responsibility of the leader. Irwin Federman, president and CEO of semiconductor manufacturer Monolithic Memories, was quoted in *The Leadership Challenge* as saying simply: "Trust is a risk game. The leader must ante up first."

POSTSCRIPT
AND THAT'S ALL
THEY WROTE . . .

The authors of this book wish that at this point it were possible to write, "And so there you have it. Follow these no-fail rules, and you will be a leader before next Thursday." It is not to be.

What we hope you've internalized is that no one is locked into a pattern from birth. Leadership skills can be studied and acquired by virtually anyone willing to make the effort. Leaders work from a tool kit and use their judgment as to which tool is appropriate in a particular situation. It's an ongoing challenge. The study of leadership never draws to a definitive close: There is always more to learn, one more way to look at things, one more tool to add to the kit.

Bennis and Nanus note that, "Leadership seems to be the marshaling of skills possessed by a majority but used by a minority." Those in the minority who decide to gather their capabilities and potential and become leaders can make rational decisions to take action, followers' reactions to those actions can be studied, and new action can be taken. Beginners develop into outstanding leaders by consciously choosing what to do across a wide spectrum of interactions with their followers.

This is not to say that anyone who wants to can, by dint of hard work and long hours of study, become a legendary leader. But anyone willing to put in the effort, and who has at least minimal skills and intelligence to begin with, can learn to become a competent leader. The proof of becoming a competent leader is the ability to pass leadership along to others.

This is our basic belief: Given time, given effort, given guidance, leadership can become so effortless that it is impossible to tell where natural ability leaves off and acquired technique begins. This view is echoed in a (possibly apocryphal) story told about a personnel evaluation of a young army officer. His evaluation contained the statement: "Jones is not yet a born leader, but he is becoming one."

WHAT'S SO NEW ABOUT TOTAL QUALITY LEADERSHIP?

Capt James F. Brownlowe

Marine Corps Gazette, December 1991

But there is an opposite viewpoint. To some, TQL seems nothing more than the latest leadership fad. To them, it is nothing more than basic, small unit leadership.

The latest buzz word in the business world today is Total Quality Management or TQM. Businesses have gone to great expense to retrain management and institute policies to enact the revolutionary changes required to adopt the "new philosophy." Books, papers, and articles have been written to examine, explain, and dissect all aspects of the changes that must be made in order to promote this new concept. Likewise, the military has been quick to jump on the TQM bandwagon, calling it Total Quality Leadership (TQL), and undoubtedly, many junior officers reading this article have already been introduced to the wonders of TQL as part of their professional military officer training.

Of course, if those officers are like me, they probably have said to themselves, "What's so new about TQL? Sounds like plain old common sense and good leadership. Why is everyone trying to convince me this is something new and revolutionary?"

I have concluded that the junior officers must be exactly right; TQL, when applied by the small unit leader, is nothing more than fundamental leadership principles. If we focus on the 14 points of TQM from which TQL is derived, as they apply to the small unit leader, we will see that it is not something new, but a reaffirmation of sound military leadership principles.

Before we begin, a quick TQM primer is in order for readers who have been fortunate enough not to have been through a long and laborious training session on the subject. TQM is the offspring of the work of Dr. W. Edwards Deming, who was sent to Japan by Gen Douglas MacArthur to assist the Japanese in their post-war recovery. Many credit Deming as being largely responsible for the emergence of Japan as a world leader in manufacturing quality and business success. The core of his philosophy is summarized in his 14 points of TQM. These points form the core of the TQM philosophy and will be central to the discussion in the remainder of this article.

At first glance, these principles may seem new. However, one can probably recognize most of them as simple leadership principles that we, as military leaders, have been using successfully for years. MajGen John A. Lejeune summarized the attributes of a leader as follows:

> The young American responds quickly and readily to the exhibition of qualities of leadership on the part of his officers. Some of these qualities are industry, energy, initiative, determination, enthusiasm, firmness, kindness, justness, self-control, unselfishness, honor, and courage.

Are the principles of TQM so radically different from those qualities Gen Lejeune used to describe a military leader? The following paragraphs will examine them point by point.

Constancy of purpose: TQM embellishes the requirement for there to be a constancy of purpose in order for the company (read unit) to survive in the competitive marketplace. A sense of direction must be created, innovation encouraged, and a long-term outlook must be maintained in order for the unit to get past day-to-day problems and forge ahead into the future.

As leaders we have always known that the successful unit does not stagnate on what is happening today, but plans for the future. As successful military leaders we have instilled in our troops the notion that there is a direction our unit must take to accomplish the mission assigned. Initiative should be encouraged from the bottom up, and everyone should know his part of the plan so the objective can be obtained with minimal supervision. To be sure, these are all TQM principles, but the average platoon leader could have recited them.

Adopt the new philosophy: American industry is scurrying to change its philosophy of management of operations that have been fraught with production mistakes, inattention to detail, and inadequately trained workers. Yet the small unit leader has always known that his only means of survival depends upon the quality and training of his troops. He knows that he alone can never achieve the mission, so his job is to foster an attitude that will enable his unit to achieve the mission. His experience has told him that he must insist on attention to detail and not tolerate mistakes born of carelessness. The successful military leader already knows the philosophy that ensures success. So what is this "new philosophy" everyone is telling us to adopt?

Cease dependence on inspection to achieve quality: Everyone will point to the military and say, "You use inspections as a matter of routine." Yet every small unit leader knows that inspections do not guarantee quality. Pride, trust, training, example, and attitude ensure quality. The inspection is merely an opportunity to exhibit this quality. Of course, the small unit leader will use the sampling techniques described by the TQM philosophy to monitor his unit's progress, but he knows that no amount of mass inspection will make the improperly trained or poorly motivated unit polished and successful. Therefore, this principle is nothing new to the military leader.

End the practice of awarding business on the basis of price tag alone: One may question the applicability of this principle to the military, since many contracts in the past have been awarded to the lowest bidder. However, let us look at this principle from the perspective of the small unit leader. The platoon sergeant usually knows the "best" way to do the job is not always the easiest or "cheapest" way to do the job. He knows that he must examine how his approach is going to ensure the success of the mission and not focus only on the immediate apparent "cost" of his plan of action. Just as the TQM philosophy promotes the use of "long-term relationships of loyalty and trust" to decrease the total cost of a job, the small unit leader knows that he must use long-term unit relationships, along with the loyalty and trust of fellow unit members, to accomplish difficult tasks with minimal expenditure of time and resources. The effective leader will cultivate and cherish these relationships and strive to foster a sense of teamwork in his unit and among adjacent units. So, while we as small unit leaders may have little to say about the cost of a piece of hardware, we have long known that the price of effective leadership is not always cheap.

Improve the system of production and service to improve quality and productivity: The philosophy of TQM insists on constant improvement of the process used to accomplish the task to avoid making the same mistakes and increase the quality of output. Of course, the small unit leader recognizes this as being fundamental to his unit's continued success. We as military leaders have long been faced with seemingly insurmountable tasks with limited resources, yet we have realized that with proper planning and efficient use of available resources, we can accomplish the mission. This is possible only when the unit leader actively seeks ways to improve his capability to complete assigned tasks. He knows that he must depend on each unit member to continually suggest better ways to improve efficiency. Most important, he must have the courage to implement the changes that are constructive and the wisdom not to change methods for the sake of change alone. Looking for better ways to accomplish a task is not new to the small unit leader. In fact, the *Marine Officer's Guide* encourages initiative in subordinates and adaptability on the part of unit leaders.

Institute training on the job: American industry has been criticized for being inflexible in its training methods and not recognizing the individual training needs of its workers. Training programs are often ill-conceived and lacking direction. Many times the programs are administered by individuals who are not adequately trained themselves. The successful small unit leader understands this point all too well. The effective leader will recognize that all of his troops have unique and varying abilities. He will structure his training program to capitalize upon these different abilities and will often use a team concept of training. Each unit member's strengths will be used to ensure every unit member is trained adequately in the tasks he will be expected to accomplish. The successful leader will recognize that his own professional expertise is crucial to the success of the program; he will be expected to set the example for the unit. He will also note that training must be meaningful and realistic to be worthwhile. On-the-job training is nothing new to the military leader, for he has long lived by the adage, "The more you train in peace, the less you bleed in war."

Institute leadership: American business has been criticized for having management consisting of supervisors, not leaders. These supervisors have been dependent upon sheer numbers for production goals, and they have been unfamiliar with their workers and their workers' tasks. Most of all, they have not insisted upon quality leadership to promote quality production of goods and services. The small unit leader knows that the success of his unit depends almost entirely upon his personal leadership and the leadership of his subordinate unit members. He knows that his loyalty must run downward to his most junior troops. The *Marine Officer's Guide* is quick to define loyalty downward as:

> loyalty to protect and foster your subordinates, to assume responsibility for their actions (their mistakes, too), and to see that they receive all credit due them.

The successful unit leader will not overly supervise his troops and will allow them to perform the tasks they are capable of with minimal supervision. He will keep in mind the leadership question posed by the proper way to erect a flagpole in which the answer is simply to say, "Sergeant, put up that flagpole." American management may currently be made up of supervisors, but the successful unit commander has always been a leader.

Drive out fear: TQM points out that fear can paralyze the work force by causing the workers to feel so insecure that they are afraid to express ideas or even ask questions. Given such fear, innovation is stifled and a "cover your behind" mentality is cultivated. The effective small unit leader realizes quickly that his unit will not be successful if its members are constantly in fear of retribution for well-intentioned mistakes. He realizes that mistakes are often inevitable and a cost of doing business, that each mistake can provide lessons learned and can often be an indicator of a hidden problem in the system itself. The successful leader will not fear innovation. For example, a decision to hand write a squadron daily flight schedule instead of typing it may be stymied by the fear of what others may think. Yet such innovations may increase the efficiency of operations greatly. The successful military leader has long known that the trait of courage does not apply only to the battlefield, but to daily operations as well. He is well aware that there is no room for fear in his unit.

Break down barriers between staff areas: TQM emphasizes that teamwork within the organization is essential to success and efficiency of operations. Dr. Deming states that too often there is a lack of communication between suborganizations within the unit, and this contributes to great losses in time and quality.

Military organizations are also broken down into suborganizations, be they departments, divisions, or fireteams. Each suborganization may be given specific responsibilities, but the successful unit leader will realize that each group does not work in a vacuum. He knows that the whole unit's success depends not on the success of any individual suborganization, but on the continued success of all. He will stress teamwork and effective communication between suborganizations. Many times this is done formally, as in department head meetings, but often informal communications is equally effective, as in a "heads-up" phone call from the operations scheduler to the maintenance chief. The effective small unit leader knows that artificial barriers must be torn down in his organization, and he knows that teamwork is key to his unit's success.

Eliminate slogans, exhortations, and targets and *Eliminate numerical goals:* American businesses have often depended upon catchy slogans demanding ever-increasing production and zero tolerance for mistakes. They have used these slogans, unsuccessfully, in an attempt to motivate workers and increase quality.

The leader knows that trendy slogans such as "Be all you can be" and "The few, the proud, the Marines" may be great for recruiting posters, but they do little to foster unit morale or mission accomplishment. He knows that the best motivator for his troops is for him to provide them with the best opportunities for success by conducting realistic training, knowing their problem areas, and exhibiting his personal devotion to the unit's success.

Likewise, he knows that demands for numerical goals are often counterproductive. Staff members (not leaders) have created goals such as cost-per-hour, maintenance-manhours, or body counts for accounting purposes. However, the successful small unit leader will not make the mistake of planning his operation around achievement of these goals in order to satisfy the bean counters. The successful leader is well aware that his troops will easily see through the veil of success that may be portrayed by clever slogans and meaningless numbers.

Remove barriers. Eliminate rating systems: American business has been accused of treating workers as commodities. Companies do not take an interest in the quality of their employees' work, listen to their complaints or problems, or make them feel a part of the team. The successful unit leader has always known that he must ensure his people know he sincerely cares about their work and well being. He will evaluate their work, not with the intent of finding fault, but with the attempt of praising them for a job well done or in an effort to find ways to improve. He will listen to their suggestions and implement them when possible. Most of all, he will let them know they are a key ingredient that will contribute to the success of the unit.

Dr. Deming views the annual rating system as a barrier to pride of workmanship in that it "nourishes short-term performance, . . . builds fear, demolishes teamwork, nourishes rivalry and politics." We in the military might be accused of falling victim to this by use of fitness reports. However, the effective leader knows that his evaluation of subordinates must not be used as punishment for bold attempts to improve operations, even when those attempts may have failed. The successful leader knows well that pride of service is a key motivator to his troops, and he will do everything in his power to let nothing stand in its way.

Institute a vigorous program of education and self-improvement: Education and self-improvement differ from training in that they directly benefit the individual rather than the organization. However, the leader knows that a program of education among his troops will foster a sense of accomplishment, promote self-esteem, and ultimately increase morale. The leader will do all he can to encourage self-improvement and, to the best of his ability, make the time available for pursuit of outside education. He knows that it will eventually benefit the unit as a whole.

Put everybody to work to accomplish the transformation: This final point implies that a change must be made to adopt the philosophy of TQM. For American businesses this may well be true. They may undoubtedly need to closely examine their management practices that have relied too heavily upon supervision and not upon leadership. However, we as military leaders recognize that TQM is just a business term for small unit leadership. Unfortunately, the farther we get from the small unit, the more likely we are to fall into the traps that the 14 points of TQM state we must avoid. We as leaders must continually guard against this as we advance through the ranks and not forget the fundamentals we learned and practiced as small unit leaders.

As the "magic" message of TQM filters throughout the military under the title of TQL, and as we are indoctrinated into its "revolutionary" ideas, keep in mind that a few years from now another management philosophy will surface and find its way into vogue. But the principles of leadership are timeless and have been proven over the years. The 14 points can be best summarized by three simple lines quoted by Maj C. A. Bach, USA in an address to new officers in 1917: *Know your men, know your business, know yourself.*

LISTS, LISTS, AND MORE LISTS . . .

Four Major Themes:

- Strategy I: attention through vision
- Strategy II: meaning through communication
- Strategy III: trust through positioning
- Strategy IV: the deployment of self through (1) positive self-regard and (2) the Wallenda factor

Five Key Skills for the Emotionally Wise:

- The ability to accept people as they are, not as you would like them to be.
- The capacity to approach relationships and problems in terms of the present rather than the past.
- The ability to treat those who are close to you with the same courteous attention that you extend to strangers and casual acquaintances.
- The ability to trust others, even if the risk seems great.
- The ability to do without constant approval and recognition from others.

—From *Leaders: The Strategies for Taking Charge* by Warren G. Bennis and Bert Nanus. Copyright © 1986 by Warren G. Bennis and Bert Nanus. Published by HarperCollins Publishers, Inc. Reprinted by permission.

Characteristics of Principle-Centered Leaders:

- They are continually learning
- They are service-oriented
- They radiate positive energy
- They believe in other people
- They lead balanced lives

- They see life as an adventure
- They are synergistic
- They exercise for self-renewal (physical, mental, emotional, and spiritual)

> —Reprinted by permission of Simon & Schuster from *Principle-Centered Leadership* by Stephen R. Covey. Copyright © 1990 by Stephen R. Covey.

Seven Habits of Highly Effective People:

Primary:
- Be proactive
- Begin with the end in mind
- Put first things first

Secondary:
- Think win/win
- Seek first to understand, then to be understood
- Synergize
- Sharpen the saw

> —Reprinted by permission of Simon & Schuster from *The Seven Habits of Highly Effective People* by Stephen R. Covey. Copyright © 1989 by Stephen R. Covey.

Five Leadership Practices Common to Successful Leaders and Ten Commitments:
(A) Challenged the process:
   (1) Search for Opportunities
   (2) Experiment and Take Risks
(B) Inspired a shared vision:
   (3) Envision the Future
   (4) Enlist Others
(C) Enabled others to act:
   (5) Foster Collaboration
   (6) Strengthen Others

(D) Modeled the way:
   (7) Set the Example
   (8) Plan Small Wins
(E) Encouraged the heart:
   (9) Recognize Individual Contribution
   (10) Celebrate Accomplishments

—From *The Leadership Challenge* by James M. Kouzes and Barry Z. Pozner. Copyright © 1987 by Jossey-Bass, Inc., Publishers : San Francisco. All rights reserved.

Nine Commandments of Leadership:

1. Thou shalt develop a personal philosophy of leadership, share part of it with thy subordinates and live by it, recognizing that thou canst fool none of the people none of the time.
2. Thou shalt view thy subordinates as the children of God and behave accordingly in the exercise of power, recognizing that power corrupts and thou art corruptible.
3. Thou shalt not bring sadness and gloom unto the workplace. Instead, thou shalt endeavor to enrich the life of each subordinate thou toucheth.
4. Thy mind shall dwell in the future whenever possible. Thou shalt not make a decision a subordinate could make just as well.
5. Thou shalt not direct thy subordinates without explaining WHY.
6. Thou shalt tolerate and even encourage some degree of conflict, disagreement and error and combat the afflictions of doppelgangeritis, numberungus, and pole vaulting over mouse droppings.
7. Thy hand shalt include both a palm and knuckles. Thou shalt reward frequently and in public BUT thou shalt also possess the innards to punish in private with blinding speed and surgical skill.
8. While thou shalt maintain some "psychological distance" from thy subordinates, thou shalt make thyself available to

those in trouble, offering thy hand, thy ear, thy heart and thy handkerchief but never thy money. In the process, thou shalt resist the temptation to play God or psychiatrist unless thou art properly anointed or qualified.

9. Thou art responsible for everything thy organization does or fails to do. When things are "gangbusters," thou shalt step back and introduce thy subordinates. When everything turns brown, thou shalt step forward and take thy licks.

> —From *Love 'Em and Lead 'Em* by Paul B. Malone III, 1986. Note that Malone restricted himself to nine commandments so as not to compete with Moses. This list is also included in Malone's second book: *Abuse 'Em and Lose 'Em* (1990). Paul Malone's two books can best be ordered by calling 703-573-0909 (they are self-published).

Essential Qualities:

Loyalty, Courage, Desire, Emotional Stamina, Physical Stamina, Empathy, Decisiveness, Anticipation, Timing, Competitiveness, Self-Confidence, Accountability, Responsibility, Credibility, Tenacity, Dependability, Stewardship

> —From *Leadership Secrets of Attila the Hun* by Wess Roberts, Ph.D. Copyright © 1985, 1987 by Wess Roberts, Ph.D. Reprinted by permission of Warner Books, Inc.

Royal Marine Corps, Canada—Qualities of a Leader:

Loyalty, Professional, Competence, Courage, Honesty, Commonsense, Good Judgment, Confidence, Initiative, Tact, Self-Control, Humour, Personal Example, Energy, Enthusiasm, Perseverence, Decisiveness, Justice

Royal Air Force College, Great Britain—Qualities of a Leader:

Efficiency, Energy, Sympathy, Resolution, Courage, Tenacity, Personality

Field Marshall Lord Slim—Qualities of a Leader:
Courage, Willpower, Initiative, Knowledge

—From *Training for Leadership* by John Adair, 1968.

Leadership is a composite of a number of qualities. Among the most important I would list self-confidence, moral ascendancy, self-sacrifice, paternalism, fairness, initiative, decision, dignity, and courage.

—From "Know Your Men, Your Business and Yourself" by Major C. A. Bach, 1917.

The following list is for pitchers and catchers [leaders and followers] alike. . . :
1. The right to be needed.
2. The right to be involved.
3. The right to a covenantal relationship.
4. The right to understand.
5. The right to affect one's destiny.
6. The right to be accountable.
7. The right to appeal.
8. The right to make a commitment.

—From *Leadership Is an Art* by Max De Pree. Copyright © 1987 by Max De Pree. Used by permission of Doubleday, a division of Bantam Doubleday Dell Publishing Group, Inc.

Ten Steps to a Courageous Conscience:
1. Be proactive.
2. Gather your facts.
3. Before taking a stand, seek wise counsel.
4. Build your fortitude.
5. Work within the system.
6. Frame your position so it will be heard.
7. Educate others on how your view serves their best interest.

8. Take collective action.
9. If you meet leader resistance, seek higher authority.
10. Have the financial and emotional cushions to exercise other alternatives.

Principles of Leadership:

1. A commander will command.
2. Summer soldiers will be transferred before the sun goes down.
3. Keep a quick line of communications.
4. Punishment for mistakes must be immediate, or a dead man does not have any ego.
5. Say what you mean and mean what you say.
6. Any man who thinks he is indispensable ain't.
7. The mission is all important! Think about standard rules later.
8. Always be alert to the source of trouble.
9. Select leaders for accomplishment and not for affection.
10. Every commander must have authority equal to his responsibility.
11. Protect the troops first! The wishes of superior officers are secondary.

Leadership Traits:

Integrity, Loyalty, Commitment, Energy, Decisiveness, Selflessness

Leadership Principles:

Know your job, Know yourself, Set the example, Care for people, Communicate, Educate, Equip, Motivate, Accept your responsibility, Develop teamwork

> —From *Air Force Leadership* (AFP 35-49), United States Air Force, 1985. The various military correspondence course material and other texts from the U.S. armed services are best obtained by cultivating a friend in the appropriate service and doing some creative begging.

Principles of Leadership:

1. Know yourself and seek self-improvement.
2. Be technically and tactically proficient.
3. Seek responsibility and take responsibility for your actions.
4. Make sound and timely decisions.
5. Set the example.
6. Know your soldiers and look out for their well-being.
7. Keep your subordinates informed.
8. Develop a sense of responsibility in your subordinate.
9. Ensure the task is understood, supervised, and accomplished.
10. Build the team.
11. Employ your unit in accordance with its capabilities.

Leadership Competencies:

1. Communications
2. Supervision
3. Teaching and Counseling
4. Soldier Team Development
5. Technical and Tactical Proficiency
6. Decision Making
7. Planning
8. Use of Available Systems
9. Professional Ethics

> —From *Military Leadership* (*FM 22-100*), United States Army, 1990.

USMC Counseling Program Student Handout

The Basic School

Marine Corps Schools, Quantico, Virginia

Guidelines for counseling techniques include the following:

A. Active Listening
   (1) Obstacles
      (a) Lack of concentration
      (b) Filters
   (2) Techniques
      (a) Listen not only for facts, but also for generalizations.
      (b) Distinguish between facts and opinions.
      (c) Listen for changes in tone of speech, rate of speech, and volume.
      (d) Watch for nonverbal clues.
B. Questioning
   (1) Closed-end questions
   (2) Open-end questions
   (3) Probing questions
   (4) Interpretive questions
C. Giving Feedback
   (1) How
      (a) Use positive reinforcement.
      (b) Focus on events—not on the person.
      (c) Relate to the junior's and the unit's targets.
      (d) Probe silent agreement.
      (e) Allow the junior to vent emotions; avoid arguments.
   (2) Feedback is most effective if:
      (a) It deals with things that can be changed.
      (b) It is timely.

(c) It is given to satisfy the junior's need.

(d) You are prepared to hear the junior's response.

D. Problem Solving

(1) Questions to ask

(a) What is happening that shouldn't happen?

(b) What is not happening that should happen?

(c) Is something about the junior preventing performance?

(d) Is something outside the junior's control impeding performance?

(2) If a junior is part of the problem, explore whether the junior:

(a) Has the required ability.

(b) Knows performance is not meeting expectations.

(c) Has the necessary knowledge.

(d) Has the necessary skills.

(e) Has the proper attitude.

(3) Tailor corrective action to the deficiency

(a) If a knowledge problem, provide information.

(b) If a skill problem, provide guidance and feedback.

(c) If an attitude problem, employ non-directive counseling.

(4) Consider obstacles to performance outside the junior's control.

(a) Inadequate definition of targets.

(b) Lack of positive reinforcement.

(c) Lack of feedback on inadequate performance.

(d) Conflicting or competing demands on the junior's time.

(e) Insufficient resources.

(f) Lack of delegated authority.

(5) Evaluate solutions

(a) Likely consequences

(b) Practicality

(c) Required resources

(d) Likely benefits

      (e) Required support and follow-through
      (f) Simplicity

E. Setting targets
  (1) Performance targets are:
      (a) Targets to shoot for.
      (b) Yardsticks for measuring performance and identifying problems.
      (c) Planning tools.
      (d) Motivational tools.
  (2) Effective performance targets are:
      (a) Stated as a result or outcome.
      (b) Measurable.
      (c) Realistic.
      (d) Challenging.
      (e) A "must."
      (f) Limited in number.
      (g) Jointly set.
      (h) Revised if circumstances change.

F. Planning for improvement
  (1) Jointly develop plan for improvement.
  (2) Use plan to track progress and identify problems.

The pocket-size *USMC User's Guide to Counseling (PCN 100 013485 00)* includes a complete discussion of the counseling function.

THE SUBORDINATE: THE ART OF FOLLOWERSHIP

Sergeant First Class Michael T. Woodward

Infantry Magazine, July–August 1975

FM 22-100, *Military Leadership* states, "The ultimate objective of leadership in a military organization will always be the successful accomplishment of the mission." Much literature, time, instruction, and effort are devoted in the military services to the vital area of leadership. Techniques of leadership, desired characteristics of leaders, various surveys, studies, data, and a multitude of printed matter focus on leaders, and rightly so.

Very little, however, has been directed towards the one element that all leaders and the difficult skill of effective leadership depend upon—the follower. Professionalism in followership is as important in the military service as professionalism in leadership.

Followership can be defined as a process in which subordinates recognize their responsibility to comply with orders of leaders and take appropriate action consistent with the situation to carry out those orders to the best of their ability. In the absence of orders they estimate the proper action required to contribute to mission performance and take that action.

Inherent in the above definition of followership is a high degree of self-discipline. The follower must have a personal commitment to the successful completion of his unit's mission. The most effective follower is the one who accepts the necessity for compliance and who is committed to placing the needs of the unit above his own needs.

A high degree of self-discipline among followers assures that they can be relied upon to contribute positively toward mission accomplishment, even in dangerous and stressful situations where personal needs might otherwise dominate. History is replete with examples of self-discipline among followers, from the ancient Hebrews at Masada to Roger's Rangers to American POWs, who spent years in Southeast Asia prisons unbroken in spirit and still dedicated to mission accomplishment.

An effective follower needs more than self-discipline. Competence is a requirement and requires continual self-development, which may take the form of training or education. The Army offers and encourages followers to take advantage of the many training and educational programs available, for acquired competence among followers leads to responsibility, an important characteristic of followership professionalism.

The responsibilities given by leaders to the followers must be realistic. The follower must be held accountable for the end result of his responsibilities, but should be given as much latitude as possible in accomplishing those responsibilities. Of course, responsibility implies more than just doing what is required—it includes an obligation to serve and perform in the best manner possible for that individual follower.

Dedication is a commitment to a system or ideal. It is the vehicle of self-discipline, competence, responsibility, and professionalism; it is the follower's guideline. For the professional follower, it is a firm belief in the nation, the Army, its mission, and his role.

Unlike the dedication of followers in other walks of life, the dedication of the follower in the Army may involve putting his life in danger for that dedication. He understands and lives with that possibility.

Any organized group activity—military or otherwise—must have followers. To succeed in whatever purpose it has, the group's followers must function effectively. This is true in politics—from the township council to national political parties. It is true from the smallest businesses to the multinational corporate giants that transcend national boundaries and economies. Most of all it is true in all military organizations, from fire team to field army level. Without followers, nothing is accomplished.

There is one major difference, however, between the military services and other activities—the consequence of failure. In politics, failure may cost votes or, at its most serious, a lost election. If followers fail in the realm of the business world it may mean financial loss or even bankruptcy. Serious consequences, certainly. But in the Army?

Depending upon the size of the organization and the importance of the operation a failure of followership can lead to unnecessary casualties, failure to take an objective, the loss of a battle, or, at worst, complete defeat of a nation and subjugation by others. Even in peacetime, the failure of an Army's followership can be somber. A soldier's failure, a unit's failure, or an Army's failure to perform its peacetime missions can reflect directly upon that individual's, that unit's, that Army's ability to perform effectively in combat.

Therefore, followership cannot be ignored. It needs to be nurtured and fostered as leadership has been. Leaders are useless without followers, marginally effective with apathetic followers, and most effective when the followers are as professional in their attitude toward followership as the leaders are about leadership.

PARTICIPATION

Followers who have the same sense of mission accomplishment as their leaders, who are aware of and actively participate in the art of followership, make leadership possible. Specific guidelines directed at followers enhance the art of followership as a separate but dependent leadership function. Effective leadership requires followers who are more than Pavlovian reactors to their leaders' influences. When followers actively contribute, are aware of their function, and take personal pride in the art of followership, then the joint purpose of leadership and followership—higher levels of mission accomplishment—is achieved effectively.

Specifically directed at followers, these "Guidelines for Followers" have been developed by the Leadership Department, USAIS [United States Army Infantry School], several of which are principles of leadership which apply equally to followers:

- Know yourself and seek self-improvement.
- Be technically and tactically proficient.

- Comply with orders and initiate appropriate actions in the absence of orders.
- Develop a sense of responsibility and take responsibility for your actions.
- Make sound and timely decisions or recommendations.
- Set the example for others.
- Be familiar with your leader and his job, and anticipate his requirements.
- Keep your leaders informed.
- Understand the task and ethically accomplish it.
- Be a team member—but not a yes man.

Finally, as an example for all those interested in the art of followership as applied to leaders who are also followers, the Creed of the Noncommissioned Officer was developed by the NCOs of the NCO Subcommittee, Command and Leadership Committee, Leadership Department, USAIS. It currently appears in the Leadership Workbook given to all students in the Basic Noncommissioned Officer courses at the Infantry School and is awaiting approval for Army-wide distribution.

The creed is as follows:

No man is more professional than I. I am a noncommissioned officer, a leader of men. As a noncommissioned officer I realize that I am a member of a time-honored corps, which is known as the "Backbone of the Army."

———

I am proud of the corps of noncommissioned officers and will at all times conduct myself so as to bring credit upon the corps, the military service, and my country regardless of the situation in which I find myself. I will not use my grade or position to attain pleasure, profit, or personal safety.

———

Competence is my watch-word. My two basic responsibilities will always be uppermost in my mind—accomplishment of my mission and the welfare of my men. I will strive to maintain tactical and technical proficiency. I am aware of my role as a noncommissioned officer. I will fulfill my responsibilities inherent in that role. All soldiers are entitled to outstanding leadership; I will provide that leadership. I know my men and I will always place their needs above my own. I will communicate consistently with my men and never leave them uninformed. I will be fair and impartial when recommending both rewards and punishment.

Officers of my unit will have maximum time to accomplish their duties; they will not have to accomplish mine. I will earn their respect and confidence as well as that of my men. I will be loyal to those with whom I serve, seniors, peers and subordinates alike. I will exercise initiative, by taking appropriate action in the absence of orders. I will not compromise my integrity, nor my moral courage. I will not forget, nor will I allow my comrades to forget, that we are professional noncommissioned officers—Leaders of Men!

Followers are potential leaders. Ambition to be a leader and proven leadership ability lead the way from followership to leadership, and the most effective follower is that individual whose goal is future leadership.

Therefore, followership must be an integral part of Army doctrine, for it is the base upon which future leaders are tempered and its enhancement among subordinates will insure that professionalism is keyed to all levels—followers as well as leaders.

Followership does not guarantee success from any group, but when combined with effective leadership, this Army will indeed be ready to win the first battle of the next war.

APPENDIX E
LOVE
AND LEADERSHIP

Major Patrick L. Townsend

Marine Corps Gazette, February 1982

The English language, so rich in variety that there is a recognized network of words for expressing virtually every nuance of any central concept, has been strangely abused in one key area—love. We have come to limit its meaning, on the personal level, to two instances—family and sex. We are uncomfortable, for instance, to hear of one man loving another, or of a married person admitting love for a member of the opposite sex other than their spouse.

Yet there are many manifestations of love, and one of the greatest is good leadership. We acknowledge this with statements such as "he really loves his men" or "they really love him," but we rarely look past the cliches. Love and leadership are not synonymous terms, but since leadership is a form of love, our knowledge and experience of the root concept can provide us with useful insights into leadership.

Perhaps the most obvious thing that leadership and love have in common is the act of caring about the welfare of others—an act that is central to both. One's love for another implies caring for the well-being, physical and mental, of the other. Conversely, a failure to notice, or to obviously care about, a decline in the quality of someone's state of existence is taken as proof that "you don't love me anymore." In the parallel case, if the "led" perceive that their leader doesn't care about the fact that, for example, their food is bad and getting worse, he will quickly be adjudged a poor leader. This idea is formalized by the fact that taking care of the troops is considered second in importance only to the accomplishment of the mission.

It is that ordering, more than anything else, that makes the words love and leadership nonsynonymous. (For other "technical" similarities and dissimilarities, see the accompanying chart.)

Marine, the biography of Chesty Puller, provides a classic example of the close tie between love and leadership. Anyone who reads *Marine* and ignores the tender love letters to his wife, written from combat, misses the point of the book and of the man. Chesty Puller loved his men, and they him, just as truly and as fiercely as he loved his wife and family. His great capacity for love enhanced immeasurably his abilities as a leader.

A person who would call himself, or herself, a leader of Marines must be capable of love, of allowing themselves to be loved, and of understanding the awesome responsibilities incurred when one seeks and accepts the love of others. To love someone is to make a commitment to them, a promise to work hard to better them and to better yourself. It is not a pledge to nag them until they finally shape up but rather a promise to work with them towards a mutual goal, a higher state.

This is not to say that I am advocating a utopian democracy for the Corps in which the leaders and the followers somehow merge into one happy, loving, homogeneous group. Remember, I said the words are not synonymous. Nor is it to say a person in a leadership position who loves the people assigned to his responsibility will automatically be a great leader. However, without the ability to love, he will not be a great, and perhaps not even a good, leader. The technical knowledge, the courage, the personal integrity so often discussed are definitely necessary. Love though is what makes it work; it is what makes the followers willingly accept the technical knowledge and treat the courage and personal integrity as something to emulate rather than just applaud.

The relationship between the leader and the follower(s) is most closely analogous to that between parent and child. The good parent listens to his child and considers both the child's desires and abilities along with outside demands and personal responsibilities before making a decision. Whenever possible, that decision is explained to the child. Also, the good parent will strive to set a good example for the child.

In both love and leadership, perception is frequently as important as reality. If someone is perceived as being a good leader or of loving, then the recipient of that leadership or love will normally react by willingly following or by returning the love. The importance of ensuring that the object of the leadership or love is aware of outward signs that are taken as positive evidence of love or leadership increases as the distance—both physical and organizational—between the leader and the follower(s), the lover and the loved one(s), increases. The possibility of successfully faking it, of making the perception different than the reality, also increases as the distance grows.

A grandparent, for instance, is perceived as loving by a grandchild if he or she is careful to never miss a birthday or Christmas. Likewise, troops rarely see their commanding general and few ever actually talk with him. Yet every Marine will offer an opinion about his general, will tell you whether he will happily follow him and give that extra effort. This assessment, largely emotional, which will translate itself into tangible performance, is based on a combination of the reputation that the general built for himself on the way up, on the individual Marine's knowledge/perception of his performance in his current job as commanding general, and on the individual Marine's perception of how well the command is "taking care" of him.

In point of fact the commanding general may be doing very little himself to see that his troops' physical and mental welfare is being attended to. He may not even be "setting the tone" but rather be simply blessed, accidentally or intentionally, with a good staff. Similarly, a child will profess his love for both grandparents—since both have been signing the cards that came with the gifts. Yet it's possible that left to his own devises, grandpa might never admit that he has grandchildren, let alone remember their birthdays.

A historical example is offered by Napoleon. His men loved him as proved by their statements and their actions. Yet Napoleon's cavalier attitude towards them was summed up in his claim that he had "an income of 20,000 men a month to spend." His troops didn't know his opinion of them. They knew only that he had led them to glory and satisfied both physical and mental needs and desires.

The reverse is also possible. A leader may be an extremely talented technician with a deep love for his people, but if that talent and that feeling are not made known to the Marines he would lead, he may as well not have them. Without a capable staff, the filter through which the enlisted and the majority of the officers see their commanding general, the fruits of his knowledge and love will be minimal.

Looking again at the parallel case of the lover and the loved ones. A grandmother's deep love for her grandchildren will not be recognized if she is unable to acknowledge special occasions, can never visit, and/or is being presented in a bad light by her "staff," grandpa, parents, and other relatives.

As the distance is decreased, the concepts of love and leadership become more obviously intertwined. A platoon commander, while laying the groundwork for the reputation that will follow him throughout his career, must truly love his men if he wishes to be known as a good leader. If he brings technical expertise and ambition, but no warmth, to his position, his troops will return his investment in like currency. They will do precisely what he says, but will not give the extra effort that is the mark of the well-led.

Another point of similarity is the willingness to forgive that is common to both loving relationships and to leading-led relationships. Not only will on-going faults be overlooked or compensated for, mistakes will be tolerated and not held against the lover. So too with the leader whose men are returning the love/leadership they perceive as being offered freely to them. Many a young lieutenant has been saved because the men under his command "covered for him." It was no accident, just as it was no accident when adjacent units chose not to cover for their lieutenants. In the former case, love is being returned in full.

As these young officers climb through the ranks and become more and more distant from the troops, they will still have a group of officers and men with whom they must deal on a person-to-person basis. At the highest levels, this will be the general's staff. As I mentioned above, success at that level will be a combination of the reputation earned, the common perception of his competence, and the perception, as seen through the filter of his staff, of his love for the troops. As long as the people who make up the staff feel loved, they will pass on to the lower levels that they too are truly loved. This explains, of course, how Napoleon could be so loose with his "income" of men and yet be loved by them. He did ensure that his staff felt loved and appreciated, and so they conveyed their feelings towards him to the common soldier.

What makes all of this threatening to many officers, young and old, is that it involves taking a rather large chance for, unfortunately, to just love your troops won't be enough. Just as the object of one's romantic love may not always be swept off her feet on schedule, so too in a leading-led relationship. As a result, you might find yourself a victim of unrequited love on a grand scale. Love is what makes it work, and the loved and the well-led will overlook and/or compensate for some weaknesses, but there must be some substance, some technical knowledge, to hang onto. Conversely, technical expertise by itself can ensure meeting minimum objectives and, if it's all you have, will just as surely doom you to having to settle for minimum performance.

It is the leader who combines a deep love, an ability to love and be loved, with technical knowledge and dedication who will rise to the top. It is the leader who makes an active effort to ensure the physical and mental welfare of those placed under his responsibility and whose people know it—the leader who blends the emotional and rational elements—who is the stuff that legends are made of.

To establish both the similarities and the differences, compare the two lists below. On the left are the principles of leadership as laid out in the *Guidebook*. On the right are the analogous "principles of love." Just as adherence to the principles of leadership—a task made impossible if the leader does not love his people (see #6 and #11 in particular)—promises success in the military, so too would adherence to their counterparts come close to guaranteeing a successful personal relationship.

Principles of Leadership

1. Take responsibility for your actions and the actions of your Marines. Use responsibility with judgment, tact, and initiative. Be loyal, be dependable.

2. Know yourself and seek self-improvement. Evaluate yourself. Be honest with yourself about yourself.

3. Set the example.

4. Develop your subordinates.

Principles of Love

1. Take responsibility for your actions and share the responsibility, if appropriate and welcome, for your loved one's actions. Treat your loved one with judgment and tact. Be loyal and dependable.

2. Know yourself and seek self-improvement so that your "team" can grow. Don't lie to yourself about yourself or your loved one.

3. Don't make demands that you wouldn't want made of you.

4. Using tact and judgment, offer to take part in your loved one's growth and invite them to be part of yours.

Principles of Leadership
(continued)

5. Ensure that a job is understood, then supervise it and carry it through to completion.

6. Know your men and look after their welfare. Share problems but don't pry.

7. Every man should be kept informed.

8. Set goals you can reach.

9. Make sound and timely decisions.

10. Know your job.

11. Teamwork.

Principles of Love
(continued)

5. Ensure that any requests that you make that are important to you are correctly understood.

6. Know your loved one's needs and wants and be concerned about their physical and mental welfare. Ensure that they know that you are available to share any problem, while still allowing privacy.

7. Always communicate. If something is important enough to you that it affects your behavior, tell your loved one about it.

8. Be realistic in your expectations. You are not going to be in Shangri-la every day.

9. Make the necessary decisions as well and as responsively as you can.

10. Know the "mechanical" aspects of your relationship, the job of building and nurturing a solid relationship.

11. Share with and work with your loved one towards agreed goals.

[This article was awarded a "Distinguished Performance Award" from the Marine Corps Combat Correspondents Association in 1982.]

BIBLIOGRAPHY

Books

Adair, John. *Training for Leadership*. Aldershot, England: Gower, 1968.

American Heritage Dictionary. Second College Edition. Boston: Houghton Mifflin, 1982.

Bartlett, John. *Familiar Quotations*. Boston: Little, Brown, 1980.

Bell, Chip R. and Ron Zemke. *Managing Knock Your Socks Off Service*. New York: AMACOM, 1992.

Bennett, William J. *The Book of Virtues*. New York: Simon & Schuster, 1993.

Bennis, Warren, and Burt Nanus. *Leaders*. New York: Harper Perennial, 1985.

Block, Peter. *The Empowered Manager*. San Francisco: Jossey-Bass, 1987.

Covey, Stephen R. *The 7 Habits of Highly Effective People*. New York: Simon & Schuster, 1989.

———. *Principle-Centered Leadership*. New York: Simon & Schuster, 1990.

DePree, Max. *Leadership Is an Art*. New York: Doubleday, 1989.

Gooding, Corporal James Henry. *On the Altar of Freedom*, ed. Virginia M. Adams. New York: Warner Books, 1991.

Greenleaf, Robert. *Servant Leadership*. Mahwah, NJ: Paulist Press, 1977.

Gullickson, Commander Gregg G. and Lieutenant Commander Richard D. Chenette. "Excellence in the Surface Navy." Monterey, CA: Naval Postgraduate School, 1984.

Hyland, L. A. (Pat). *Call Me Pat*. Virginia Beach, VA: Donning Company, 1993.

Kakabadse, Andrew, Susan Vinnicombe, and Ron Ludlow. *Working in Organisations*. Aldershot, England: Gower, 1987.

Keirsey, David and Marilyn Bates. *Please Understand Me*. Del Mar, CA: Prometheus Nemesis, 1978.

Kelley, Robert. *The Power of Followership*. New York: Doubleday Currency, 1992.

Kouzes, James M. and Barry Z. Posner. *The Leadership Challenge*. San Francisco: Jossey-Bass, 1987.

Leckie, Robert. *The Wars of America*. New York: Harper & Row, 1968.

Malone, Paul B. III. *Love 'Em and Lead 'Em*. Annandale, VA: Synergy Press, 1986.

―――. *Abuse 'Em and Lose 'Em*. Annandale, VA: Synergy Press, 1990.

Peacock, William E. *Corporate Combat*. New York: Facts on File, 1984.

Peters, Tom, and Nancy Austin. *A Passion for Excellence*. New York: Random House, 1985.

Peters, Tom, and Robert H. Waterman. *In Search of Excellence*. New York: Harper & Row, 1982.

Roberts, Wess. *Leadership Secrets of Attila the Hun*. New York: Warner Books, 1990.

Reynolds, Debbie. *Debbie, My Life*. New York: Pocket Books, 1988.

Rogers, Ginger. *Ginger: My Story*. New York: Harper-Collins, 1991.

Simmons, Brigadier General Edwin H. *The United States Marines, 1775–1975*. New York: Viking Press, 1976.

Simonsen, Major Jerry A., Captain Herbert L. Frandsen, and Captain David A. Hoopengardner. *Excellence in the Combat Arms*. Monterey, CA: Naval Postgraduate School, 1984.

Spector, Robert and Patrick D. McCarthy. *The Nordstrom Way*. New York: Wiley, 1995.

Sun Tzu. *The Art of War*, trans. Thomas Cleary. Boston & London: Shambala, 1991.

Townsend, Patrick L. and Joan E. Gebhardt. *Commit to Quality*. New York: Wiley, 1986.

————. *Quality in Action*. New York: Wiley, 1992.

Trulock, Alice Rains. *In the Hands of Providence*. Chapel Hill: University of North Carolina Press, 1992.

U.S. Marine Corps. *Guidebook for Marines*. Quantico, VA: Marine Corps Association, 1984.

Weigley, Russell F. *History of the United States Army*. New York: Macmillan, 1967.

Williamson, Porter B. *General Patton's Principles for Life and Leadership*. Tucson: Management and Systems Consultants, 1988.

Woodham-Smith, Cecil. *Florence Nightingale*. New York: McGraw-Hill, 1951.

Government Publications

U.S. Air Force. *Air Force Leadership* (AFP 35-49—AS 300 lesson plans). [Washington, D.C.]: U.S. Air Force, 1985.

U.S. Army. *Military Leadership (FM 22-100)*. [Washington, D.C.]: U.S. Army, 1983.

U.S. Army. *Military Leadership (FM 22-100)*. [Washington, D.C.]: U.S. Army, 1990.

U.S. Coast Guard. *Leadership Across the Curriculum* (Superintendent Instruction 5351.1). [New London, Conn.]: U.S. Coast Guard, August 23, 1995.

U.S. Marine Corps. *Counseling for Marines (MCI 01.12b)*. [Washington, D.C.]: U.S. Marine Corps, 1993.

U.S. Marine Corps. *Fundamentals of Marine Corps Leadership (MCI 03.3m)*. [Washington, D.C.]: U.S. Marine Corps, 1989.

U.S. Marine Corps. *Leadership (MCI 7002A)*. [Washington, D.C.]: U.S. Marine Corps, 1992.

U.S. Marine Corps. *Leadership (MCI 7106B)*. [Washington, D.C.]: U.S. Marine Corps, 1990.

U.S. Marine Corps. *Leadership for American Army Leaders (FMFRP 12-17)*. [Washington, D.C.]: U.S. Marine Corps, 1988.

U.S. Marine Corps. *Leading Marines (FMFM 1-0)*. [Washington, D.C.]: U.S. Marine Corps, 1995.

U.S. Marine Corps. *Marine Corps Leadership (MCI 7404)*. [Washington, D.C.]: U.S. Marine Corps, 1990.

U.S. Marine Corps. *User's Guide to Marine Corps Leadership (NAVMC 2767)*. [Washington, D.C.]: U.S. Marine Corps, 1984.

U.S. Marine Corps. *USMC User's Guide to Counseling (NAVMC 2795)*. [Washington, D.C.]: U.S. Marine Corps, 1986.

U.S. Navy Senior Enlisted Academy. *Student Readings, Unit Two*. [Newport, Rhode Island]: U.S. Navy, 1993.

Articles

Bach, C. A. "Know Your Men, Your Business and Yourself." *Air Clues,* March 1917; 114–117.

Brownlowe, Captain James F. "What's So New About Total Quality Leadership?" *Marine Corps Gazette,* December 1991; 19–21.

Conger, Jay A. "The Dark Side of Leadership." *Organizational Dynamics,* Autumn 1990.

Dempsey, James. "Admiral 'Popeye' Did it All." [Worcester, MA], *Telegram & Gazette*, 18 September 1995; B1.

Dowling, Carrie. "Flight Attendant Returns to Crash Site." *USA Today*, 25 August 1995; 3A.

"Feuerstein Extends Malden Mills Salaries." [Worcester, MA], *Telegram & Gazette*, 12 January 1996; A2.

Jones, Del. "Open-Book Policy Can Motivate Employees." *USA Today*, 14 December 1995; 1B–2B.

Juran, Joseph M. "The Upcoming Century of Quality." *Quality Progress*, August 1994; 29–37.

"Malden Mills." *USA Today*, 11 January 1996; 9B.

"Mill Owner's Heart Is Fabric of Mass. Town." *USA Today*, 29 January 1996; 3A.

"News Notes." *Retired Officer Magazine*, July 1994; 18.

Seiler, Andy. "Government Has a Hand in Filmmaking." *USA Today*, 9 June 1995; 1C.

Stuller, Jay. "Alcatraz: From Penitentiary to Parkland." *Smithsonian*, September 1995; 84–95.

" 'That's unbelievable. It's unexpected. It's a miracle'." [Worcester, MA], *Telegram & Gazette*, 15 December 1995; A2.

Townsend, Major Patrick L. "Love and Leadership." *Marine Corps Gazette*, February 1982; 24–25.

Townsend, Pat and Joan Gebhardt. "Beyond Charging the Hill and Demanding Excellence." *The Journal for Quality and Participation*, January/February 1994; 22–24.

Valente, Judith. "United's Crew Credits Special Training for Helping to Save Plane During Crisis." *The Wall Street Journal*, 3 March 1989; C16.

Will, George F. "D-Day—The Bloody Beginning of Europe's Liberation." [Worcester, MA], *Telegram & Gazette*, 5 June 1994; C3.

Woodward, Sergeant First Class Michael T. "The Subordinate: The Art of Followership." *Infantry Magazine*, July–August 1975.

Miscellaneous

Ashcraft, Ray and Kevin Rohan. Interviews with authors, May 1996.

Basaraba, Bruce. Interviews with authors, May 1996.

Byrnes, Joe and Mary Ann O'Mara. Interviews with authors, May 1996.

Conner, Sharon. Interviews with authors, May 1996.

Davenport, Sally. Interviews with authors, May 1996.

Hazelwood, Gunnery Sergeant William E., Gunnery Sergeant Michael Walker, Gunnery Sergeant Edward T. Sax, and Gunnery Sergeant Robert E. Farmer. Interview with author, 8 January 1995.

Hollywood Public Library. Query to information desk, 17 January 1996.

Jepson School of Leadership Studies. *Leadership Studies Program*. Booklet, University of Richmond, 1992.

Kelly, Commander Patrick, and Doctor John Gibson, "We Hold These Truths: The Development & Assessment of Character." Unpublished paper, U.S. Coast Guard Academy, 1995.

Knezovich, Bob. Interviews with authors, May 1996.

Manoogian, Paul. Interviews with authors, May 1996.

Marvil, Joel. Excerpt from CEO speech, Ames Rubber Company, 21 January 1993.

Mellecker, John. Interview with author, 28 July 1994.

Posk, Joe and Jeff Dennard. Interviews with authors, May 1996.

Price, Mary. Interviews with authors, May 1996.

South Grafton Elementary School. *School Improvement Plan*. South Grafton, MA, Fall 1995.

Thompson, Karen and Mary Imbornone. Interviews with authors, May 1996.

INDEX

246

surveys, 175. *See also* Ernst & Young;
  Harris Poll; South Grafton
  Elementary School, surveys

taking responsibility, 47, 52, 79, 123
Taylor, Frederick, 4–5, 13, 31, 43
Taylor, Keith, 133
teamwork. *See also* Marine Corps, teamwork; participation options
  benefits of, 44
  examples of team building
    outside job description (*see* Ames
      Rubber Corporation)
    within job description (*see*
      Devereux Center)
  impact of information on motivation,
    164–165 (*see also* communica-
    tions)
  psychological barriers to, 163–165
  team leadership, 162
  team membership, 41, 48, 78 (*see also*
    Army, "Guidelines for
    Followers"; Marine Corps,
    leadership principles)
  underlying philosophy, 153
Ten Commandants, 107–108
The Book of Virtues. See *Book of Virtues,*
  The
Thompson, Karen, 165–166
Timothy School, 127
Toastmasters Club, 89, 135
tolerance for error, 35, 94, 100, 200–201
Total Quality Leadership, 39
Total Quality Management, 6, 39
traits. *See* Marine Corps, leadership traits
Truett, W. Melvin, 199
Trulock, Alice, 25, 114
Truman, President Harry S., 22–23
trust. *See also* Army, trust; Marine
  Corps; trust
  and achieving goals, 119, 172
  basis for mentoring, 200–201
  basis for teamwork, 153
  and delegative leadership (*see* Air
    Force, delegative leadership,

conditions for use; Army, delegative leadership)
Fourteen Points, analysis of, 40 (*see*
  also Deming, Dr. W. Edwards)
glue binding units, 30
in Jepson curriculum, 193
between leader and led, 53–55
by leaders, 81
in leaders, 21, 24
possibility of mistakes, 10
as risk game, 201
and self-confidence, 9

United Airlines, 157–158
United States Air Force. *See* Air
  Force
United States Army. *See* Army
United States Coast Guard. *See* Coast
  Guard Academy
United States Coast Guard Academy. *See*
  Coast Guard Academy
United States Malcolm Baldrige National
  Quality Award. *See* Malcolm
  Baldrige Award
United States Marine Corps. *See* Marine
  Corps
United States Naval Academy. *See* Naval
  Academy
United States Naval Postgraduate
  School. *See* Naval Postgraduate
  School theses
USA Today, 20–21, 126, 131

value analysis, 176–177
values. *See also* Marine Corps, leadership traits, comparison with *The
  Book of Virtues*; Ten
  Commandments
  impact on leadership, 107–110
Victoria (queen of England), 109
Vinnicombe, Susan, 59
von Steuben, Baron, 103, 168

Wal-Mart, 133
Walton, Sam, 133

ABOUT THE AUTHORS

Pat Townsend's association with the military began as a military dependent and continued as a member of the United States Marine Corps.
Growing up as the son of an army sergeant meant a seminomadic life living in Minnesota, Hawaii, Virginia, Washington, D.C., Germany, and
Texas, attending eight grade schools and two high schools. After graduat-
ing from Marquette University in Milwaukee, Wisconsin, with a B.S. in
mathematics, he had an unusual twenty-year career in the Marine Corps,
with assignments ranging from commanding an artillery battery in Vietnam to teaching college ROTC, running a refugee camp, writing docu-
ments for an R&D project, acting as a Public Affairs officer, and directing
a drug and alcohol rehabilitation unit. Along the way he earned a Master's degree in computer science at the U.S. Naval Postgraduate School
in Monterey, California.

On retiring from the Marine Corps, Townsend became the director of
Quality Team Central for the Paul Revere Insurance Group in Worcester,
Massachusetts, a job that led him to co-author his first book, *Commit to
Quality*. Following its publication, he abandoned all pretense of a real
job and became a full-time speaker and author on the topics of leadership, innovation, and quality. He is also the co-author of *Quality in Action* and a steady stream of articles on a wide variety of topics. For three
years, he and his wife Joan wrote a current events column for the
Worcester Telegram & Gazette.

Pat is now a resident of Holden, Massachusetts, and the very proud
father of two talented sons named Michael and Brady. In his free time he
enjoys traveling with his family and—when he's feeling strong—going to
Red Sox games.

As the daughter of a Navy chief, **Joan Gebhardt** was raised in Col-
orado, Hawaii, Illinois, Utah, and California, attending sixteen schools
in the process. She graduated with a B.A. in history from Lewis and
Clark College in Portland, Oregon, taking part in its Freshman Abroad
Program in Mexico and touring the Orient with a USO-sponsored musi-

cal as a junior. During the tour, she met her future husband Patrick on duty with the United States Marine Corps in Okinawa. While Patrick was in Vietnam, she attended California Polytechnic Institute in Pomona, earning a Lifetime Teaching Credential from the State of California.

Joan is an expert on packing household goods, moving eleven times in the first sixteen years of marriage before settling down in Holden, Massachusetts. She is also pretty good at finding a variety of jobs: dorm mother, teacher, office worker, saleswoman, editor, and public relations. In the heyday of game shows, she created a school to advise potential contestants on how to pass the interview; her zaniest job was decorating eggs for a boutique. She is the co-author of two books, over 200 articles, and a Malcolm Baldrige National Quality Award application.

The mother of two grown sons, Michael (an artist) and Brady (a soon-to-be high school mathematics teacher), Joan now devotes her work time to writing and her play time to planning peripatetic vacations for family and friends. Joan is old enough to remember when Wakiki Beach had less than a half-dozen hotels and California was mostly orange groves.